# Shaping the Future:

## New directions for legal services

edited by
Roger Smith

 Legal Action Group
1995

This edition published in Great Britain 1995
by LAG Education and Service Trust Limited
242 Pentonville Road, London N1 9UN

© Legal Action Group 1995

British Library Cataloguing in Publication Data

A CIP catalogue record for this book is available from the British Library.

ISBN 0 905099 61 3

Phototypeset by J&L Composition Ltd, Filey, North Yorkshire
Printed by Bell & Bain Ltd, Glasgow

# Shaping the Future

# Contents

# Introduction

This book is intended to excite debate and stimulate innovation. It explores new ways in which legal services may be provided for those unable to afford lawyers' traditionally high fees. The diversity of the answers suggested reflect the varied backgrounds of the 18 different authors. They report on experience from five continents and their contributions have been arranged within six major themes. The book is intended to challenge the conventional parochialism of much domestic debate on legal services. The demands on the various parts of the English legal system, particularly the courts and legal aid, are stretching available resources to breaking point. Other jurisdictions face similar problems and, not surprisingly, have in some cases developed responses from which we can learn. To do this, we must not only be open to experience from abroad. We must be prepared to cross the conceptual barriers within which we traditionally compartmentalise different areas of policy. For example, we must cease to regard reform of legal aid as raising one set of issues and reform of court processes another.

Contributions from domestic authors have deliberately been placed among those from other countries. Some major issues of domestic concern, such as the organisation of publicly funded legal services, have been treated only obliquely, through discussion of the situation in other jurisdictions. This is deliberate. The aim is to seek a kaleidoscopic vision from which new approaches to old problems may emerge. Short introductions preface the parts of the book that include coverage of overseas experience. These draw out some of the themes of particular relevance in England and Wales. The final chapter summarises the main arguments put forward by the contributors and seeks to explain the way in which the very varied subject-matter of the different chapters fits together and suggests themes which should be explored further.

1

Behind this book is an assertion of optimism. The first three chapters document the crisis widely felt by those working within the legal system in England and Wales at the time of writing. However, despite the present threats to legal service provision to the poor, there are still opportunities to shape the future so as to improve access to justice. It is hoped that this book will help to clarify objectives, broaden thinking and inspire practice.

The book concentrates on civil justice. This mirrors current British government concern. An eminent Law Lord, Lord Woolf, is in the course of producing what is expected to be an important report on the future of civil litigation. In relation to legal aid, the Lord Chancellor has indicated that he is concentrating on the problems relating to civil cases. Criminal justice has recently received significant attention, including the report of the Royal Commission on Criminal Justice, to which LAG responded in *Preventing Miscarriages of Justice*, published in 1993. Accordingly, it seemed right to focus on issues that are particularly relevant to civil cases. Some matters, however, such as the organisation of legal aid practice, unavoidably involve discussion of criminal issues as well.

The three chapters in the first part of the book give a general analysis of the current state of civil legal services in England and Wales, thus providing the context for any innovation, experiment or reform. The following parts describe a variety of ways in which new directions and approaches, largely developed in other countries but some suggested by British authors, might provide a way forward. This is discussed in the final chapter.

There is, of course, considerable inter-connection between the various chapters. For instance, Terry Purcell's contribution in Part II concentrates on the use of new technology by lawyers but also discusses his Law Foundation's innovative CourtGuide project, which itself could have been located in Part III under legal education and information. In any event, the division into themes is necessarily somewhat arbitrary. The index should help those interested in following discussion of a particular issue through different parts of the book.

Two points of detail may be helpful for readers outside the UK. First, legal aid is administered separately in each of the three jurisdictions of England and Wales, Scotland and Northern Ireland. Hence, statistics relate only to England and Wales unless otherwise stated. Second, legal aid is administered in England and Wales by a Legal Aid Board appointed by the Lord Chancellor, the government minister with responsibility for the legal system. The Lord Chancellor at the time of writing is Lord Mackay of Clashfern.

The book's origin lies in a project funded by the Nuffield Foundation. For this, the Legal Action Group (LAG) expresses its gratitude, particularly for the assistance given beyond the call of duty by Robert Hazell and Irene Hall. Nuffield's grant allowed LAG to select eight people at the cutting edge of various aspects of the development of legal services and to bring them to London for a week in the autumn of 1994. A degree of randomness was unavoidable in such a process. The articles in this book are based upon the papers that these guests presented at a conference and series of seminars. Thanks are due to them and to all the domestic participants in these discussions, particularly those whose papers are also contained in this book.

LAG does not necessarily endorse the ideas of those who have contributed to this book. It does, however, consider them stimulating enough to promote further debate. Those who would like a clear statement of LAG's own policies in the field of publicly funded legal services should read *A Strategy for Justice*, published in 1992 at £9.95 plus £2 postage and packing.

Roger Smith
Director, Legal Action Group

# Part I

# The domestic context

# CHAPTER 1

# Current trends

ROGER SMITH

The future of civil litigation and of legal aid is attracting the language of crisis from government, practitioners, academics and clients. Much of this sense of crisis has been precipitated by the government's concern with cost. The government makes enormous direct contributions to the legal profession through legal aid, the Crown Prosecution Service, the court service and the Government Legal Service. The process of undertaking 'fundamental reviews' of expenditure has now reached the Lord Chancellor's Department. This has focused on legal aid. Cash-limiting of the civil legal aid budget is now very firmly on the government's agenda.

The government has also shaken the legal profession by its attack on its monopolies, of which it is the regulator. One effect of the Courts and Legal Services Act 1990 will be to bring unprecedented competition to both of its branches. The Bar is already finding it difficult to maintain its past rate of expansion: it is likely now to begin to contract. Solicitors face the potential diversion of significant amounts of money for publicly funded legal advice to voluntary sector lay advisers.

As a result, ministers, and those appointed by them, have for some years tolled a steady knell. In 1991, the Lord Chancellor told an audience of legal aid practitioners: 'we are just about at the limit of what is possible without radical change'. In 1995, matters had advanced further and he announced to a seminar: 'There must be change.' Lord Woolf, appointed by the Lord Chancellor to examine civil litigation, echoed the same refrain in his comments to the press: 'To create a system for the twenty-first century, one is forced to the conclusion that one has to make fundamental change'.

Such pronouncements understandably dismay lawyers. More than their income is at stake. Developments such as franchising,[1] and the mooted block contracting of legal aid cases, threaten the conventional organisation of solicitors in private practice. Franchising may also threaten a good deal of the traditional self-image, however true it ever was, of a liberal and independent profession developed in the nineteenth century. Cyril Glasser, author of chapter 15, has argued in another context that separating out those lawyers specialising in publicly funded work from those involved in other kinds of work may have deep implications: 'The primary issue for lawyers over the next decade will be that of professional coherence, that is to say, the way in which people identify with, or call themselves lawyers, re-interpret their role and function and claim a common ideology and social purpose'.[2]

The disconcerting effects of change are also being felt by lay advisers in the voluntary sector. Unparalleled pressure on local authority budgets has squeezed grants to many advice agencies. The extension of franchising by the Legal Aid Board to the voluntary sector would involve such agencies in the provision of a statutory service for the first time. This is likely to alter both their own sense of identity and their perception by the public.

Meanwhile, despite record numbers of clients for both legally aided lawyers and lay advice organisations (see next chapter), a gap is opening up in the provision of legal services. Access is increasingly restricted to those rich enough to pay lawyers' private client rates on the one hand or those poor enough to qualify for free legal aid and advice on the other. Eligibility for public legal assistance is increasingly being restricted to those on levels of income around those applicable to minimum social security 'safety net' benefits. Those just above such minimum income levels are squeezed out of assistance by the escalating contributions required from them and by declining levels of eligibility that may threaten any entitlement at all. Such people have been christened 'Minelas' by the Consumers' Association (middle incomes, not eligible for legal aid). As cuts in legal aid bite more and more severely, the Minelas are increasingly being supplemented by 'Linelas' (lower incomes, not eligible for legal aid).

## Common themes

A prevailing sense of crisis can also be identified in other jurisdictions. 'The American legal profession stands at the crossroads of change . . . The predominant sense seems to be that lawyers, both individually and collectively, have lost control over forces that are reshaping the markets in which they compete . . . and their status in society', begins the introduction to one recent study.[3]

The structures that have supported the legal profession and the courts for more than a century since the last great period of reform in the mid-nineteenth century are being overwhelmed by powerful economic and political currents. Much of the law itself is based on nineteenth century notions of individual economic liberalism. The legal system as a whole has found it difficult to adapt to the issues of collective rights raised, for example, by mass torts and multi-party actions. The last major reform of the structure of the civil courts was in 1875. By that time, the legal profession had organised itself in very much its current form. The Law Society in London had assumed control of entry into the solicitors' profession: the Inns of Court, also in London, were governing the Bar. Legal problems following the great influx of public money that accompanied the creation of the welfare state after the second world war largely poured into the existing moulds of both lawyers and courts.

Few other jurisdictions have placed such reliance on private practitioners to deliver publicly funded legal services. In countries like the United States, Canada and Australia, the provision of funds for publicly funded legal services came later than in Britain, reaching sizable proportions only in the 1960s and 1970s. More use was made of salaried lawyers employed by organisations like legal aid societies, public defender organisations or legal aid commissions. Legal services were also seen in a broader context, as necessarily involving the provision of legal education and information as well as individual casework. This is well illustrated in Gordon Hardy's discussion of such activity in British Columbia in chapter 6.

Eligibility for public assistance remains lower in most other common law jurisdictions than in England and Wales for most types of cases (see *A Strategy for Justice* for details). This has probably led to more injustice but it has also, of necessity, stimulated more innovation from private practitioners in meeting need. It has led to developments such as the 'unbundling theory' discussed by Forrest Mosten in chapter 4. All common law jurisdictions have, however, encountered the same problems with court structures and patterns of litigation that are a legacy of British influence. Carrie Menkel-Meadow discusses the consequent developments in alternative, or better, 'appropriate' dispute resolution with which courts in the United States are experimenting.

The future of civil justice and of provision of legal services for the poor are both causing concern in many countries. Many contributors refer to recent or current reviews and initiatives in their own jurisdictions. Such activity is shared by other countries unrepresented in the unavoidably arbitrary selection of this book. The government of Ontario, for instance, established a civil justice review in April 1994 at the same time as reviewing the fundamentals of its Legal Aid Plan.

Government-inspired investigations of the civil justice system often have potentially conflicting aims: saving cost and widening access. This may well be due to developments common to the economies, societies and politics of many countries in the late twentieth century; there is a polarisation within many societies which results in increasing divergence between the interests of generally richer taxpayers and generally poorer benefit-consumers. The impact of this on legal aid in England and Wales is discussed in chapter 2.

Another common trend, pulling inexorably away from containing expenditure and in the direction of causing greater cost, is the onward march of 'legalisation' in modern societies. Law is increasingly used to regulate relationships within society, giving rise to an increasing need for lawyers, legal information and legal assistance. This has been widely observed by academic commentators in the UK and abroad. Professor Galanter recently discussed the phenomenon in the context of the United States: 'A larger, more educated, more diverse population enjoying higher incomes, more social services, and longer life expectancies is situated in a greatly expanded, more service-driven, more internationalised economy. Recent accounts suggest declining confidence in major institutions'.[4] The amount of law grows, whether measured in volume of statutes, law books or litigation.

As the amount of law grows, so, continues Professor Galanter, does the number of 'legal voices' – for example, 'in the family area . . . organisations have appeared and taken legal action on behalf of battered wives, divorced fathers, adoptive children, natural parents of adoptive children, parents of cult members, and the families of the victims of the Pan American flight that crashed at Lockerbie in December 1988'. Furthermore, he says, law now has an ever-extending reach over areas not previously seen as in need of 'close articulation with legal principles', such as the conduct of the police, juvenile justice, schools, mental hospitals and welfare agencies.

These proliferating legal voices, combined with the extending reach of law and, thereby, greater legal conflict are manifested in England and Wales in rising legal aid expenditure. Of this, legal regulation of police conduct, one of Professor Galanter's examples, provides a very clear illustration. The police station duty solicitor scheme, introduced at the same time as statutorily based rules governing suspects' rights, now accounts for over 5 per cent of all legal aid received by solicitors. This source of expenditure hardly existed before 1 January 1986. More examples of increased legalisation giving rise to higher legal aid costs are given in the next chapter.

Legalisation often tends to be overlooked as a cause of the rise of legal aid expenditure. It was, for instance, completely ignored in a recent Social Market Foundation paper on legal aid produced by authors close to the government's fundamental review.[5] As a result, the debate about legal aid tends to be narrowed to only some of the factors causing an increase in expenditure. It is directed away from general trends in society that contribute to the growth in legal aid expenditure. Discussion needs to be widened to include cause as well as effect.

## Access to justice

One of the central ideas motivating the legal activism of the last decade has been the idea of increasing 'access to justice'. This has struck an international chord. The phrase gave the title, for instance, to a chapter in a domestic Civil Justice Review in 1988; to an Australian government-appointed Access to Justice Advisory Committee which reported in 1994; to another report published by a government-appointed working group in Quebec on the accessibility of justice in 1991; and to a major Canadian conference, co-sponsored by the federal government in the same year.

Appropriately for such an internationally useful phrase, it was initially promoted in an international survey organised by two academics, one from Italy and the other from the United States, as the result of a project based at the European Institute in Florence and sponsored, among others, by the American Ford Foundation and the Italian government. In a much-quoted introduction, Professors Cappelletti and Garth announced what has proved a potent typology:

The recent awakening of interest in effective access to justice has led to three basic approaches, at least in the Western-orientated countries. Beginning about 1965, these approaches have emerged more or less in chronological sequence. We can say roughly that the first access solution – the 'first wave' in this new movement – was *legal aid*; the second concerned the reforms aimed at providing *legal representation for 'diffuse' interests*, especially in the areas of consumer and environmental protection; and the third – and most recent – is what we propose to call simply the *'access to justice approach'* since it includes, but goes much beyond, the earlier approaches, thus representing an attempt to attack access barriers in a more articulate and comprehensive manner.[6]

At one level, the idea of 'access to justice' has proved so successful because it makes such obvious sense. The problems of providing justice for all will not be solved just by legal aid, by funding private practitioners to undertake individual cases, nor even by the creation of bodies representing disadvantaged or diffuse groups, such as the Commission for Racial Equality or the Office of Fair Trading. Any coherent strategy must involve the wide range of elements identified by Professors Cappelletti and Garth as examples of a comprehensive approach – reform of general litigation procedures, alternative dispute resolution outside the courts, special procedures and institutions to meet particular social needs, changes in the delivery of legal services and simplification of the law. Such a concept underlies the 'legal services approach' which LAG set out in *A Strategy for Justice*. This called for acceptance of the need for 'equal access to justice' and argued that there were at least three means by which it might be attained: 'advice, assistance and representation' (defined as the statutory goals of legal aid in the Legal Aid Act 1988); legal education and information; and the reform of law and procedure'.[7]

The dominance of the idea of 'access to justice' and, indeed, LAG's modification of it has not gone unchallenged. Professor Rod MacDonald neatly illustrated his general criticism in memorable aphorisms which he used as sub-headings to a powerful critique. Among these was the thought-provoking 'Before "Access to Justice" there was just justice'.[8] He argues that the concept has tended to obscure the objective of the provision of services, the attainment of justice, by focusing on a range of means of achieving it. Another explicit dissenter from LAG's position called for an opposing approach which 'would emphasise the political, participative, democratic and collective aspects of problems of law as opposed to the apolitical, representative, non-democratic and individual manner in which legal problems are channelled through the legal system.'[9]

There are three responses to such criticism. First, 'legal services' can be defined widely enough to encompass approaches other than those involving lawyers and litigation. The chapters in Part III of this book, for instance, are specifically designed to advance the argument that public legal education and information must be a serious component of any coherent legal services strategy. Second, the practical dangers of stressing substantive justice, however attractive in tapping the idealism of providers, can be read into Gerry Singsen's analysis of US experience in chapter 11. In the US, civil legal aid has become identified with a particular political programme and, even more damagingly in terms of security of funding, with a particular political party. This may yet prove fatal to its long-term future. Third, LAG has modified the usual phrase to a demand for 'equal' access to justice precisely to emphasise the need for an equalisation of power within the legal process which can sometimes be lost in demands simply for 'access'.

Nevertheless, the concept of 'access to justice' presents difficulties. It was originally formulated by radical critics of the *status quo* outside government. The danger of co-option by those within was evident to the early proselytisers: 'The access-to-justice approach tries to attack . . . barriers comprehensively, questioning the full array of institutions, procedures, and persons that characterise our judicial systems. The risk, however, is that the use of rapid procedure and inexpensive personnel will produce a cheap and unrefined product. This risk must continually be kept in mind.'[10]

In England and Wales, the issue is very clearly illustrated by the fate of the Civil Justice Review, discussed in chapter 3. Implementation of its recommendations has largely been limited to the allocation of cases lower down the adjudication process. This was promoted as a good thing in itself but the real picture was more complicated. One recommendation called on the government to compensate for lack of representation in these lower courts by suggesting that 'those agencies whose staff maintain a regular presence at courts, and which provide representation and other services to litigants, should be eligible for funding by the . . . Legal Aid Board in respect of such services'.[11] The board drew up plans for such a duty scheme, but they were vetoed by the Lord Chancellor on grounds of cost. As a result, only the potentially cost-saving elements of the package were implemented.

The issue cannot be avoided: there must be some statement of the *purpose* of funding the legal system. The terms of reference of the government's fundamental review of legal aid include a commitment to 'consider whether public expenditure by the legal departments in England and Wales has a clear purpose [and] whether the purpose is right for the 1990s'. In LAG's view, the purpose is clear: it is the provision of equal access to justice. Discussion should focus on the means by which this might be achieved.

Articulation of the objective of government policy in such terms contrasts strongly with the current 'fundamental aim' of the Lord Chancellor's Department. This is 'to ensure the efficient and effective administration of justice at an affordable cost'.[12] Such a formulation LAG believes to be wrong, because it stresses the means above the end. The interests of members of society must be considered before the means by which those interests will be met. Failure to do this begins a policy trail that results in narrowing of consideration to how cost might be controlled. This is evident from the department's own 'strategic priority': 'to control legal aid costs and contain expenditure on court services, while maintaining proper standards by means consistent with this priority'. Cost considerations may constrain the means by which a policy objective may be achieved, but cost control should not be elevated to a goal in itself.

## Shaping the future

Thus the crisis faced by the English system of justice has broader dimensions than those in which it normally tends to be seen. The causes are complex, reflected in a deep-seated malaise which is international in scope.

Any adequate response must recognise these dynamics. Neither legal aid nor reform of the courts can any longer by themselves provide, if ever they could, an acceptable level of access to justice. Policies must be developed which call upon experience elsewhere and mobilise all the mechanisms available in providing access to justice. Nevertheless, the effectiveness of such an approach depends upon a clear understanding of the current state of legal aid, as discussed in chapter 2, and of lawyers, the courts and their alternatives, which are the subject of chapter 3.

## References

1 See ch 3 (p30).
2 'The Legal Profession in the 1990s – images of change' *Legal Studies*, March 1990, p2.
3 R Nelson and D Trubek, 'New Problems and New Paradigms in Studies of the Legal Profession' in R Nelson, D Trubek and R Solomon, *Lawyers' Ideals/Lawyers' Practices: Transformation in the American Legal Profession*, Cornell University Press, 1992, p1.
4 M Galanter, 'Law Abounding: Legislation around the North Atlantic' *Modern Law Review*, January 1992, pp3–4.

5 G Bevan, A Holland, M Partington, *Organising Cost-Effective Access to Justice*, Social Market Foundation, 1994.

6 M Cappelletti and B Garth, *Access to Justice, Volume 1: A World Survey*, Sijthoff & Noordhoff, 1978, p21.

7 LAG, *A Strategy for Justice*, 1992, p150.

8 R MacDonald, 'Access to justice and law reform', *The Windsor Yearbook of Access to Justice: Tenth Anniversary Volume*, University of Windsor, 1990, p326.

9 M Cousins, 'The Politics of Legal Aid', *Civil Justice Quarterly*, April 1994, pp130–131.

10 Cappelletti and Garth as above, p 124.

11 *Civil Justice Review: Report of the Review Body on Civil Justice*, HMSO, Cm 394, p66.

12 *Departmental Report of the Lord Chancellor's and Law Officers' Departments: The government's expenditure plans 1994–95 to 1996–97*, HMSO, Cm 2509, 1994, p3.

# CHAPTER 2

# The changing nature of legal aid

ROGER SMITH

In England and Wales, the availability of legal aid will be a major factor in shaping the future of civil litigation, as it has been since 1950.[1] The government wishes to cap the civil legal aid budget. Such a move is likely to have profound effects that cannot be ignored, both on those who currently provide services and on those that receive them.

Legal aid is so embedded in the operation of civil justice that potential reform of any part of the legal system must be considered in relation to its impact on legal aid. As discussed in *A Strategy for Justice*, legal aid has largely remained in the form in which it was devised, a way of funding lawyers to undertake cases of certain defined categories in courts. Public funding of legal services in the UK predominantly funds solicitors and barristers for a wide range of criminal, divorce and personal injury cases contested in the courts, while tribunals, forms of mediation and non-lawyer advisers have received minimal assistance.

The result has been to create something of a paradox. One of the movements to grow out of the explosion of legal services in the 1970s was directed against lawyers and courts. The initial impetus of this movement was a radical thrust towards the empowerment of individuals and hitherto marginalised groups. 'First, we kill all the lawyers', has provided a well-worn radical slogan. In the short term, however, any move towards informality, for instance, through extension of the small claims procedure in the county court, usually also entails loss of legal aid and of any effective assistance. This creates a happy situation for a cost-conscious government. It can profitably steal some clothes. Reforms such as increasing the small claims limit of the county court or establishing mandatory mediation in divorce proceedings can be presented in terms of increasing access to justice as well as saving money. Their effect can, however, also be to leave people bereft of help that they desperately need.

Any prospective change needs, therefore, to be considered in a double context. It is necessary not only to ask what is the proposal's intrinsic merit in potentially increasing access to justice. Also necessary of consideration is whether the proposal adversely affects legal aid in its current form. For instance, a proposal to increase the number of cases dealt with as small claims may have advantages from the point of view of the courts and some litigants. Implementation would, however, imply the removal of legal aid from the cases affected because small claims do not attract legal aid. A reform which might be beneficial in another jurisdiction can become more problematic where legal aid is lost as a result. This may account for some of the greater caution exercised by professional bodies and interest groups in proposing alternatives to the current situation than has been the case in jurisdictions where reform is not seen against the background of so broad a coverage of legal aid.

## Justice and society

Increased use of lawyers, the courts and legal aid follow a trend more widespread in society as a whole than is often acknowledged. The increasing use made by people of diverse sources of assistance in many different aspects of their lives is recorded in official government statistics. People are reaching out for help in ever increasing numbers, in relation both for the material and the psychological aspects of their problems, as can be seen from Table 2.1 (p18).

The rise in legal aid has, thus, paralleled the increased use of a wide range of helping organisations over the last 20 years.

The most recent figures for the use of legal aid are as in Table 2.2.

Another relevant factor, often ignored, in the use and perception of legal aid is the changing pattern of wealth. Over the last decade and a half, there have been major shifts in income between different sectors of society. 'Whichever way you measure it,' reported the Child Poverty Action Group in 1993, 'poverty has grown significantly over recent years and by 1988/89 between 11 and 12 million people in the United Kingdom – about a fifth of our society – were living in poverty.'[4] In 1979, 14 per cent of the population were living at or below supplementary benefit levels: by 1989, the equivalent proportion was 20 per cent.

Government statistics reveal how the poor have stayed poor but

**Table 2.1: Numbers using various sources of assistance[2]**

| Organisation | 1971 | 1981 | 1991 |
|---|---|---|---|
| Alcoholics Anonymous | 6,300 | 30,000 | 45,000 |
| Citizens advice bureaux | 1,500,000 | 4,514,600 | 7,648,900 |
| Relate | 21,600 | 38,300 | 70,000 |
| Young People's Advisory and Counselling Service | 89,000 | 314,700 | 470,000 |
| Samaritans | 21,600 | 38,300 | 70,000 |
| Civil legal aid | 201,072 | 174,795 | 256,000 |
| Crown Court criminal legal aid | 52,575 | 100,720 | 137,175 |
| Magistrates' court criminal legal aid | 71,618 | 296,134 | 477,170 |
| Legal advice | n/a | 649,496 | 1,230,000 |

**Table 2.2: Numbers using legal aid (1993-94) [3]**

| Category | 1993-94 |
|---|---|
| Civil legal aid | 359,000 |
| Crown Court criminal legal aid (1993) | 116,477 |
| Magistrates' court criminal legal aid | 432,000 |
| Magistrates' court duty solicitor scheme | 239,000 |
| Police station advice scheme | 658,000 |
| ABWOR* | 37,000 |
| Legal advice (green form) | 1,230,000 |

* Assistance by way of representation (before certain tribunals)

the rich have got richer since 1979. The richest 20 per cent of the population have increased their slice of the national income more than any other group. Only the bottom 20 per cent have seen no improvement in their absolute income.

Table 2.3: Net weekly income after housing costs: distribution of household income as percentages of total income of all households[5]

| Quintile | 1979 (per cent) | 1988-89 (per cent) |
|---|---|---|
| Bottom fifth | 9.6 | 6.9 |
| Lower fifth | 14.1 | 12.0 |
| Middle fifth | 18.1 | 17.0 |
| Upper fifth | 23.1 | 22.9 |
| Top fifth | 35.3 | 41.1 |

Table 2.4: Net median weekly income after housing costs: at 1992 prices

| Quintile | 1979 (£) | 1988-89 (£) |
|---|---|---|
| Bottom fifth | 81 | 81 |
| Lower fifth | 112 | 124 |
| Middle fifth | 143 | 176 |
| Upper fifth | 183 | 234 |
| Top fifth | 253 | 355 |

Confirmation of the relative drop in income for the poor and growth of income for the rich comes from the 1995 Rowntree Inquiry into income and wealth. This was reported as proving that 'Britain is now a more divided society than it has been at any time since the Second World War . . . divisions between the bottom tenth of the population, who are 17 per cent worse off than they were in 1979, and the top tenth, who are more than 60 per cent better off . . .'[6] Will Hutton, influential *Guardian* financial correspondent, argues that changes in relative prosperity are bringing about a 'thirty, thirty, forty society': 'the first 30 per cent are the *disadvantaged* . . . the second 30 per cent are made up of the *marginalised* and the *insecure* . . . The last category is the *privileged*.'[7]

Table 2.5: Percentage of households
eligible for civil legal aid on income
grounds[8]

| Year | Per cent |
|---|---|
| 1979–80 | 77 |
| 1992–93 | 53 |
| 1993–94 | 48 |
| 1994–95 | 47 |

Table 2.5 shows legal aid eligibility in civil cases. It shows steady
decline in entitlement.

Estimates by at least one independent statistician suggest an even
more dramatic fall.[9] There is evidence that legal aid is increasingly
available only to those with income at the lowest levels. The
percentage of recipients that are required to pay a contribution,
which would reflect higher incomes, has dropped significantly over
the last 30 years (Table 2.6).

Table 2.6: Percentage of all civil legal aid certificates which are granted
on the basis of no contribution from the recipient

|  | All courts | All except magistrates' courts | Magistrates' courts only |
|---|---|---|---|
| 1962–63 | – | 49 | 79 |
| 1973–74 | 78 | – | – |
| 1983–84 | 78 | – | – |
| 1993–94 | 86 | – | – |

Thus, the essential character of legal aid is changing: it is no
longer a benefit for which the majority of the population is eligible. Cuts have limited it to the poorest section of society, a group
which is itself increasingly detached from those who pay for it
through taxation. Reflecting this, a recent Lord Chancellor's Department's document defined legal aid in such terms as 'a form of
conditional financial support, provided by the taxpayer, for individuals whose financial circumstances would prevent them from taking
or defending proceedings without assistance with their legal costs'.[10]

In 1993, the Lord Chancellor took this process to its logical conclusion in relation to legal advice. Eligibility was reduced to only those at levels of income giving entitlement to the basic means-tested social security benefit, income support. Those paying for the benefit through taxation were largely divorced from the group receiving it. This split is accentuated by the move from indirect to direct taxation: the poor are paying more for their own poverty.

A concern with the cost of legal services for the poor should not, therefore, be taken as reflecting some level of objective reality. It is, in some measure, the consequence of political, economic and social shifts in society that create a far greater polarity of interest than has hitherto been the experience of our society.

## The cost of legal aid

A memorandum from the right-wing Social Market Foundation sets out the alleged horror story in relation to legal aid cost:

> Since 1979, legal aid has been the fastest growing programme of public expenditure, having increased fivefold in real terms since 1979–80. During the same period, total Government expenditure increased by 29 per cent, and Gross Domestic Product by 24 per cent . . . Since 1987–88, public expenditure on legal aid has doubled in real terms, whilst total Government expenditure increased by 14 per cent and Gross Domestic Product by 4 per cent.'[11]

Expenditure has, indeed, risen sharply, as can be seen from the figures over the last five years in Table 2.7.

Table 2.7: Net legal aid expenditure in £m (inc. administration)[12]

|  | *1989–90* | *1990–91* | *1991–92* | *1992–93* | *1993–94* |
|---|---|---|---|---|---|
| Total | 569 | 685 | 906 | 1,090 | 1,257 |

The net cost may be broken down further, as in Table 2.8 (p22).

There has been considerable fluctuation in the proportions of expenditure over the five-year period covered by these statistics. The proportion spent on crime dropped by 14 per cent: that on matrimonial and family proceedings rose by 9 per cent. Comparison over a ten-year period shows further changes. In 1984, criminal expenditure accounted for 54 per cent of the net total. In all probability, however, spending on crime has remained relatively constant. Passage of the Children Act 1989 has led to reclassifica-

Table 2.8: Percentages of total legal aid expenditure[13]

| Category | 1989–90 | 1990–91 | 1991–92 | 1992–93 | 1993–94 |
|---|---|---|---|---|---|
| Crime | 58 | 56 | 52 | 46 | 44 |
| Civil non-matrimonial | 24* | 26* | 27 | 29 | 29 |
| Civil matrimonial | 18* | 17* | 21 | 25 | 27 |

* estimated

tion of child care proceedings from criminal to the more logical heading of matrimonial and family civil legal aid.

The authors of the Social Market Foundation report asserted that the main determinant of legal aid expenditure was what they called 'supplier-induced inflation'. Yet government policy and client need may be to blame as much as the entrepreneurial enterprise of solicitors. For example, the cost of criminal legal aid has been affected by the introduction of a statutory legal advice scheme in police stations in 1986. In 1986, this cost £12m: by 1993–94, the cost was £67m (just under 6 per cent of the total paid to legal aid practitioners). In addition, the Criminal Justice and Public Order Act 1994 will remove a defendant's right of silence and increase the use of prison. No thought appears to have been given to the likely cost implications of either. A memorandum from an academic expert in legal aid suggests, however, that the cost of the former can be predicted at between £36.6m and £47.6m in the increased use of lawyers and legal aid.[14]

The Legal Aid Board indicated another reason for expenditure increases in its annual report for 1993-94. The rise in cost of matrimonial and family matters was the consequence of changes to children's legislation 'as increasing numbers of Children Act certificates issued since 1991 began to reach a conclusion'.[15] The number of applications for legal aid certificates for matrimonial matters has actually dropped over the last five years – from 173,735 to 150,045 between 1988–89 and 1993–94. However, the number of applications for certificates in relation to the Children's Act has risen from zero to 18,368.

## Contributions and cuts

The government's initial response to concern at the escalating cost of legal aid was to make cuts while retaining the existing overall structure. Eligibility was cut, and contributions were increased. Eligibility for criminal legal aid was, however, preserved at a high level. In the light of the discovery of a series of miscarriage of justice cases, there was probably little political opportunity to cut criminal defence representation. The police station 24-hour duty solicitor service remained free and non-means tested. Legal aid representation rates in Crown Court trials remain between 99–100 per cent.

The government's approach to civil eligibility has been inconsistent. In response to controversy over the research findings on eligibility levels, an enhanced upper level of eligibility for personal injury cases was introduced in April 1992. In April 1993, it was effectively cut because it was not uprated.

Repeated attempts have been made to raise contributions from recipients but this has apparently stalled in both criminal and civil cases (Table 2.9).

**Table 2.9: Contributions and costs in criminal cases (in £m)[16]**

| Year | Magistrates' courts | | Crown Courts | |
|------|---------|----------|----------|----------|
|      | Receipts | Payments | Receipts | Payments |
| 1993 | 2.8 | 191 | 1.3 | 232 |
| 1992 | 3.0 | 209 | 1.6 | 216 |
| 1991 | 1.8 | 199 | 1.4 | 172 |
| 1990 | 3.4 | 173 | 1.9 | 155 |
| 1989 | 2.2 | 141 | 1.1 | 137 |

In April 1992, in the hope of increasing revenue, the Lord Chancellor's Department (LCD) issued a circular to magistrates' clerks requiring strict proof of earnings, usually over 13 weeks, from defendants prior to grant of a legal aid certificate. This proved completely unworkable and embarrassingly had to be rescinded. Very few legal aid certificates are, in any event, revoked for failure to pay contributions required. In 1992, for instance, legal aid was revoked in only five out of the 1,842 cases where legal aid was granted subject to a contribution for a Crown Court trial.[17]

Particularly in criminal cases, the court has an interest in seeing that the defendant is legally represented. English courts can only operate at their current levels of throughput with significant levels of representation provided by lawyers. The catastrophic effect in long serious fraud trials of a defendant who has no legal representation has been such that the LCD has consulted on the idea that this might be forced upon such a person, as an *amicus curiae*, where 'the defendant has been offered but has refused legal aid; and where in the opinion of the judge, the interests of justice require it'.[18]

Contributions in civil cases are more significant than in criminal, raising significant sums (Table 2.10).

Table 2.10: Contributions from civil legal aid cases in £m[19]

| 1989–90 | 1990–91 | 1991–92 | 1992–93 | 1993–94 |
|---------|---------|---------|---------|---------|
| 13.3    | 13.4    | 14.3    | 14.9    | 15.4    |

These figures remain, however, a very small percentage of overall expenditure. In April 1993, the percentage of disposable income taken from people required to pay a contribution was increased from 25 per cent to 33 per cent. This is likely to reinforce the trend noted earlier for civil legal aid to become available only to those in receipt of the lowest levels of benefit because litigants will refuse to pay the contributions demanded. Commendably, the Legal Aid Board has commissioned research on a related problem – the high numbers of those who are offered legal aid subject to a contribution and decline the offer.

Table 2.11: Percentages of civil legal aid applicants required to make contributions[20]

|         | Nil | Under £150 | £150–299 | £300–499 | £500+ |
|---------|-----|------------|----------|----------|-------|
| 1983–88 | 78  | 9          | 6        | 5        | 2     |
| 1992–93 | 86  | 3          | 3        | 3        | 6     |

In civil cases involving damages or property, legal aid in a successful case is simply a loan, the cost being recouped from awards of costs against the losing party or from property or money recovered, upon which the Legal Aid Board has a statutory charge. As a result, the fund receives money back from most cases for which it has provided legal aid to one of the parties. In matrimonial cases, the sum involved was £37m in 1993–94 and in non-matrimonial cases the sum was £11m. The overall figures disguise the relative importance of this provision for some types of case. Disputes over the matrimonial home or personal injuries can cost the Legal Aid Board relatively little. A suggestion was made in the 1970s that eligibility for legal aid for plaintiffs in personal injury cases could be extended to everyone on a suitably calculated administration charge, then estimated to be £50. Provided the fund maintained a suitably high success rate, it would be reimbursed its cost by awards payable by losing defendants.

## Remuneration

Lawyers' remuneration has been curbed in three ways: hourly rates, where applicable, have not been increased at all or by less than inflation and have, in some cases, been reduced; standard fees are being introduced; finally, 'franchising' (see below) is intended to bring down costs either by the imposition of average rates of payment to all practitioners or by the more draconian introduction of competitive tendering for blocks of cases.

Standard fees were introduced into the magistrates' courts in April 1993 following a long battle with the profession. They were designed to combat the phenomenon of 'cost creep', whereby practitioners allegedly compensated for low or no annual increases on their hourly rates by making cases take longer. This had indeed been a problem, as the figures in Table 2.12 demonstrate.

Table 2.12: Rise in cost of a magistrates' court criminal case[21]

| Year | Percentage rise on previous year |
|---|---|
| 1988–89 | 10 |
| 1989–90 | 13 |
| 1990–91 | 14 |
| 1991–92 | 12 |
| 1992–93 | 3 |
| 1993–94 | 0 |

The reason for the dramatic halt in the increases, which took place a year before fixed fees were introduced, is obscure. Analysis of detailed breakdowns of solicitors' bills undertaken by the Legal Aid Board suggests that the cause might be improved cost control – or practitioners' fear of it – by the board.[22] Fixed fees were introduced in such a panic that the LCD's own consultants criticised the lack of any link with the standard of work undertaken.[23]

Fixed fees are now being introduced in civil cases.

## The search for alternatives

Legal aid in England and Wales has been the subject of three major reviews since 1986. The range of alternatives to legal aid suggested in these included loans, legal expenses insurance and arrangements relating to contingency fees.[24]

The potential of these within England and Wales seems, however, limited. The legal expenses insurance market has all but collapsed since the late 1980s, suggesting that it is no real alternative.[25] Conditional fees, although soon to be permitted with up to 100 per cent additional mark-up, seem unlikely to be of much overall effect in expanding access to justice; they are only appropriate where a sum of money may be won as a result of the action. A crucial defect in an English context is that they offer no indemnity in relation to the costs of an opponent. Insurance schemes exist to cover these but it is likely that insurers will back only those cases where success is virtually guaranteed. The result of the introduction of conditional fees may, therefore, be simply to increase lawyers' fees, not to extend access to justice for their clients. However, their existence may be used to justify the removal of legal aid.

All these alternatives would involve little change in the form in which legal services are delivered. Increasingly, however, attention has shifted to reforms that are much more fundamental. These are discussed in the following chapter.

## References

1   See Legal Action Group, *A Strategy for Justice*, 1992, ch 1.
2   Throughout, some percentages will not total exactly 100 due to rounding errors. *Social Trends 23*, HMSO, 1993, table 11.22; Criminal Statistics: England and Wales 1972 and 1981 (the figure for Crown Court legal aid in 1971 is in fact the number of certificates given in 1972); *Judicial Statistics 1991; Legal Aid Reports* 1971–72 and 1981–82 and *Legal Aid Board Annual Report 1991–92* (all legal aid statistics except those for the Crown Court are in fact for 1991–92). The figures for civil and Crown Court criminal legal aid are for certificates granted. The other figures are for bills paid. The apparent drop in civil legal aid grants in 1981 is due to reclassification of categories. There was, for example, no advice scheme ten years earlier.
3   *Judicial Statistics 1989* and *1993*, Legal Aid Board *Annual Reports 1989–90* and *1993–4*. Figures are for bills paid.
4   C Oppenheim, *Poverty: The facts*, CPAG, 1993, p29.

5 *Social Trends 23*, HMSO, 1993, table 5.18, p77.
6 'To have and have not,' *Independent on Sunday*, 12 February 1995.
7 W Hutton, *The State We're In*, Jonathan Cape, 1995, pp106–8.
8 Written Answer in *Hansard* (21 April 1994) col 590.
9 M Murphy, 'Civil legal aid eligibility estimates,' published as Appendix 1, LAG *A Strategy for Justice*, 1992, p161.
10 Lord Chancellor's Department, *Review of Financial Conditions for Legal Aid: Eligibility for civil legal aid*, LCD, 1992, p5.
11 G Bevan, A Holland and M Partington, *Organising Cost-Effective Access to Justice*, Social Market Foundation, 1994.
12 *The Government's Expenditure Plans 1993–94 to 1995–96: Departmental report*, The Lord Chancellor's and Law Officers' Departments. HMSO, Cm 2209, 1993, p8, and LCD press office.
13 The figure for crime includes the cost of legal aid in the higher courts, for which separate statistics are given, and all other legal aid and assistance on crime funded by the Legal Aid Board.
14 L Bridges, 'The Financial Costs of Limiting the Right of Silence', *Parliamentary Briefing*, February/March, 1995.
15 Legal Aid Board, *Annual Report 1993–94*, HMSO, 1994, p2.
16 Annual Judicial Statistics.
17 *Judicial Statistics 1992*, HMSO, Cm 2268, p94.
18 The Lord Chancellor's Department, Home Office, Legal Secretariat to the Law Officers, *Consultation Paper on Long Criminal Trials*, Lord Chancellor's Department, 1992, p9.
19 Legal Aid Board, *Annual Report 1993–94*, p103.
20 Legal Aid Board, *Annual Report 1992–93*, p70.
21 Legal Aid Board, *Annual Report 1992–93*, p81.
22 Legal Aid Board, *Annual Report 1992–93*, table criminal 11, p68.
23 Price Waterhouse, *Advice and Survey on Criminal Legal Aid in the Magistrates' Courts*, 1992, p37.
24 *Review of Financial Conditions for Legal Aid Eligibility for Civil Legal Aid: a consultation paper*, Lord Chancellor's Department, 1991.
25 See, eg, F Betson, 'Down – But Not Out' *The Lawyer*, 6 April 1993.

# CHAPTER 3

# Lawyers, courts and alternatives

ROGER SMITH

Legal aid in England and Wales was the creation of the Law Society, the professional body of solicitors. The society dominated the Rushcliffe Committee that recommended a national legal aid scheme in 1944 and even assisted the Lord Chancellor's Department in the detailed statutory drafting.[1] Solicitors, and to a lesser extent barristers, have dominated the scheme ever since. The strength of the legal aid sector within private practice in the 1970s accounts for why salaried provision in the form of law centres never took off in the way that it did in other jurisdictions such as the United States, Canada, Australia and the Netherlands. There are currently only 55 law centres in England and Wales. In 1993–94, they received in total £3.7m from the Legal Aid Board.[2] This represented 0.3 per cent of all legal aid expenditure.

The deployment of private practice so overwhelmingly to deliver publicly funded legal services has undoubtedly affected what services are delivered. Around three-quarters of all legal aid expenditure still goes on crime and matrimonial work.

## The legal profession

The importance of legal aid as a source of income for the legal profession can be seen from Table 3.1.

Total solicitors' annual turnover is estimated by the Law Society as £6.4bn for 1992–93.[4] Legal aid contributed just over 12 per cent of all solicitors' income. Total turnover for the Bar is not published but the Bar Council estimated that legal aid accounted for 27 per cent of the total income of the Bar in 1989–90.[5] Legal aid has, therefore, helped to succour a legal profession that has expanded massively since the 1960s in parallel with legal aid (Table 3.2).

There is evidence that the growth of both branches of the profes-

Table 3.1: Gross income from legal aid 1992–93 in £m[3]

| Source of legal aid income | Solicitors | Barristers |
|---|---|---|
| Magistrates' courts criminal | 176 | 17 |
| Higher courts criminal | 92 | 117 |
| Civil family | 248 | 32 |
| Civil other | 269 | 57 |
| Duty solicitor schemes | 72 | – |
| Legal advice (green form) | 119 | – |
| TOTAL | 976 | 223 |
| Total less VAT | 831 | 190 |

Table 3.2: Numbers of practising lawyers[6]

| Year | Solicitors | Barristers |
|---|---|---|
| 1960 | 19,069 | 1,919 |
| 1970 | 24,407 | 2,584 |
| 1980 | 37,832 | 4,589 |
| 1990 | 57,167 | 6,579 |
| 1993 | 61,329 | 7,735 |

sion is under pressure. A report from the Bar Council confirms that 'it is likely that the Bar will decline in size' as there is insufficient income to sustain the vastly increased numbers of barristers called in recent years.[7] In 1994, around one-third of all those successfully completing the Law Society's legal practice course, about 2,000 people, were unable to obtain traineeships within solicitors' offices. There is little information on any characteristics specific to legal aid solicitors and barristers. If they are typical of the rest of the profession, an increasing number will be women. The proportion of solicitors who are women has risen from 21 per cent in 1988 to 29 per cent in 1994.[8] They will also tend to be young. Forty-five per cent of male solicitors and 79 per cent of all female solicitors are under 40. A similar pattern exists at the Bar. A recent study indicated that 'almost one quarter of the Bar is within 5 years of call'.

A remarkable feature of legal aid at the present time is the extent to which it permeates the work of the legal profession as a whole. Statistics on this are inadequate. Legal Aid Board figures, for example, suggest that legal aid was paid to 105 per cent of all practising barristers in 1993–94.[9] Board statistics suggest also that a legal aid cheque was received by 82 per cent of all solicitors' offices. These figures then cannot be entirely accurate but they suggest correctly enough the breadth of the legal profession's involvement in legal aid.

A much smaller number of barristers and solicitors are legal aid specialists. Only 3,849 offices – around a quarter of the total of solicitors' offices – received more than £60,000 from the Legal Aid Board in 1993–94, suggesting that they would have employed the equivalent of one full-time solicitor or more on legal aid matters. Information is too limited on the extent of barrister involvement to be very helpful. However, in 1993–94, 2,280 barristers received more than £14,000 from the Legal Aid Board. The Lord Chancellor recently estimated that 50 barristers received more than £100,000 (inclusive of VAT and travelling expenses) for criminal cases and 100 more than £100,000 (exclusive of VAT and travelling expenses) in criminal cases.[10]

## Franchising

Solicitors face major change under the influence of the Legal Aid Board's development of the idea of 'franchising' providers. The first franchising contracts were offered in August 1994. These are contracts between the board and legal aid practitioners binding them to work to the practice management standards set for the whole profession by the Law Society but which are otherwise advisory only. The contract also gives power to the board to monitor the quality of individual cases undertaken by way of compliance with 'transaction criteria'.

Most major legal aid providers are likely to become franchised within a short period of time, even if unfranchised providers are still able to practice. It is clear that this may happen simply because practitioners are scared of the consequences of not being franchised as the government begins to suggest that franchised providers be given certain privileges such as increased rates of pay. As a result, the present wide distribution of legal aid throughout the profession is likely to contract.

A further result may be that increasing tension is manifest in the role of the Legal Aid Board. On the one hand, as a bulk purchaser of legal services, it will continue to be the voice of the consumer, developing guarantees on quality. On the other, the board may be increasingly instructed by the government to tighten up on spending. With the board playing a leading role in setting quality standards, self-regulation, one of the hallowed hallmarks of a profession, will, in consequence, be threatened. Professional control over services, and indeed clients' choice of lawyers, would be further challenged if the Lord Chancellor implemented the idea of competitive tendering for contracts to carry out legal aid work.[11]

Such a development raises the serious issue of potential conflict between the government's twin roles as guardian of the consumer's interests and as the largest single purchaser of legal services.

## New technology

One of the side effects of franchising has been to increase the computerisation of legal aid solicitors' offices. Computerisation as such is not necessary in order to obtain a franchise but the management requirements are such that, in practice, it would be difficult to operate without it.

Use of new technology in England and Wales appears to lag behind that in the United States. One author noted recently: 'In the US, 70 per cent of attorneys have PCs on their desks, but . . . only 33 per cent of partners and fee earners in the UK have their own workstation', though he argued that in the US such workstations were largely 'corporate jewelry'.[12] His figure is compatible with that produced in 1993 by the Law Society's research department. Its

Table 3.3: Personal use of computers (percentages of Law Society sample)

| Use | Sole practitioner | Senior partner | Managing partner |
|---|---|---|---|
| Word-proccessor | 37 | 44 | 48 |
| Electronic diary | 6 | 7 | 24 |
| Spreadsheets | 8 | 11 | 23 |
| Database | 9 | 16 | 24 |
| Any of above | 40 | 52 | 52 |
| Has computer or terminal in own room | 15 | 19 | 16 |

figures indicate, however, the very limited use made of computers as yet.

There has been very little use of new technology for the purposes of increasing legal information and education. To the extent that it has been harnessed, this has been done by the legal profession for its own needs, and computer programmes have been developed for lay advisers, largely in the field of welfare benefits. Although interactive video and computer-assisted information systems are beginning to make their appearance in art galleries, banks and travel agents, there has been no use at all of such aids in the legal profession comparable to that described by Terry Purcell in chapter 5 as happening in the United States or Australia.

## Lay advisers

There is evidence of a steady growth in the number of lay advisers or paralegals within and outside the institutions of the legal profession. An indication of this is given by the number of non-solicitor fee-earners disclosed in insurance returns as employed in solicitors' firms. This figure has grown from 20,511 in 1988 to 23,816 in 1992, a rise of almost a fifth.[13] The actual rise may be larger since solicitors may not consistently categorise all their paralegals as fee-earners. A commercial paralegal sector is also growing up to compete with solicitors. Independent Legal Practitioners franchises 50 paralegals around the country with a head office of ten. Its members undertake largely personal injury and employment work on a contingency fee basis. A number of paralegal groups, such as the Institute of Legal Executives, have applied for rights of audience or the right to commence litigation under the Courts and Legal Services Act 1990.

The largest group of paralegals remains, however, in the advice sector. The network of citizens advice bureaux[14] contained 724 main offices and 803 linked outlets in 1994. Increasingly, these operate with a core of paid officials together with the volunteers who have been their base since their establishment in the second world war. Around 55 per cent of main bureaux now have a full-time paid manager and 20 per cent now have a full-time paid deputy. In 1994 the bureaux dealt with 7.6 million enquiries (see Table 3.4). 

The other network of advice agencies, the Federation of Independent Advice Agencies (FIAC), has a somewhat more disparate membership but many of its members have a similar pattern of work. A recent estimate of the staffing of advice and law centres

Table 3.4: Categories of CAB enquiries (per cent)

| Social security | 24 |
|---|---|
| Debt | 24 |
| Employment | 11 |
| Housing | 10 |

gives the following figures: 'FIAC members employ a total of 2,523 staff (1,721 full-time, 802 part-time) and have 5,288 volunteers. Law Centres employ around 350 staff, with an unknown number of volunteers. CABx employ 2,500 staff (a substantial proportion of whom are part-time) and have 14,500 volunteers.'[15]

The work of the advice agencies is very sensitive to changing patterns of need. The CAB service did not even have a category explicitly for recording debt cases before 1990–91. The annual numbers of consumer and debt cases now regularly equal social security cases. The number seeking assistance with debt reflects the aftermath of the credit boom of the 1980s, during which personal consumer credit quadrupled and mortgage borrowing rose fivefold.[16] As a result, a whole new group of people are encountering the legal system. A report from the Policy Studies Institute suggested that in 1989 around 330,000 mortgage holders may be in arrears and quoted earlier evidence that up to a third of all council tenants may be in arrears with their rent. It calculated that perhaps one million summonses were issued in relation to personal debt in any one year.[17] The debt explosion has largely been dealt with by the advice agencies though it has made some impact on legal aid. Legal advice on debt cases cost the fund £8 million in 1993–94. Five years earlier, its cost had been only £2.7 million.

## Switching resources

An efficiency scrutiny in 1986 recommended the large-scale transfer of legal advice from solicitors to lay advisers. The idea was eventually abandoned in the face of opposition from those working in the agencies concerned. In 1993, the government returned to the theme: 'The legal aid scheme is currently provided almost entirely by lawyers in private practice. The Lord Chancellor intends that they should continue to be the principal providers of service under the scheme. However, he wishes to encourage law centres, CABx and others to take on an increasing proportion of work which it is appropriate for them to handle.'[18]

In furtherance of this approach, the Legal Aid Board announced in 1994 a £100,000 research project into different methods of delivering service and has announced a pilot franchising project with non-solicitor agencies. This is to test the idea of franchises for areas of social welfare law with 42 advice agencies. The board and the Lord Chancellor are contemplating the idea that work on welfare benefits, debt, housing, employment, consumer and immigration could be safely transferred from solicitors in private practice to paralegal organisations without lawyers. This would involve around £50m in annual spending at currrent levels. Such a move has implications both for lawyers and the non-solicitor advice agencies. Lawyers would potentially lose an involvement in social welfare law which they have, globally, been reluctant to accept but in which a small minority have developed a formidable expertise. The agencies would become, for the first time, firmly part of the statutory sector. They would be delivering services under contractual standards though still relying largely on volunteers. This raises the questions of the agencies' continuing voluntary sector ethos and of their continued ability to attract volunteer recruits.

## Civil litigation

In February 1985, Lord Hailsham, then Lord Chancellor, established a civil justice review. The review's report was, as Cyril Glasser describes in chapter 15, hailed as little short of revolutionary. However, its terms of reference were narrow and it did not address the problems found in earlier research on the difficulties encountered in gaining access to justice. They had been exposed by an international survey conducted in the mid 1970s under the direction of Professors Cappelletti and Garth. The authors dwelt on the problems of delay, cost, and complexity, but also discussed other barriers to attaining justice. These included a range of issues relating to the unequal capacity of different parties in relation to finance, capacity to recognise and pursue the essential points in dispute and the advantages available to 'repeat-player' litigants over those who had only 'one shot' as one individual involved in one case. The authors also considered the problem of how a wide spread of litigants could be represented, eg, by representative or class actions.[19]

The review's terms of reference were simply 'to improve the

machinery of civil justice in England and Wales by means of reforms in jurisdiction, procedure and court administration and in particular to reduce delay, cost and complexity'.[20] No mention was made of other considerations. Its final report noted that there had been 58 reports on civil procedure and the organisation of the civil and criminal courts since 1851. The sixtieth soon followed with the publication in June 1993 of *Civil Justice on Trial – The case for change* from a joint Bar/Law Society working party. It was clear that the civil justice review had not been as effective as its initial publicity suggested. The following spring, Lord Woolf, appointed by the Lord Chancellor to head a further examination of civil justice, pronounced what appears to be a damning judgment: 'Five years ago, we had the civil justice review: most of its recommendations have been implemented. Yet costs are still out of control, and the time litigation is taking is out of control.'[21]

The civil justice review's principal recommendation was that cases should be devolved from the High Court to the county courts. Judicial statistics reveal some success in shifting personal injury cases. In 1986, 24,180 such cases were commenced in the High Court. By 1993, this was reduced to 1,555. Overall, there has, however, been surprisingly little reduction in the number of cases commenced in the High Court. In 1986, a total of 234,780 cases were begun in the Queen's Bench Division. In 1993, the comparable figure was 211,275. The overall drop largely reflects the diversion of a high proportion of personal injury cases to the county court. The effect of this has been masked by the continuing preference of many commercial lenders to pursue debtors in the High Court.

One reason for reluctance to use the county court may be delay. Interestingly, the annual Judicial Statistics offer no information on delay at this level. Their indication of the situation in the High Court is not, however, encouraging. The Court was manifestly less efficient in 1993 than 1986 (see Table 3.5).

Practitioners report that the county courts are suffering badly in

**Table 3.5: Average waiting times from issue of writ to disposal or start of trial in weeks**

| 1986 | 126.8 |
|------|-------|
| 1993 | 152.6 |

their attempts to cope with the much-increased workload. In 1993, 3 million cases were commenced as opposed to 2.3 million in 1986.

A very small proportion of cases comes to trial in either the High Court or county courts. Only 650 cases were determined by trial in the Queen's Bench Division of the High Court in 1993, with a further 250 settled during the trial. The county courts decided 25,258 cases by trial and 105,843 by arbitration. As a result, the major function of the court system might be portrayed more as the provision of a method of enforcement than a forum for adjudication.

## Group actions

The need for some adjustment of current procedures in relation to group actions has been apparent since the problems encountered by the Opren cases in the mid–1980s. The civil justice review ducked the issue by calling for further study by the Law Commission. Lord Mackay responded to continuing pressure by requiring the Legal Aid Board to examine the issue in 1988. The board produced an interim report in 1990 and a final report in 1991. Its recommendations, however, referred only to co-ordinating the legal aid aspects of such cases.

LAG argued in its 1989 submission to the board that the issues of procedure and funding were 'so closely interlinked they cannot and ought not to be separated'.[22] Subsequent experience suggests that this was correct. Incensed at losing between £30 and £35 million in abortive litigation in relation to the tranquilliser Benzodiazepene, the board has now issued yet another consultation paper on future reform in which it has finally realised that not only were legal aid changes required but that 'the Lord Chancellor's Department should address the procedures for handling these actions in the courts'.[23]

There are indications of an acceptance of the need for reform. The Supreme Court Procedure Committee, responding to the very practical problems of taking multi-party actions, has produced a guide to procedure. It notes, however, that 'the existing law is in some respects uncertain'.[24] The English legal system is manifestly not finding it easy to adapt to one of the characteristics of modern society: the development of mass markets leading to mass obligations.

Actions involving a large number of people can cover a wide spectrum of subjects. The most obvious examples are litigation over allegedly defective drugs, such as that which involved Opren or Thalidomide, and 'disaster' litigation, such as the sinking of the

*Herald of Free Enterprise* off Zeebrugge. The Supreme Court Procedure Committee listed eight different examples of situations in which group actions might arise. They were all based on private law claims and included such matters as environmental pollution and mass claims by tenants against their landlords.[25] The range of potential cases is, however, enormous. They are not limited to private law. The Law Commission has recently raised the related issue of the role of group and public interests in the context of legal standing to take actions for judicial review.[26]

A number of other jurisdictions are feeling their way to a solution of the problems surrounding group actions. Both the Canadian province of Ontario and Australia have recently introduced legislation to deal with procedure and, in Ontario's case, funding.

## Alternative dispute resolution

In a Hamlyn lecture delivered in 1993, Lord Mackay set out his view of the possibilities of alternative dispute resolution. He showed himself aware of the problems of definition that have beset discussion of this topic and, in particular, the differences between court-annexed arbitration or mediation and out-of-court services that were more truly 'alternative' to the courts. He also revealed the attraction of cost-saving of ADR: 'The proposition that ADR is cheaper and quicker than litigation, and therefore might effect substantial savings, including legal aid savings, must be specifically examined.'[27] This approach is reflected in his policies as Lord Chancellor. A major shift to mediation in divorce was proposed by a Green Paper published in 1993, and is likely to be taken further in a white paper to be published in the summer of 1995.[28]

## Small claims

In the late 1970s, a campaign by consumer interests led to the establishment of a small claims jurisdiction within the county court. This was seen as alternative dispute resolution from normal court adjudication. Hearings were informal; legal aid was not available. As the ceiling for cases required to enter this procedure rose, so the lack of any legal aid for poor people became more of a problem. Also, some types of case, such as housing possession and debt cases, were processed more as routine administrative operations than as judicial determinations. Both these problems were recognised by the civil justice review. As noted on p13, one of its recommendations was that 'litigants in small claims cases and in debt and housing cases which are proceeding in a county court should have a statutory right to be assisted or represented by a lay representative of their choice, subject to the discretion of the court'.[29] It led to research commissioned by the Legal Aid Board[30] but implementation of a scheme was vetoed on the ground of cost. The rigid demarcation line that divides 'proper cases' from others as eligible for legal aid remains in place.

## Tribunals

Various tribunals decide many aspects of the life of people on low incomes. These are 'alternative' only in the sense that they are not courts: applicants have no choice but to use them. Statistics show increased use (Table 3.6).

Table 3.6: Cases received[31]

|  | 1988 | 1992 |
| --- | --- | --- |
| Industrial tribunals | 26,127 | 67,025 |
| Immigration adjudicators | 14,508 | 26,226 |
| Criminal Injuries Compensation Board | 36,285 | 55,993 |

Tribunals exist in an enormous variety. The Council on Tribunals is responsible for supervising well over 60, ranging from the major ones listed above to the Wireless Telegraphy Tribunal, which has never been convened since its establishment in 1949.

Intended to be informal, accessible and open to individuals without the need for lawyers, some of their early promise has been lost. A recent study of the industrial tribunals begins: 'The industrial tribunals have been in operation for over 21 years. In that period, they have changed from being administrative tribunals, dealing with appeals against industrial levies and selective employment tax, into quasi-labour courts, adjudicating in disputes between employers and employees under 13 different Acts of Parliament and a variety of statutory instruments.'[32] Just like courts, the industrial tribunals have become a forbidding arena dominated by legalism and lawyers, with both sides frequently represented by barristers who are experts in the expanding case law relating to employment matters.

The Independent Tribunal Service (ITS) runs other tribunals a little more faithful to the original conception. Formed out of the discredited supplementary benefit appeal tribunals in the mid-1980s, the ITS has a president, a corporate management structure, an enabling philosophy, and a coherent training programme for its legally qualified chairs and its lay members (see ch 18). Even so, research commissioned by the Lord Chancellor's Department suggests that representation, not necessarily by a lawyer but certainly by a specialist, significantly affects the statistical chances of a claimant's success.[33] This is a finding with enormous implications in terms of the resources required to balance the parties.

In today's cost-conscious world, a tribunal must beware of being too successful. The Home Secretary has been trying to abolish the Criminal Injuries Compensation Board and replace it with a tariff-based compensation system, but has so far been frustrated by the courts. The board had been giving increasing amounts of compensation. Similarly, the establishment of the ITS was not without consequences. The social security appeal tribunals improved immeasurably in the early 1980s but found that they lost jurisdiction over single payment appeals. Their cases received, as a result, declined from 274,614 in 1988 to 169,836 in 1992. However, the ITS is now in danger of being overwhelmed by child support appeals.

## Ombudsmen

One form of dispute resolution that appears to be gaining favour with government and business is the ombudsman. Use of both the Parliamentary Commissioner for Administration and the Local Government Ombudsman has increased in recent years. Cases before the PCA increased from 741 in 1983 to 945 in 1992. Complaints received by the LGO rose from 4,229 in 1987–88 to 13,307 in 1992–93. In March 1993, the United Kingdom Ombudsman Association was established to represent ombudsmen in the public and private sectors, where their numbers have recently proliferated. Private ombudsmen now bestride such areas as the banking and insurance industry. The Courts and Legal Services Act 1990 introduced the legal system's own legal services ombudsman as a final resource for those with complaints against lawyers.

Ombudsmen have, however, their limitations. Cases before many ombudsmen, including the LGO, face increasing delay. The personal attention inherent in the idea makes this almost unavoidable. In addition, many ombudsmen have advisory powers only. They cannot impose a solution on a dispute or mandate the payment of compensation.

## The way forward

The following five parts discuss various developments in other parts of the world as well as what is happening or could happen in England and Wales. The final chapter seeks to bring out the lessons and to begin to chart a way forward.

## References

1 Legal Action Group, *A Strategy for Justice*, 1992, ch 1.
2 Legal Aid Board, *Annual Report 1993–94*, p33. Most law centre funding comes from other sources.
3 Written Answers, *Hansard* (28 April 1994) cols 237–242, and Legal Aid Board *Annual Report 1992–93*. These figures are net of disbursements except in relation to legal advice and duty solicitor fees.
4 Law Society *Annual Statistical Report 1994*, to be published.
5 Bar Council Strategy Group, *Strategies for the Future*, 1990, p18.
6 R Abel, *The Legal Profession in England and Wales*, Blackwells, 1992; The Law Society, *Annual Statistical Report 1994*, to be published; and General Council of the Bar, *Annual Report 1993*.
7 Joint Working Party of the Young Barristers' Committee and Legal Services Committee of the Bar Council, *The Work of the Young Bar*, 1993, p7.
8 Law Society *Annual Statistical Reports* 1988 and 1994.
9 The Legal Aid Board's *Annual Report 1993–94* discloses payment to a total of 8,136 barristers. As at the 1 October 1993, the General Council of the Bar's *Annual Report 1993* discloses that there were only 7,735 barristers in independent practice.
10 *Parliamentary Written Answers (HL)* vol 560, col 100 (30 January 1995).
11 Lord Chancellor's Department, *Management Statement for the Legal Aid Board*, HMSO, 1994.
12 B Onswusah, 'The Technology Leapfrog,' *New Law Journal*, 14 October 1994, p1418.
13 *Annual Statistical Report 1993* p27.
14 Information comes from National Association of Citizens Advice Bureaux *Annual Reports for 1993 and 1994*.
15 D Perry, 'Legal Aid – a suitable case for treatment?', *Legal Action*, October 1994, p7.
16 M Wolfe and J Ivison, *Debt Advice Handbook* CPAG, 1993, p1.
17 R Berthoud, *Credit, Debt and poverty*, Social Security Advisory Committee, HMSO, 1989, ch 3.

18 Lord Chancellor's Department *Management Statement for the Legal Aid Board*, HMSO, 1993, p13.

19 M Cappelletti and B Garth *Access to Justice: a world survey* volume 1, Sijthoff and Noordhoff, 1978, ch 1. See further ch 1 of this book.

20 *Civil Justice Review: Report of the Review Body on Civil Justice*, HMSO, 1988, Cm 394, p1.

21 *Observer*, 29 May 1994

22 Legal Action Group *Response to the Legal Aid Board's Consultation Paper on Multi-Party Actions*, 1989.

23 Legal Aid Board, *Issues arising for the Legal Aid Board and the Lord Chancellor's Department from Multi-Party Actions*, May 1994, p1.

24 Supreme Court Procedure Committee, *Guide for use in Group Actions*, May 1991, p4.

25 Ibid p5–6.

26 Law Commission, *Administrative Law: judicial review and statutory appeals*, HMSO, 1993, section 9.

27 Lord Mackay, *Hamlyn Lectures*, Sweet & Maxwell, 1995.

28 *Looking to the Future: mediation and the ground for divorce*, HMSO, 1993, Cm 2424.

29 Recommendation 48.

30 L Bridges *The Provision of Duty Advice Services in County Courts*, 1991.

31 Council on Tribunals, *Annual Reports* 1988–9 and 1992–93; Criminal Injuries Compensation Board, *Annual Reports* for years ending 31 March 1989 and 1993.

32 Justice, *Industrial Tribunals*, 1987, p7.

33 H Genn and Y Genn, *The Effectiveness of Representation at Tribunals*, Lord Chancellor's Department, 1989, p70.

## Part II

# Issues in legal practice

# Issues in legal practice

The two contributions in this part cover different but related issues. Both Forrest Mosten and Terry Purcell are concerned with reducing the cost of legal services from a common recognition that lawyers are becoming too expensive for a large part of the population. Forrest Mosten refers to this potentially excluded group as people with 'middle incomes', above eligibility for state-assisted provision but unable to afford lawyers' current expectations of their charges. The British equivalent is the 'Minelas' referred to on p8.

Forrest Mosten recounts how he has developed his legal practice in line with unbundling theory, a term taken from the early development of computers. He has striven to strip down legal services into their component parts so that he can offer clients a choice of the full package or parts of it. Terry Purcell also wants to deconstruct legal cases into their component transactions so that he can use the possibilities of new technology to bring down cost. Appended to Forrest Mosten's account is a draft contract which brings home the implications of his idea in a very precise way. He presents a persuasive argument for what amounts to little less than a reconceptualisation of the usual lawyer-client relationship.

Mr Mosten practises matrimonial law in Beverley Hills, California with a largely middle-class clientele. The potential of client libraries and expectation of more do-it-yourself might be less relevant in a more working class or ethnically mixed community. Terry Purcell's article considers technology in essentially two different ways. Technology can be used in the service of the legal profession or, perhaps more radically, directly to impart information and skills to individual people. The potential for both is enormous. A striking feature of the approach of his Law Foundation is its closeness to that of the Legal Aid Board in England when it developed transaction criteria to monitor the quality of legal aid work. Cases are broken down into 45 their components and, in the board's case, measured against standards and, for new technology's purposes, processed into a computer program. The transaction criteria must be the ideal start to a process of computerisation in this country.

The second aspect of his paper is how technology can be used more directly to demystify the law and the legal process so that it helps to empower people in contact with it. He discusses two important projects that have used interactive video – the New South Wales CourtGuide programme, and QuickCourt, developed in the United States. The development and widening distribution of CD-ROM players opens up a fertile field in this area. Information could be made available in public libraries, courts, solicitors' offices and elsewhere to help people with the skills necessary to conduct a case or be a witness; it could forewarn them of procedure in courts and tribunals through showing, as the Australian programme does, short clips of film; it could impart knowledge about the law and even, as QuickCourt does, draft the appropriate documentation. Terry Purcell's paper also deals with other technological developments such as the use of sophisticated telephone systems.

All use of new technology has to be measured against what people actually want. Terry Purcell does not hide the fact that some people would prefer to talk with other people rather than machines. Nor does he conceal the practical problems that arise from the need to update material and repair hardware. Nevertheless, his account provides a stimulating introduction to some of the possibilities to be explored.

# CHAPTER 4

# The unbundling of legal services: increasing legal access

FORREST S MOSTEN[1]

*Forrest S Mosten is a Certified Family Law Specialist and Mediator in Los Angeles, California. He is an Immediate Past Member of the American Bar Association Standing Committee on the Delivery of Legal Services, Chair of the Beverly Hills Bar Association's Alternative Dispute Resolution Committee, Trustee of the National Center for Preventive Law, Executive Chairperson of the International Bar Association's Louis M Brown International Client Counseling Competition, and Adjunct Professor of Law, Pepperdine University.*

Today, law clients are more active, more educated in the art of clienthood, more questioning, and more demanding in the control of the purchase and supervision of legal services. The roles of client and attorney are undergoing major evolution.[2]

Indicative of this change is a handbook recently produced by the California Bar Association expressly 'for lawyers who wish to expand their practice by helping clients help themselves'. An introduction addressed to practitioners sets out the purpose of this guide: 'Potential clients simply cannot afford your services if they are structured in the traditional way. You can help by changing the way you view your professional practice. We propose that you allow these clients to do as much of their own work as they are prepared to do and provide only the advice and support they require to handle their own cases as [litigants in person]'.[3]

Competent lawyers understand that a client is more than the sum total of a 'case file'. Economics, social relationships, emotional and psychological concerns, moral values and pragmatic factors affect how a client can move on with life after a lawsuit is resolved. Unbundling legal services (alternatively known as discrete task representation or alternatives to full-time representation) is a con-  47 ceptual model for the lawyer-client relationship that may transform legal practice in the twenty-first century. Much unbundling already occurs in the law practice. While the examples of unbundling in this chapter focus on private law practice in family law, unbundling can be applied successfully in other areas of law and in a variety of practice settings.

## Definition of unbundling

Lawyers generally offer a full service package of discrete tasks that encompass traditional legal representation. More specifically, the lawyer implicitly or explicitly undertakes the following services on behalf of a client:

- gathering facts;
- advising client;
- discovering facts of opposing party;
- researching law;
- drafting correspondence and documents;
- negotiating;
- representing the client in court.

When a client hires a lawyer, generally both client and lawyer understand (or assume) that the lawyer will perform those services in a full-service package. The lawyer believes (because of training and experience) this is necessary to represent the client's interests adequately. Unbundling these various services means that the client can select the lawyer's services for only a portion of the full and usual package and contract with the lawyer accordingly. Further, the client may, in some cases, specify the depth or extent of each service. For example, a client may want representation at trial but may wish to handle court filings, discovery and negotiations without the lawyer. Conversely, a client may seek the advice and support of a family lawyer in negotiating a settlement, but may choose to self-represent or retain another attorney for actual court representation.

The concept of unbundling is far richer than a mere series of practical suggestions or practice tips. Because lawyers have been schooled in practising with the full package of services, breaking up the package may require major rethinking about the lawyer/client relationship. Consumer motivations are evident in unbundled services. Instead of retaining a lawyer for full-service representation in which total fees often cannot always be predicted accurately, lawyers are becoming available to perform only *part* of the job for *part* of the total fee. The lawyer's hourly rate may not differ in discrete task representation, but the cost to the client will be more controlled and generally far less.

Historically, one can trace the origins of unbundling from the development of legal clinics. When legal clinics were first established in the early 1970s, the merging interests of law clients and a wider consumer movement took hold. The public began demanding more control over accessibility of attorneys, the demystification of legal jargon and arcane court procedures, and alternatives for lower and moderate income people to the high costs of legal services. Private legal clinics provided an elementary form of unbundling through legal consultations for a specific time, length and price without any further obligation on the part of the client or the lawyer. The middle income client's access to a lawyer to consult and obtain significant legal advice for a known, set and reasonable price was a revolutionary development. It received significant and positive consumer reaction.

Building on the success of private legal clinics in the 1970s and 1980s, legal access models, including a variety of prepaid and group legal health plans, navigated the marketplace with mixed results. Due to the growth in lawyer advertising, contingency fees, surplus of lawyers, the proliferation of non-lawyer practices, and the development of publicly funded legal aid schemes, lawyers became easier to find and less unaffordable. This steady trend towards consumerism took a major step forward with the growth of mediation and other forms of ADR. Citizens facing legal trouble were offered the opportunity to maintain increased control over the content of case resolution and the decision-making process. In mediation, opposing parties in a lawsuit negotiated directly with each other and retained the discretion as to whether to involve lawyers and to determine the scope and role of consulting attorney.

Unbundling is, therefore, a natural outgrowth of the twin developments of legal access arising from mass marketing *and* client control stemming from mediation. Cost savings and informed consumer choice are common themes, and unbundling provides both clients and attorneys with an opportunity to utilise these trends in a traditional law office setting.

## Unbundling at work in the legal profession

In order to explore unbundling and its potential for the practice of law in the future, three unbundling models in the setting of family

### Table 4.1: Legal counsellor for the litigant in person

| *Counsellor for the litigant in person* |
| --- |
| Unbundle discrete lawyer services |
| Educate client |
|     Legal rights |
|     Court procedure |
|     ADR options |
|     Spousal communication |
|     Litigation and negotiation strategy and role play |
| Client controls extent and depth of services |
| Coach available for full-service representation |

law are explored in this chapter followed by a discussion of unbundling in other substantive areas and other practice settings.

Litigants in person are the unwanted prodigal children of the court system.[4] Litigants in person often do not speak the language, dress in appropriate costume or prepare adequately. They are unfamiliar faces. They are perceived as unprepared and taking too much court time. Family lawyers and judges (often former family lawyers) too often feel that a litigant in person symbolises one more lawyer being cut out of a fee. These prejudices toward litigants in person may be difficult to alter, but the drumbeat of increasing representation in person, coupled with general lawyer-bashing, makes it economically imperative for lawyers to understand the in-person movement and respond to it positively.

First, the rapid growth of litigants in person replacing lawyers in the USA is remarkable. In 1980, 76 per cent of the cases involved at least one lawyer, generally two. This means that in only 24 per cent of the cases were both parties unrepresented. In 1985, in fully 47 per cent of the cases, both parties were unrepresented. In only a six-year period, the number of families handling their entire divorce without any lawyers doubled! A 1993 study of Maricopa County, Arizona indicated that the trend toward self-representation in family law had not only solidified, but had increased. In 1990, 52 per cent of families obtained a divorce without any attorney, and in 88 per cent of cases, at least one party was either self-represented or had defaulted.[5]

If a lawyer is willing to offer discrete services, clients are generally

more than willing to pay for general services such as legal counselling, help with forms, coaching for negotiations, ghost-writing
letters, preparing settlement documents, and reviewing proposals
and drafts.

In such models, clients are afforded access to a family lawyer and
the opportunities to contract for discrete necessary services. Some
examples are:

– the lawyer can educate the litigant in person about options, inside
  or outside the courthouse, for resolving the case without adjudication;
– the lawyer can advise the client and offer an experienced assessment of proposed settlements or other courses of action. The
  lawyer can role-play strategies and techniques in a simulated
  negotiation to prepare the client for actual negotiations;
– the lawyer can offer a psychological or negotiating profile to help
  the client deal with the other spouse and/or opposing counsel;
– the lawyer can assess legal strengths and weaknesses in the client's
  case, helping the client formulate positions for negotiations and/or
  court hearings;
– the lawyer can provide computer printouts on child and spousal
  support guidelines, develop budgets, analyse available income and
  perquisites, and help the client develop a realistic economic plan;
– the lawyer can refer the client to necessary ancillary professionals such as accountants, therapists, appraisers, or vocational
  counsellors.

In addition to gaining increased legal knowledge, clients often feel
empowered and relieved to handle their own case and control their
own destiny with the assurance that the lawyer can be brought in for
future full-service representation if the client so chooses.

Two major barriers currently exist which limit lawyer availability
for unbundled legal services to litigants in person: malpractice
exposure and pejorative attitudes by lawyers, court staff and judges
toward litigants in person.

## *Malpractice and ethical exposure for unbundling legal services*

In most American jurisdictions, a lawyer who is involved in only part
of the case may still face malpractice liability from a disgruntled
client who later claims that the lawyer should have advised about
rights and obligations that are ancillary to the problem presented by

the client. A lawyer/client relationship (with or without compensation) is usually imputed from the most limited meeting. Lawyers who offer discrete task unbundling to litigants in person do not presently have a safe harbour for incorrect or incomplete advice rendered due to the limited scope of employment. The client may have chosen to retain the lawyer for two to three hours only. Yet when faced with a subsequent tax assessment, omitted asset, or prejudicial custody order, the lawyer may be the scapegoat. Currently, no special legislation or rule of professional responsibility exists to protect the lawyer in a limited engagement.

## Civil immunity and official encouragement for unbundling lawyers

It is proposed that civil immunity be granted from liability when they provide limited-scope discrete-task representation. In California, all third-party neutrals have such immunity due to the public policy benefits of rendering mediation and arbitration services. If the need for ancillary legal services for litigants in person is also in the public interest, then civil immunity is necessary provided that there is a proper lawyer-client contractual foundation limiting the scope of services rendered. Contracts would set forth the nature and scope of the services to be rendered, compensation, and adequate disclosures and waivers.

Regardless of one's view as to granting complete immunity for mediators (even in extreme cases of fraud, conflicts of interest, or self-dealing), it is not suggested here that complete immunity for unbundled lawyering malfeasance should be enacted. Rather, it is proposed that liability should attach according to the contracted scope of lawyer engagement. Just as many jurisdictions provide model attorney-client engagement contracts for traditional full-service lawyering, it is also proposed that such 'official models' be developed for unbundled engagements. A proposed model limited scope for a discrete attorney counseling service agreement is included in the Appendix (see p62).

Until immunity or limitations on malpractice exposure are enacted for task representation, the best protection is the same that exists in all lawyer/client relationships, bundled or unbundled: clear communication and a positive personal relationship between lawyer and client. The risk of malpractice should dwindle if there is clear client understanding as to the scope of legal work to be done and what is *not* being done. Further, clients who *feel* well treated and held in high personal regard by their lawyers are far less likely to sue if problems develop down the line.

## Disincentives for unbundling in the current British legal aid scheme

From my brief exposure to public funding for legal services under current British governmental regulations, it appears that systemic barriers are built into the scheme that preclude or greatly discourage solicitors from offering unbundled legal services.

The essence of unbundling is the solicitor offering legal advice and/or coaching to the litigant in person. It is my understanding that legal aid pays *less* for legal advice under the green form scheme than it does for court representation. Also, there are procedural difficulties for a solicitor to offer continuous advice/coaching to a client who chooses to self-represent throughout the negotiation and/or litigation stages following an initial consultation.

In respect to a solicitor serving as a consultant during mediation, it is my understanding that the current legal aid scheme will not pay for solicitor services if a client selects mediation or other tribunal option as opposed to court representation. Such governmental policy hurts clients in two ways. First, if a solicitor is certain to lose revenue by recommending the use of mediation, it would be the rare solicitor who would make such a recommendation at his/her economic detriment. Second, as ADR options are increasingly 'lawyer-friendly', it is common for parties to opt for mediation *and* have the protection and advice of their lawyers, who are present in the mediation or tribunal session (approximately 50 per cent of the divorcing parties who come to me as a mediator also have their lawyers in the mediation room.)

Finally, I learned of the concern regarding solicitors who have attempted to take a pro-active preventive approach in providing legal check-ups to members of the public who may have undetected (asymptomatic) legal needs. While the motives of solicitors who go out to pubs or shopping malls and obtain several completed green forms in an afternoon may be susceptible to conflicting conclusions, solicitors should be encouraged to provide preventive wellness check-ups and other planning techniques to clients in their offices.

The financial savings to the government in encouraging conflict prevention should be the subject of focused research. I believe that the overall financial benefits of employing preventive techniques to avoid problems and maximise opportunities will far outweigh the payment of fees to solicitors for such preventive work.[6]

## The consulting attorney in mediation

As mediation enjoys increasing acceptance, client participation in one or more forms of mediation inside and outside the courthouse is becoming commonplace. In the early stages of the development of alternative dispute resolution, mediation was viewed primarily as a consensual tool for the two divorcing parties working alone with the mediator. In fact, a major client motivation in opting for mediation was to cut out lawyers and their resulting fees. Since highly conflictual cases stayed in the adversarial court system, cases involving

**Table 4.2 Discrete tasks of consultant during mediation**

| |
|---|
| Advice re substantive rights and legal procedures |
| Assessment of options to litigation |
| Selection of mediator |
| Review and/or negotiation of rules and terms of mediation |
| Determination of client's financial needs |
| Advice re overall objectives and negotiation strategy |
| Monitoring progress of mediation |
| Attendance at mediation sessions |
| Selection and monitoring of outside experts |
| Evaluation of estate planning needs |
| Review mediator progress letters |
| Review legal and financial documents |
| Limited negotiation with opposing party, opposing counsel and mediator |
| Review/draft marital settlement agreement |
| Advice re tax consequences |
| Availability to represent client in court proceedings |
| Preventive planning |
| Legal wellness checkup |
| Monitor compliance with marital settlement agreement |

more amicable couples with generally modest estates were the primary early users of mediation. Most family lawyers generally ignored mediation as a viable option for their clients, rendered cautious warnings, or tacitly remained on the sidelines while their clients attempted to mediate.

As mediation has grown and increased in acceptance, clients with large and complicated estates and/or those with highly adversarial interpersonal dynamics have also begun opting for mediation. In order to meet this demand, more family law specialists are choosing to serve as mediators, either full-time or as an ancillary part of their practices. Since the law office remains the gateway to most legal decision-making, many clients are increasingly seeking the services of lawyers who are knowledgeable in and supportive of ADR goals and practices and who are skilled to represent them throughout the mediation process. Mediation is often favoured because it allows clients the opportunity to order their own lives privately by negotiating directly with each other, basing their settlement on their own goals, needs and values, and using creative possibilities for solutions that go well beyond the limitations of the law and court jurisdiction.

Some clients who use mediation will negotiate the whole of their own deal and only talk with their consulting lawyer after a written settlement agreement has been prepared. Others want their lawyers to be intimately involved in a number of discrete tasks such as helping identify, interview and select the mediator; reviewing and/ or negotiating the terms of the mediation contract; advising or arranging the agenda or procedures; reviewing the progress of each session; coordinating outside experts; negotiating with, and educating, the mediator; drafting, reviewing, and approving any final marital settlement agreement; and generating documents such as deeds, corporation records, and loan applications.[7]

Lawyers and clients are both concerned with keeping control. The submission of a decision to a judicial officer is the ultimate loss of control. Lawyers who want to render unbundled services to mediation clients must be willing to give up some of their customary views of control over the negotiating process, and over case strategy as a whole. Clients seeking mediation often want more power over their own lives; they want to be full and active participants in their cases. In addition, the active presence of a third-party neutral (even non-binding) requires increased accountability on the part of the lawyer to his/her client; the attorney needs to be responsive to the observations, interventions and proposals of the mediator. A skilled mediator may often provide legal knowledge and options to the client that the lawyer may have missed. What at first blush may seem to be loss of control may, in fact, result in more control for both lawyers and clients. In mediation, the result is wholly consensual.

Another advantage of the consulting role for a lawyer is that mediation clients pay their bills. If settlement is reached through consensual mediation, clients tend to have greater satisfaction. Satisfied clients generally pay faster so that fewer fees are written off. Also, because bills do not skyrocket so fast and lawyer work is better understood and appreciated (the client is actually with the lawyer for much of the time billed), accounts do not become so out of control.

Attorneys who sign on for the discrete task of legal consultant in mediation may find greater personal satisfaction and congruence with their personal values than in the bloodletting of a courtroom. A lawyer's belief in the creative opportunities, efficiency, and cost benefits of mediation can often inspire and steady a client to persevere through the often bumpy and painful process. That inspiration and belief alone may help clients achieve satisfactory resolution.

## Preventive action

Preventive law is the conceptual forerunner of unbundling. Preventive lawyers counsel a client, investigate potential legal soft spots and advise a client as to whether the soft spot needs immediate attention.

Table 4.3: The preventive legal health care provider

| SYMPTOMATIC |
| --- |
| Monitor compliance with court orders |
| Provide for future dispute resolution |
| Adjust documents based on terms of settlement |
| ASYMPTOMATIC |
| Anticipate trouble |
| Maximise opportunities |
| Encourage harmonious relationships |
| Regular client legal check-ups |
| Non-litigation calendar to monitor client's life events |

If solutions are required, the preventive lawyer helps the client decide *if* a professional is needed, *what professional* is best suited to treat the problem, and *how* to locate, engage and work with that professional. Therefore, the preventive lawyer is not necessarily the same lawyer who performs the needed services. The lawyer rendering preventive advice might limit work to problem diagnosis and legal counselling. The preventive counselling function may be unbundled from the role of the service provider.

Similarly to mediation, preventive lawyering is more than a service of techniques and practice tips. Preventive law is an attitude that can permeate a lawyer's entire outlook toward clients. As one of its early advocates explained:

> Preventive law presents a different atmosphere. Preventive law seeks, among other things, to forecast future legal trouble. The legal difficulty, if any, has not yet occurred. Future legal trouble does not present as bold a picture as does present legal trouble. Incipient difficulty is not as 'obvious' as is actual difficulty. The practice of preventive law requires that methods be found and used to bring inchoate legal trouble to the attention of the lawyer. Preventive law requires that techniques be available to discover legal trouble early so that incipient legal trouble can be prevented from becoming actual legal trouble.[8]

This preventive approach is particularly applicable in the family law context at all stages of representation. Two of its overriding maxims are that the attorney-client relationship should not end when the file closes, and that the client should never leave the lawyer's office without knowing when the next client-lawyer contact will occur. Some preventive lawyers merely contact the clients and offer them an opportunity to come in for a preventive legal wellness check-up. Others routinely schedule an appointment several months in advance, planned out on an office non-litigation calendar, when no symptoms of legal trouble are yet present.

As clients are accustomed to seeing lawyers only at the later stages of legal disease, client education is imperative to develop this preventive relationship. Some preventive lawyers, including this writer, have installed client libraries in their offices to help with the client education process and for the client to be a collaborative partner in the attorney-client relationship. As the National Center for Preventive Law and other providers are publishing legal checkup questionnaires, the family lawyer now has a ready supply of tools to perform this unbundled service.

Lawyers are overcoming their own reluctance to suggest such preventive advice, particularly as their role evolves to that of a preventive legal care provider. As the client's partner in insuring legal health, the lawyer is expected to advise and diagnose incipient legal trouble – not necessarily to do all the routine work. In turn, clients are learning to view their lawyer as a preventive legal health care provider, a helper and a resource to be consulted with regularity or upon important life events (eg, marriage, birth of a child, retirement).

## Unbundling – beyond family law

Within private law practice, unbundling is, at present, successfully in operation in a variety of substantive fields. A few examples from different areas of law are given below.

### Purchase and sale of property

Lawyers are available to counsel clients as needed in making or accepting offers, drafting and reviewing sales documents, negotiation with parties and/or real estate agents, financial institutions or zoning planning bureaucrats and, of course, handling disputes.

### Wills

With the growth of statutory form wills available in stationery stores and in computer programs, lawyers can offer an accessible, low-cost unbundled review of client efforts. Presently, most people drafting their own will choose to do so alone. However, as the public continues to view the law office as more accessible, in addition to consulting lawyers to draft wills initially, purchasers of commercial wills might be more prepared to see a lawyer to review the will and, at the same time, the client can discuss the need for a durable power of attorney or other estate planning vehicles as well as obtain a legal checkup.

### Commercial disputes

With the proliferation and judicial approval of adhesive arbitration and mediation clauses in consumer contracts, clients can benefit from lawyers who serve as coach and as consultant in these ADR procedures that pre-empt court action. These non-court processes often reduce the need for full service representation.

*Health care and other governmental benefits*

As vital human services increasingly meld private providers, insurance companies, and governmental regulation, lawyers willing to offer unbundled services will be in increasing need and demand. Currently, many hospitals have staff social workers, financial counsellors, and ethicists (to assist patients in voluntary life termination procedures and protect hospital liability) and the opportunity for private lawyers to fill this need should increase steadily.

## Unbundling in other law practice settings

This chapter has focused on the use of unbundling in private legal practice for middle-income persons. However, this concept transfers well in a wide range of settings and other substantive areas ranging from public legal service programmes for the poor to multinational companies.

*Legal service programmes*

Due to a variety of factors, the unmet legal need gap for low income persons continues to grow. Legal service lawyers have long provided coaching to litigants in person who do not qualify for services or when full-service representation is not otherwise available. The major contribution of unbundling to legal service programmes is an infusion of positive client-centred attitudes and utilisation of techniques to improve the quality of self-representation.

As indicated above, many moderate income litigants choose to self-represent for non-economic motives: mainly distrust of lawyers, belief in the do-it-yourself philosophy, and desire for control and reduced conflict. The poor generally self-represent out of economic necessity, not choice. This resignation may be transmitted to legal services attorneys who coach out of desperation rather than inspiration. It is also possible that many legal services attorneys are attracted by the large public impact case and/or are overwhelmed in their representation of their full-service clients. Therefore, many legal service attorneys pressed for time and other demands do not devote sufficient time or thought to improving their service to clients who desire but are rejected for full service representation.

Some illustrations of the infusion of the unbundling approach in legal services are:

– client libraries in legal services offices or in nearby public libraries such as the Legal Information and Access Centers (LIAC) in

Sydney, Australia sponsored by the Law Foundation of New South Wales;

- lawyer coaches who are trained in and assigned to unbundled service departments within the legal service office;
- referral procedures for affordable coaching services in the private sector.

## Corporate legal departments

The last decade has seen shifts in the allocation of functions between in-house lawyers and outside law firms. After a surge in growth of in-house legal staff to maintain control and lower costs, the trend appears to have reversed, with added vigilance by companies to monitoring and limiting fees as well as encouraging use of ADR to cut corporate legal costs. The values and techniques of unbundling can meet these corporate goals in a number of ways. Case referral criteria can be refined so that referral of a case may not be limited to a single practitioner. Firms may be hired solely to strategise a plan; consult for a settlement possibility; offer second opinions; or other limited-scope functions. There may be corporate self-help through routine legal audits and compliance reviews to determine the legal health of a company. Legal education of management by outside firms and consultants may teach conflict resolution and prevention in regulation of compliance, intra-company policies and relationships with counsel, competitors and governmental entities.

## Governmental agencies

As national and local government are often a nation's largest employer as well as the largest purchaser of goods and services, government officials have a built-in incentive to reduce the costs of government legal bills. Unbundling may be explored by government agencies in monitoring legal costs in some of the following ways. Dispute resolution may be assessed by independent settlement specialists (on staff or private consultants) before any governmental agency files a lawsuit or regulatory proceeding; prevention of future litigation should be considered routinely before promulgation of new government regulations; advice can be given in prevention of inter-governmental disputes; public awareness and understanding of government activity should be assessed routinely and used as criteria for continued funding of governmental progress; the promotion of a society's legal health should be measured and assessed (much like a population census) and a national legal health strategy developed and implemented.

## Conclusion

Unbundling is an emerging trend in America's legal environment which developed in response to consumer demand and has taken hold with surprising tenacity. Unbundling meets the public's demand for increased availability of legal services in a user-friendly environment at lower cost. By modifying its emphasis from court-room advocacy to adaptable dispute avoidance, management and resolution, family lawyers are responding to actual legal needs as they have evolved in society. The exploration, development and commitment to unbundling offers the family law bar the opportunity to redefine and develop new legal service products well into the twenty-first century.

## References

1 This article contains excerpts from Forrest S Mosten, 'Unbundling of Legal Services in Family Law Practice,' *American Bar Association Family Law Quarterly*, vol 28, no 3, Fall 1994, p421. The author wishes to express special gratitude to Louis M Brown (the 'Father of Preventive Law') for his friendship and inspiration and to Jody Grotzinger for her gentle and tireless support.

2 See James Podgers, 'Rediscovering the Middle Class', *American Bar Association Journal*, December 1994 at 61. This article profiles eight innovative practitioners who serve a middle income clientele.

3 State Bar of California's Legal Services Section's Standing Committee on Legal Services to Middle Income Persons, *The Pro-per Counselling Handbook*, 1994.

4 See Justice Donald B King, 'No Justice in Family Court', *California Lawyer*, vol 14 no 11, November 1994 at 43.

5 See Bruce D Sales, Connie Beck and Richard K Hahn, *Self-representation in Divorce*, 1993; and see *Responding to the Needs of the Self-Represented Divorce Litigant*, 1994, American Bar Association Standing Committee on the Delivery of Legal Services.

6 See Thomas Gonser and Forrest S Mosten, 'The Case for National Legal Health Strategy', 12 *Preventive Law Reporter* at 32, Summer 1993.

7 See Penelope Eileen Bryan, 'Reclaiming Professionalism: the lawyer's role in divorce mediation', *Family Law Quarterly*, vol 28, no 2, Summer 1994 at 177.

8 Louis M Brown and Anne O Kandel, *The Legal Audit, Corporate Internal Investigation*, 1990 at p5.

# Appendix

## Model limited scope engagement attorney counselling service agreement*

This Agreement is made between Attorney and Client as designated at the end of this agreement.

1. *Nature of Agreement.* This Agreement describes the relationship between the Attorney and Client. Specifically, this Agreement defines:
   (a)  the general nature of Client's case;
   (b)  the responsibilities and control that Client agrees to retain over the case;
   (c)  the services that Client seeks from Attorney in his/her capacity as attorney at law;
   (d)  the limits of Attorney's responsibilities;
   (e)  the immunity from civil liability granted to the Attorney for services not provided by Attorney;
   (f)  methods to resolve disputes between Attorney and Client;
   (g)  the method of payment by Client for services rendered by Attorney.

2. *Nature of Case.* The Client is requesting services from Attorney in the following matter:

........................................................................................................

........................................................................................................

3. *Client Responsibilities and Control.* The Client intends to handle his/her own case and understands that he/she will remain in control of the case and be responsible for all decisions made in the course of the case. The Client agrees to:
   (a)  co-operate with Attorney or office by complying with all reasonable requests for information in connection with the matter for which Client is requesting services;
   (b)  keep Attorney or office advised of Client's concerns and any information that is pertinent to Client's case;

(c) provide Attorney with copies of all correspondence to and from Client relevant to the case;

(d) keep all documents related to the case in a file for review by Attorney.

4. *Services Sought by Client.* The Client seeks the following services from Attorney: [*Check off services to be provided.*]

(a) Legal advice: office visits, telephone calls, fax, mail, E-mail;

(b) Advice about availability of alternative means to resolving the dispute, including mediation and arbitration;

(c) Evaluation of Client's self-diagnosis of the case and advising Client about legal rights;

(d) Guidance and procedural information for filing or serving documents;

(e) Review correspondence and court documents;

(f) Prepare and/or suggest documents to be prepared;

(g) Factual investigation: contacting witnesses, public record searches, in-depth interview of client;

(h) Legal research and analysis;

(i) Discovery: interrogatories, depositions, requests for document production;

(j) Planning for negotiations, including simulated role playing with Client;

(k) Planning for court appearances made by Client, including simulated role playing with Client;

(l) Backup and trouble-shooting during the trial;

(m) Referring Client to other counsel, expert or professional;

(n) Counselling Client about appeal;

(o) Procedural assistance with an appeal and assisting with substantive legal argumentation in an appeal;

(p) Provide preventive planning and/or schedule legal check-ups;

(q) Other:

................................................................................................

................................................................................................

5. *Attorney's Responsibilities.* The Attorney shall exercise due professional care and observe strict confidentiality in providing the services identified by a check mark in Paragraph 4 above. In providing those services, Attorney SHALL NOT:

(a) Represent, speak for, appear for, or sign papers on the Client's behalf;

(b) Provide services in Paragraph 4 which are not identified by a check mark; or

(c) Make decisions for Client about any aspect of the case.

6. *Method and Payment for Services.*

(a)  *Hourly fee.* The current hourly fee charged by Attorney for services under this agreement is as follows:

Senior Partner:        $____
Junior Partner:        $____
Associate:             $____

Unless a different fee arrangement is specified in clauses (b) or (c) of the Paragraph, the hourly fee shall be payable at the time of the service. . . .

7. *Resolving Disputes Between Client and Attorney*. . .

8. . . .

9. *Civil Immunity for Counsel.* Client hereby waives any right to prosecute a claim of professional negligence against Attorney for any service not specifically set forth by a check mark in Paragraph 4 of this Agreement. The Client grants to Attorney complete immunity from civil liability arising from all aspects of the case not specifically undertaken by the Attorney. Client acknowledges that many attorneys will not offer limited scope representation due to the fear of malpractice claims by clients who later find or believe that the limited scope representation was not sufficient to protect the client properly. The Client acknowledges that retaining an attorney for limited scope representation is a consumer choice by the Client based on Client's desire to lower fees, maintain client control and belief that the Client can competently handle all issues and tasks not specifically undertaken by Attorney. Client agrees to bear the full risk of any damage caused to the Client due to the Client handling the matter without specifically requested legal services from the Attorney. Such waiver of malpractice claims does not extend to those services which the Attorney undertakes to render on behalf of the Client as instructed by the Client. The Attorney represents that the law firm carries Professional Liability Insurance as required by the State Bar of California.

10. *Statement of Client's Understanding.* I have carefully read this Agreement and believe that I understand all of its provisions. I signify my agreement with the following statements by initialing each one:

I have accurately described the nature of my case in Paragraph 2;

I will remain in control of my case and assume responsibility for my case as described in Paragraph 3;

The services that I want Attorney to perform in my case are identified by check marks in Paragraph 4. I take responsibility for all other aspects of my case;

I accept the limitations on Attorney's responsibilities identified in Paragraph 5 and understand that if I make mistakes in handling my own case, I have granted the Attorney immunity from being sued for professional malpractice. This means that I cannot sue and/or recover from the Attorney regardless of the damage I might suffer;

I shall pay Attorney for services rendered as described in Paragraph 6.

I will resolve any disputes I have with Attorney under this Agreement in the manner described in Paragraph . . .;

I understand that any amendments to this Agreement shall be in writing, as described in Paragraph . . .

I acknowledge that I have the right to consult another independent Attorney to review this Agreement and to advise me on my rights as a Client before I sign this Agreement.

Dated:_____ Signed:_____
                         CLIENT

Dated:_____ Signed:_____
                         ATTORNEY

\* The Model Agreement is derived from an agreement contained in Stephen Elias, *Lawyers' Guide to Being a Coach* (Draft, 1994) for publication by California State Bar Committee of Delivery of Legal Services for Middle Income Persons. This updated version will appear in Forrest S Mosten, 'Coaching the Pro Se Litigant', *ABA Compleat Lawyer* (awaiting publication). Copyright Forrest S Mosten 1994.

# CHAPTER 5

# Technology's role in access to legal services and legal information

TERENCE PURCELL

*Terence Purcell has been director of the Law Foundation of New South Wales since 1972. During this time, the foundation has established a reputation for being one of the most innovative funding bodies in the world in the field of legal services. Its projects have ranged from the creation of a Public Interest Advocacy Centre and a Communications Law Centre to the foundation of a research centre on civil justice. Working with the NSW's Attorney General's Department, it funded an interactive video programme known as 'Court-Guide'. More recently, it has commenced an ambitious project aimed at making lawyers more efficient. This involves an electronic network linking solicitors' firms with each other, the courts and other sources of information.*

The catalyst for legal change is the placement of information in electronic form and the widespread availability of information as well as the means for accessing, communicating and manipulating information in this form. These technologies constitute the seeds of legal change. . .

M Ethan Katsh

## The challenge of survival

Small law firms, that is, those that have been the traditional providers of personal legal services, are facing extinction. To survive they must face the challenge of achieving a greater level of economic viability through greater efficiency and an expanded client base. Only by meeting this challenge will we see, in the Australian legal services context, greater accessibility for people with ordinary legal problems. Government funding is not the solution to increasing access to legal services. In Australia, at least, we have to find ways of handling low economic value legal problems at a price the community can afford, and in a way service providers can get a reasonable return. The profession's steady diet of high economic value legal matters is drying up as firms become more competitive and traditional clients more discerning. While there are many forces pushing the profession in this direction, there is a real chance that many in the profession will not be able to move with the times and they will be overwhelmed and made irrelevant to the great bulk of the community.

*Tomorrow's Legal Services*, a recent report of the Law Foundation of New South Wales, has addressed this issue of the survival of many in today's legal profession and has concluded that solutions can be found. It is clear that the management techniques of many firms can be improved but simply making the old methods a little more efficient is a short-term response. There are three related challenges: the need for research and development in relation to legal practice and the market for legal services; the need to understand and better manage innovation as a business tool; and the need to realise the benefits of technology. In comparing this situation with that of many other industries we realise how far behind the legal services industry is. We have all seen that competitively successful industries and business enterprises usually have the following attributes:

− a commitment to research and development;
− an understanding and management of innovation; and
− the good application of available technology to re-engineer processes and not simply to automate the old ways of doing things.

While all three issues are relevant to the legal profession, the crucial element which will make meaningful change possible is technology. However, before exploring that issue in more detail the issue of the adaptability of the profession requires consideration. Unlike other professions such as engineering and medicine, there is no profession-wide initiative or support driving the development and adoption of new approaches to service delivery in the legal profession. The legal profession does not have a commitment to innovation and lacks an understanding of, and skills for, innovation processes. As with market research and other essential industry information, it is primarily left to individual practices to identify and develop new approaches, relying on their own limited skills and resources. Similarly the profession appears slow to adopt and adapt advanced management practices. There is a big gap between well managed and not so well managed firms.

The development of new approaches to service delivery such as 'unbundling' and 're-engineering' inevitably raises issues about the accepted norms of the profession. Issues of rules of professional conduct, statutory regulation and relations with the courts and government agencies are also raised. Such issues cannot be dealt with at the level of individual practices but must be dealt with on an industry-wide basis in the broadest possible sense. This observation also holds true for approaches which involve changing the role of lawyers, for example, from adversary to mediator. It is almost impossible for individual practitioners to expand or change their role on their own. As indicated earlier, even if the profession is willing to adopt new ideas, there are many individual practices which lack the management skills and resources to do so.

The Law Foundation's central position, with links to all key stakeholders in the legal system, has given it an opportunity to be the catalyst for promoting the need for a commitment to innovation among those stakeholders and, in particular, the practising profession. The foundation is committed to developing initiatives which are designed to help the legal profession adopt new and different ways of providing services more rapidly, more cost effectively, and to wider markets than they have previously served. As noted earlier, technology is the key to the required transformation. A description of initiatives taken by the foundation follows.

## Clever systems

In the late 1960s, lawyers around the world began to wonder how computers could be applied within the legal system. Early versions of word processors were being marketed by IBM, which was building on its near stranglehold, in Australia at least, of the office equipment market through its ubiquitous 'golf ball' electronic typewriter. By the early 1970s IBM magnetic card machines heralded the arrival of the word processor. Some lawyers in the late 1960s were also interested in another IBM development, namely its STAIRS software program, which, for the first time, harnessed the power of computers for the purpose of storing and retrieving full-text legal information. This United States development stimulated considerable interest in Canada, the United Kingdom and Australia and led fairly quickly to various legal databases being established.

For reasons which are not difficult to understand, greater success was achieved with this new information technology in North America than elsewhere. Certainly the experience in Australia with developing full-text databases containing legal information has enjoyed limited success largely due to lack of a tradition of cooperative activity and the inability of commercial interests to understand the profession's real needs.

Nevertheless, progress has been made in applying technology in other ways. Besides widespread use of word processing applications, headway has been made in developing comprehensive computerised accounting packages for law firms, which have gained fairly wide acceptance. There are also some interesting moves in the areas of sophisticated document preparation and litigation support, although mainly within the larger firms. Such firms are also developing their own precedent databases, some of which are computerised. Furthermore, computer-based office management systems offering more than accounting have come to the fore in recent years but would appear to be tailored to servicing the needs of larger law firms and thus do not meet the needs or budgets of smaller firms.

Another area of law and technology yet to penetrate the mainstream but which has intrigued some, mainly academic, lawyers, is the development of so-called expert systems and other applications of artificial intelligence. Despite some interesting experiments over the last 20 years, little has emerged which can be readily used in day-to-day legal practice. This is an area of particular interest to the foundation, as we believe it shows the greatest promise of being a catalyst in transforming the way lawyers provide personal legal services.

One of the major disadvantages facing practitioners in most law firms is the start up time it takes to get a matter underway. This is unlikely to be a problem if the practitioner is dealing with a matter which is of frequent occurrence and which is within his or her speciality. If it is not something that falls into this category, considerable time may be expended on researching the law and procedure, and because the lawyer is uncertain, he or she may approach the matter with considerable caution, all of which adds up to considerably more time being taken, and thus cost, than would be taken by a specialist. Traditionally, in Australia, many smaller practices simply refer such matters to counsel for advice, which sees both cost and time being added in a different way.

We believe that a new model of legal services delivery will only occur if we, the profession, can take advantage of current technology to speed up the way such matters are handled. One of the barriers preventing the ready availability of such software outside areas of high volume work such as conveyancing, personal injury litigation, debt collecting and will preparation, where quite a few products are available, is the substantial cost involved in developing more sophisticated and intelligent matter-handling software.

Transaction analysis, breaking the process down into its component parts, will provide the first step towards developing such programmes which capture applied knowledge. The results of such analysis, combined with expert system software, will quickly guide practitioners through unfamiliar procedures. One immediate benefit of this approach will be to reduce the start up cost of undertaking cases. The service in question can, therefore, be offered at a cheaper price. A good start has already been made in applying transaction analysis in the United Kingdom by the Legal Aid Board with the various transaction criteria, although it is using it for a different purpose. There is only a relatively short step to computerising the management of matters using those criteria.

The foundation is working with the developers of an Australian expert system software program which they recently created for a number of federal government agencies. We believe their system, E-STATUTE, can be applied in helping practitioners gain access to a range of different information sources when dealing with a matter. In one government agency, an application of this software has enabled a wide range of information, previously only available in different locations and in different forms, to be brought together in one computerised database, allowing decision-makers the opportunity to make almost instant review of the relevant legal, factual and expert information and relate it to the particular claims lodged with the department.

The foundation has direct links with the developers of this ground-breaking program through a grant made some years ago to enable the development of an earlier version of the program to assist welfare rights centres to deal quickly with clients with complicated social security appeals. With their legal centre backgrounds, the developers are very keen to see their expert system software applied to a wide range of legal issues.

The overall goal will be to provide practitioners with the ability to deal quickly and cheaply with a much wider array of client problems than has been feasible to date. However, while expert system technology is the key to such developments, we do not underestimate the cost of developing prototypes. This, of course, is the reason why software developers, both from within the profession and outside it, have been reluctant to move beyond the 'boilerplate' document-preparation, information-retrieval and lower-level matter-tracking systems which are still today's leading edge technology for the legal profession.

# First Class Law – the network

Another initiative identified by the foundation as being a likely catalyst for a wider use of technology within the profession is the role a communications network facility might play in addressing the need for the profession to transfer electronically documentation between firms and between legal institutions and their clients more efficiently. No matter where our investigations and deliberations concerning technology went, we kept coming back to this issue as the key matter that needed resolution if significant breakthroughs were to take place allowing for a new legal services delivery model.

Electronic communication with other practitioners and with government departments and agencies was among the subjects mentioned most frequently in discussing the problems that practitioners face in gaining full advantage from their investments in technology. To be able to use currently available hardware and software technologies in exchanging information, data and documents is considered to be one of the conditions precedent to the profession being able to maintain viability in the environment of heightened competition and consumer demand. The quick dissemination of data, information and other necessary materials will make the profession more responsive to market needs.

Solving this problem stood out as being the one most likely to have a significant effect on the way solicitors provide their services in the future. E-mail is already being used internally for communication and, in some cases among medium- and large-size firms, for client communication. Given the wide and diverse spread of the Australian profession, the issue we faced was: 'Is there a way of linking the already installed computer capacity of practitioners in a way that builds a communications bridge for the profession?'

A communications highway linking the profession will help with usage of, and provide access to, data and information needed in everyday legal practice pursuits. This will start a process of change in the profession through the better use of available technology and will empower the profession to seek out better ways of providing legal services. As a minimum, it will encourage the management process of reviewing how tasks could be performed in future. As a direct benefit, clients ought to get better quality service. Depending on how many practitioners could be brought on to the network and how user-friendly any such network highway could be made, the dynamics resulting from this could be considerable.

Because the new communications technology permits almost limitless access to information, the wider community would also be able to gain access to much of the information which has, in the past, only been available to legal professionals. They, in turn, can become better informed about the legal market and be in a better position to make decisions about whom they will use for whatever legal problem confronts them and what is likely to be involved. The predictions of writers as diverse as M Ethan Katsh[1] and Howard Rheingold[2] are becoming realities in commercial, professional and domestic environments alike.

A communications highway will cause the synergetic effect of opening up the significant knowledge base of the profession, while fostering a change in the orientation of those who choose to embrace the possibilities created for them. It will add real strength to the future positioning of the profession in modern society as a provider of information and legal services. We were aware that attempts both here and overseas had been made to establish networks, but with limited success. This was probably due to the fact that technology with a level of utility that would lend itself to answering lawyers' communications needs was not previously available.

We believe that for a network to be successful in the legal environment it must:

– have a low cost of entry and of use;
– be capable of access by a large number of potential users;
– provide relevant information in quantity and quality;
– address the fundamental needs of lawyers;
– be responsive to market demands;
– be secure;
– be versatile in the documents that can be transferred and read;
– be very simple to use;
– use the services of those already in the market;
– not invent a system for lawyers when other industries have already solved the problem; and
– have standards for handling all forms of communication.

A communications highway with these features is now possible, and the foundation's First Class Law Network meets this standard. Following the foundation's decision in early April 1994 to adopt the strategies outlined in *Tomorrow's Legal Services*, the establishment of the network facility was seen as the first priority. Thus, following the identification and testing of a suitable network software program, the foundation has established a pilot network which will operate until early 1995 before becoming fully operational.

The network software being used is FirstClass™, an electronic mail, conferencing and on-line system developed by SoftArc Inc in Canada. FirstClass Client, which is the software actually loaded onto a user's computer, is freely-distributable software for connecting to FirstClass file servers by network or by modem. The software can handle communication between Macintosh and Windows PCs, and between different word processing programmes, such as WordPerfect and Microsoft Word. Before finally choosing the FirstClass approach, the foundation's computer consultant and the writer visited SoftArc and ensured that it fully met the foundation's specifications and expectations in relation to ongoing support. As FirstClass was to be the cornerstone of the network, we believed that this additional investment was justified.

The foundation will operate and support fully the network during the pilot developmental phase. We see this as a key element in the process of learning about the real information and communication needs of the profession. Additionally, the foundation is in an ideal position, as a statutory-based independent organisation within the legal environment, to work with practitioners and relevant information-providers to ensure that the information sources available through the network are relevant. The foundation's emphasis on increasing the profession's efficiency and accessibility and non-profit status removes the need to take short cuts which might lead yet again to disillusionment within the profession about this new technology.

The network offers the following facilities:

- electronic mail
- document transfer with other firms and agencies
- public and private conferences
- bulletin boards
- online 'chat' facilities
- access to information databases.

The strength of the software is particularly evident in its ease of use for document transfer and electronic mail. This has been demonstrated by several users who have conducted negotiations about contracts over the network. One very complex negotiation concerning the acquisition by the Law Society of New South Wales (the solicitors' professional association) of an entire new computer system was concluded in a matter of days, compared with a previous similar process of personal meetings and using fax and courier to exchange drafts of documents, which took more than three months to finalise. Considerable use is already being made of the network to transfer documentation between solicitors and barristers and in some instances between solicitors and their clients. The lawyers involved in a Royal Commission have established their own secure 'conference' which they use to transfer documentation between one another. Another function of the software which has attracted considerable interest is the history feature. This allows each party to track the progress of communications between them. A high level of security is also an integral part of the transfer process and it satisfies the most stringent test.

In terms of the type of information databases to be provided, we are currently able to provide the New South Wales Supreme Court's daily lists. Other daily court lists will follow shortly, as will the ability to file documents. As well as increasing the number of users, we will be constantly adding new sources of information throughout the pilot. In this regard, we will be keen for practitioners to suggest information that they feel it would be useful to include.

We have advised the profession that to participate in the network pilot, they will need to be using either Macintosh or Windows software in their office. They will also need access to a modem, preferably operating at 9600 baud or better. During the current pilot phase, the foundation is making the network software available to users free of charge. Users are able to obtain a copy of the user manual for $10 (about £4.75), and training and online support processes are being developed. At the completion of the pilot, software and access charges will be introduced, with the latter being based on analysis of usage statistics during the pilot phase. We will be seeking feedback about the accuracy of our assessments of usage from those participating in the pilot, as well as their views about charging rates and what can be supported.

Agreements are being settled for both users and service providers, such as database managers or suppliers of various services to the profession. We have already hired an experienced network manager who will assist with installations, customer support and maintaining the network. While we are consciously taking our time to get things right during this pilot phase, we formally launched the network at a legal industry trade show (LEXPO) in late October 1994. A business plan has been formulated which sees the foundation maintaining the network operating on a commercial level around the 'user pays' principle.

We have also retained a business development consultant to help us plan marketing and the ultimate day-to-day management, as we are becoming concerned that we will be overwhelmed by demand to participate in the network. Every time information goes out about it, we get more requests from the profession wanting to become users. The Law Society is becoming enthusiastic about getting all Presidents of its Regional Law Societies involved and also to put a range of membership related information on bulletin boards.

The pilot phase has made us more confident that the network will be a vital agent for change within the legal profession. Already there is evidence of willingness to upgrade equipment to ensure participation on the network, which is complemented by an endless flow of suggestions from the pilot users as to the best way of tailoring it to their needs by adding new databases and creating new bulletin boards and conferences.

A timely forecast comes from another American scholar, Ronald V Staudt, a law teacher at Chicago-Kent Law School, who sees communication technologies as the key to the future. When addressing a conference in June 1993 on the future of the legal profession, Staudt said: 'The advances in the use of litigation support databases, expert systems, automated practice systems and artificial intelligence are developments of computational power. There are indications that the communications capabilities of the computer will be more important in changing the practice of law during the next ten to twenty years.'

## Access through telephony

Another major access initiative of the foundation has been its support for a free telephone advice and information service operated by the Law Society of New South Wales' Community Assistance Department. Experienced solicitors were hired with funds from the foundation and they handled a wide range of telephone inquiries covering many different issues such as, 'Do I have a legal problem?', 'Where can I find a solicitor?', 'Is my solicitor overcharging/handling my matter the right way?', as well as 'How do I make a complaint against my solicitor?'

Public response to this service, initiated in the early 1980s, was dramatic and by the early 1990s over 80,000 calls a year were being handled, but at a considerably growing cost. There was also some

concern about the efficiency and quality of the service. Consideration was given to finding an alternative method of conducting such a
service. We were aware that similar services elsewhere had been
replaced by a combination of recorded information on a large range
of legal topics, with an operator referring those needing a solicitor
to someone in their area. In the case of complaints about their
solicitor, these were referred to the relevant professional association
or regulatory body.

A review of the department indicated that it was likely to be more
cost-effective for its service to become technologically based and we
investigated the alternatives with the assistance of consultants. The
result was a decision to develop a new computer-based system using
technologies which have only recently come of age. At the time of
writing, the new system had only been going for six months, so it is
a little early to judge its impact. A similar service operated by the
Law Institute of Victoria has been in existence for almost five years.
It claims to have had no drop-off in the number of callers once it
switched to recorded information, and they received relatively few
complaints about not getting to talk to a lawyer.

Telephone advice is 'flavour of the month' in Australia. A typical
example is the service offered by Legal Expense Insurance Ltd (LEI),
a company established by the Law Foundation and a large general
insurer, GIO Australia, to develop and market legal expense insurance. LEI offers those covered by its policies a telephone advice
service, which it has found extremely beneficial as a way of getting
very early notice of potential claims under the policy. The telephone
service has enabled LEI to adopt a preventative role with many
matters. A number of other insurers have offered telephone advice
services to their policyholders, and legal advice is one of the major
services promoted. Entrepreneurs have now entered the field and one
company has invested heavily in computer-based equipment to
enable it to service a large number of inquiries on behalf of insurers.

Similarly, Telecom Australia has only recently offered a service
allowing information providers to sell their services over the phone
at premium rates. This service, known as Infocall, is aimed at large
institutions and professional groups such as lawyers and is different
from the much cheaper recorded information services already being
offered, referred to as 0055 Services. These services range between
35c per minute (budget) to 70c (17–33p) per minute (premium) and
cover the gamut of human interests including astrology (with 14
separate offerings) to foreign news services (11 offerings including
Cambodian and Macedonian news).

The more expensive Infocall listings include 'Racing Fields and Forms', with about a dozen providers, some offering recorded information with others offering only a fax service. There is only one listing in the latest directory (August 1994) for Legal Services – Law Hotline (live answer 190 226 3510). However, several other entrepreneurs and lawyers are planning to use this latest telephone technology, with one now advertising a charge rate of $5.00 (£2.40) per minute, which is comparable with the hourly charging rates of many of the larger Australian law firms. Only time will tell whether services offered at this price have any real prospect of market acceptance, particularly when quality will be so difficult to monitor. Despite reservations which many in the profession have about such services, they do represent an innovative approach to reaching new markets for legal services.

On a lower level, telephone technology has reached a stage when it is now possible for even small law firms to have access to some very sophisticated communications systems. The Law Foundation itself is in the process of installing a new telephone system. We have decided to use it in order to see how far its capacity can be developed for small firms. We have been offered several systems which complement the latest telephone hardware, including voice mail and other fairly widely used telephone technologies in the large commercial and professional environment.

We have selected an NEC NDK 9000 system connected to 12 exchange lines with 20 digital and eight analogue extension circuits, two of which will be dedicated fax lines. Complementing this 'hardware' will be Orator Voice Processing Software which promises 'fast, efficient communications, allowing a smooth flow of information between internal extensions and from inbound callers to various personnel and departments; this frees your staff from repetitive, time-consuming transactions by automating routine operations, thereby reducing operating costs and human resource requirements'. Key features of the software which attracted us to it and which we believe have the potential to increase productivity in even small offices, include 'Automated Attendant'.

Orator answers the incoming call and sends a greeting message. The caller can then enter an extension number or a single digit selection from their own phone. The Auto Attendant will then transfer the call to the required extension or department. This saves valuable reception time and frees personnel for other duties. Another valuable feature which we are anxious to explore in the context of a professional office is Voice Mail. This facility allows incoming callers to receive an announcement or leave a message in private Voice Mail Boxes. In a law office context, Orator is then able to notify the solicitor (the mail box owner) that a message has been received, allowing prompt response. We see this as a very useful feature for a busy professional keeping in touch with clients, with messages and information able to go both ways. Such transfers can also be made secure so that only the lawyer and his/her client can hear messages.

Other features which are offered by Orator include Audiotex, an Interactive Voice Response (IVR) application in which a caller answers a series of multi-choice questions to access the information required. This feature is at the heart of the Law Society's Community Assistance service and we are keen to explore its practicality in a law office context and the uses to which it can be put to assist clients. Another interesting feature is the capacity to leave bilingual voice messages, with the system programmed to offer voice prompts in different languages. While such software was developed for large institutions and has been applied to great effect, the issue for us is to test how effective it can be in a small professional office. We will be working with our Orator supplier to tailor the software in a way that would greatly enhance the typical small law firm's communications with its clients. We see great potential for sophisticated applications of the recorded information facility which can help the client become much better informed, not only about what the particular law firm can do for him or her, but also about progress of the matter as well as instructions about things the lawyers would like the client to follow up.

It has been long established that lawyers and clients who work closely together get better outcomes. We believe applying the latest telephone technology has an important part to play in that process. The price of such technology is falling and it would appear to be simple to use for both the service provider and the client.

## Public access technology

The foundation has also pioneered the development of public access terminals using interactive video technology. In 1983, the Board of the Law Foundation concluded that magistrates' courts represented a forgotten area in the New South Wales court system. Such courts had been operating under various names since the time of the first white settlement in Australia when Governor Arthur Phillip was appointed Justice of the Peace for New South Wales by the British

Government. While the modern magistracy dates from the turn of the century and the central role played by justices' courts dates from the colony's earliest days, the latter has left indelible marks on the public perception of these people's courts. Unlike in the United Kingdom, the magistrates are all full-time 'stipendiary magistrates'. Thus, when the foundation decided that it was time to put the spotlight on local courts (as they are now called), it did so because of the very large number of cases dealt with by the courts throughout the state and the very large number of people who had some dealings with their 100 locations throughout the state. Well over 800,000 cases a year were being dealt with at that time, requiring many hundreds of thousands of people coming into local courts each year. Needless to say, a heavy police presence in the court precincts also added a further level of intimidation to an already pretty inhospitable environment.

Against this backdrop, we decided to raise with the Attorney General's Department (responsible for their administration) the question of doing something about improving the courts' 'user-friendliness'. Our aim was to see whether we could develop a model court which would set new standards for all local courts in terms of the way court users were treated by creating a much stronger consumer focus as well as increased efficiency in the court's operations. The department had long been concerned about these questions and readily agreed to participate with the foundation in developing a new model court, and over the next six or seven years a two-court suburban complex was transformed into the 'Model Court'.

One of the key aims of the Model Court Project was to use the opportunity to explore the application of modern communications technology. So besides rather prosaic technological applications, such as computerising the court office and developing a voice-activated system for recording proceedings which also incorporated better sound distribution, there were several major high tech innovations. One involved the use of interactive video technology to provide a wide range of helpful information to assist those unfamiliar with the court, and the other, the development of public information video display terminals, not unlike those used at airports and railway stations for arrivals and departures. In the court situation, the intention was to give those attending court information about the current status of the court list and an indication of how long it would be before their case was heard.

Interactive video offered a way of addressing one of the major problems facing the local court system, namely the provision of relevant information and advice to the public attending court. Limited staff resources were available for this purpose and the changing times highlighted the need to assist individuals properly, particularly prior to any unrepresented court appearance. Our response was the development of CourtGuide, an interactive video information system, as a major Project initiative. CourtGuide is an early example of multimedia technology and consists of several basic components. It married laser disc technology (similar to a large CD) to a normal PC which controls the information appearing on the screen. The PC's database also contributes text information which complements the video replays sourced from the laser disc via a separate video disc player (again not unlike a large CD player).

Initially, the foundation funded the creation of 10 CourtGuide systems, which were located in court foyers in specially built kiosks. Later another 20 CourtGuide systems were acquired with a further allocation of $173,380 (£82,560) by the foundation and located at Local Courts throughout the state. Regrettably no programme of ongoing maintenance was put in place by the department, so that only a few CourtGuides are currently operational. However, we have recently negotiated with department officials the institution of a system of regular maintenance. The only downside is that the video content of the system is becoming dated and it is clear that there may only be a relatively short life left in the video disc. When the original video disc was made it cost well over $100,000 (£47,600) in 1987, although it is probable that a replacement multimedia system using CD ROM could be made at a much reduced cost.

CourtGuide was a first for Australian courts and perhaps elsewhere, and it is normally found in the court foyer, where it permits users access to a wide variety of information in a series of simple, screen-directed steps. The user selects the required area of information from a menu through the video display terminal's touch-sensitive membrane. The database contains video material in docu-drama format, with re-creations of court proceedings, presenters who address the user, and static images or text coupled with voice-overs. Users are able to retrieve information covering a variety of contingencies, ranging from appearing as a witness, or commencing or defending proceedings, to answering police charges and potential penalties. Listings of community agencies and court facilities relevant to users' more particular purposes are also included. These can be regularly updated by keyboard without interfering with the body of the database.

The 'onboard' computer monitors use of the system and the frequency with which users refer to individual areas. Future modification and development of the directory can be attuned to evolving community needs. Having regard to the promise of the CourtGuide technology, it was agreed as a matter of policy that the initiative would be monitored and independently reviewed. Therefore, in July 1990 consultants were retained to collect information from court users on the CourtGuide system. The consultants were to test the adequacy of the level and range of information provided presently by the system; the access and acceptability of the system to the serviced community; the category of users and non-users of the system; and the impact of promotional campaigns.

The report of the survey found:

The majority of visitors to the court on list days are there for the first time and require assistance and encouragement to use the system.

Young males are more likely to adapt to this type of information provision than other sex/age groups. They tend to hang around the system after use. Other groups would use the system if there were more signs, publicity and court staff to assist them.

The consultants observed that the enquiry desk was crowded whilst CourtGuide was not being used. One user remarked that the system 'was much quicker than waiting at the enquiry desk'.

Once a system is up and running and people do begin to use it, they increasingly use secondary menus and expect more detailed information. Users appreciate the immediacy of the information, but they need to know the limitations of the system as well as (have) handouts of screen notices.

The consultants concluded that the installation of the CourtGuide interactive video information system requires considerable back-up support to encourage usage. They said courts tend to have a majority of people who are unfamiliar with their surroundings and are unlikely to take the initiative of using resources provided by the court.

The standard of performance of the CourtGuide was found to be very high and this was based on standards of the assessment of other systems. Users confirmed that the system was well presented and provided the information they were seeking. The lack of a sound control was a problem for users. The consultants suggested that while we live in a technological age, it seems that the majority of people prefer human contact and need reassurance and encouragement to get used to the system.

Overall, we were pleased with the public's response to CourtGuide.

However, a high frequency of system malfunctions, compounded by a lack of experienced technical support from a multimedia specialist, meant that it was difficult to maintain all 30 CourtGuides. This was complicated further by the fact that the first 10 CourtGuides were controlled by a Sony-developed operating system which rapidly became obsolete and unsupported. Despite the maintenance problems common with systems using the latest technology, there is enough evidence to suggest that CourtGuide multimedia interactive technology can play an important role in providing public access to such information about the court process and the law.

Recent American developments have added considerable value to the CourtGuide-type information system through including the capacity on similar systems to accept the user's personal details and produce documentation ready for filing in court. This has been done for the Arizona Supreme Court through the QuickCourt system developed by North Communications of Santa Monica, California. QuickCourt has been, by all reports, a great success in helping do-it-yourself divorce applicants. It demonstrates how innovative use of the latest information technology can be an excellent way for courts to demonstrate a genuine desire to become much more consumer-oriented.

North Communications, which has supplied QuickCourt and other public information access systems to a range of federal, state and local administrations, confirms our experience that public access terminals can play a valuable and cost-effective role in public administration. The strength of such technology is in providing a neutral source of easily understood (multilingual, if required) information about what may otherwise seem to the public to be complex and incomprehensible procedures with which they are required to comply. One Sydney law firm specialising in communications law recently developed a highly sophisticated 15-minute promotional (and educational) multimedia CD ROM (including video, text and sophisticated graphics) married to a music soundtrack, for around $10,000 (£4,760). With CD ROM technology for both making and playing discs falling dramatically in price, this would appear to be the direction in which this type of interactive system will move, without the level of outlay required to create our original CourtGuide.

## Conclusion

The foundation has been interested in applying computer-based technology to increase access to legal services for over 20 years.

We played an important role in the mid–1970s in the development of Australia's first operational computerised legal information storage and retrieval system which we developed in conjunction with IBM Australia Ltd. Prior to that, as the foundation's representative, I was a member of the Computerisation of Legal Data Committee, established by the late Senator Lionel Murphy, Federal Attorney General, and which mapped out a strategy for developing a national system. Eventually, the Federal Government established a system which has had limited impact on the delivery of legal services and certainly never fulfilled Lionel Murphy's dream of a highly automated and computerised legal services industry. Despite this setback, the foundation has been in the forefront of supporting innovative use of technology, and, for example, all New South Wales Law Schools have student computer laboratories partly funded by the foundation.

After many false starts (partly due to the inadequacy of available technology, most of which never lived up to the marketeer's promises), it is clear from what has been described in this chapter that there is now a convergence of information technology and workable solutions. To many of us who have been looking to technology to help the legal services industry out of its nineteenth-century style of operation and into the late twentieth century, the long road through the desert of technological disappointments appears to be at an end.

Only time will tell whether we are entering the promised land. Nevertheless, it is time to rely on different media for transacting and recording our laws and legal processes, media that allow for more justice, equity, flexibility and accessibility than do laws written in 'stone'.

## References

1   M E Katsh, *The Electronic Media and the Transformation of Law*, Oxford University Press, New York, 1988.

2   H Rheingold *The Virtual Community: Homesteading on the Electronic Frontier*, Addison-Wesley Publishing Company, 1993.

# Part III

# Legal education and information

# Legal education and information

Three contributions are included in this part of the book. Gordon Hardy describes public legal education and information in British Columbia and, in particular, the work of the People's Law School, Jan Newton discusses the work of the Citizenship Foundation and John Richardson details his experience of law centres. Aspects of legal education and information are, however, also discussed in Terence Purcell's chapter on the use of new technology (p66), Forrest Mosten's on unbundling theory (p47) and Indira Jaising's description of the functions of India's unimplemented Legal Services Authorities Act (p184).

Australia and Canada have been leaders in this field. *A Strategy for Justice* described the work of Quebec's Commission des Services Juridiques, which provides another example of innovative use of various media to communicate information about the law. One of the conclusions of that book was that we should accept that legal education and information must form part of any coherent programme of publicly funded legal services.

These chapters confirm the importance of that argument but they also take it further. It is apparent that both the Citizenship Foundation and the People's Law School see their roles as wider than simply providing information about the law. They recognise that this leads inexorably to discussion of, and training about, the wider role of the citizen, hence the name of the former organisation. The video, *Where's Winston?* referred to by Gordon Hardy in ch 6, tells the story of a boy who commits a gang murder and ends up in prison. It is accompanied by teaching materials designed to develop beyond discussion of the law into consideration of behaviour.

Legal education and information can, therefore, take various forms. It has a major role in training for citizenship. Indeed, the reason why British Columbia has, historically, placed such emphasis on this area of work may be the large number of new immigrants from the countries of the Pacific rim that it has had to absorb. The Citizenship Foundation has shown a similar analysis of the value of legal education in its concentration on young people.

There remains, however, a need for straightforward information about aspects of the law. Developed societies are increasingly complex, increasingly based on legal rights and duties. Since ignorance of the law is no excuse, the state needs to take responsibility for the general legal knowledge of all its citizens. General information may, however, be poorly targeted. People are more likely to want legal information when they need it. This has been where the work of the law centres has been particularly important. John Richardson's examples of their use in housing cases in relation to the poll tax show how valuable it is to consider legal cases as also giving rise to a need for information and education. At the ultimate, it may be possible for solutions to be based more on an education model than on the model of classic legal casework. For instance, some Australian Legal Aid Commissions deal with people seeking child support or going through bankruptcy by holding classes rather than allocating lawyers. This leads to a greater emphasis on skills and empowerment.

British legal aid systems have never paid much attention to information and education because they were developed specifically as a way of funding lawyers to take cases. These chapters suggest that legal education and information should be accepted as integral to the provision of publicly funded legal services. Particularly striking is the close connection between the kind of work undertaken by the People's Law School, for which it receives significant government recognition and funding, and that of the Citizenship Foundation, which struggles for both.

# CHAPTER 6

# Pioneers in public legal education

GORDON HARDY

*Gordon Hardy, a former journalist, is executive director of the People's Law School in Vancouver, British Columbia. This has a staff of 13 and is funded by a variety of government and other agencies to provide public legal education and information.*

Canada inherited English laws and the English legal system, and the principles on which they are based. But, along with Australia and America, we have, over the past 25 years, devised a new element in our shared justice systems. That new element is public legal education. It is one thing to make just laws, and, of course, we expect compliance with our laws, citing the often-repeated phrase that ignorance of the law is no excuse. But can we really say that? If we fail to educate those people subject to the law about their rights and responsibilities under the law, can we in fairness expect their compliance? When we talk about the rule of law being the underpinning of our legal systems, can we truly expect the respect of those ruled for a web of laws which, if anything, becomes more complex and intrusive in the lives of ordinary citizens every day?

In Canada, the answer is no. Over the past quarter century, federal and provincial governments, as well as private organisations, have increasingly recognised that it is a duty of law-makers to provide information and education about the laws they make to those whose lives are affected. The reasons why they have done so are several, as are their methods of providing public legal education.

## The People's Law School: pioneers in public legal education

The People's Law School was the first sole-purpose public legal education organisation in Canada. Created in 1972, it pioneered many of the public legal education activities now routinely practised 89 throughout Canada. Its relatively small staff of 13 people manages to provide information about the law to a great many British Columbians, some 111,000 in 1994 alone.

The school does this in large measure through free law classes organised in about 60 towns and cities scattered throughout a mountainous province the size of England, Scotland and Wales combined. It also distributes large numbers of plain language pamphlets on law-related topics to targeted readerships. It produces videotapes on topical legal subjects, largely for use in schools, such as the prize-winning *Where's Winston?* aimed at preventing gang recruitment of youth at risk. It also stages a major theatre exhibit once a year on legal topics ranging from wife assault to discrimination in the workplace. Its target audiences range from the general population to specific ones – such as the poor, immigrants, youth and senior citizens. Its vision of public legal education is a broad one which encompasses social issues such as family violence, poverty, human rights and crime prevention.

## Growth of a national network

Since its inception 22 years ago, the People's Law School has been gratified to see similar organisations spring up in every province and territory in Canada, many through the intervention of the Federal Department of Justice. Each of these organisations uses a combination of free law classes, school programmes, pamphlets, videos or telephone lines to bring information about the law to people in their own jurisdictions. As in British Columbia, specific audiences in each jurisdiction require specific kinds of information delivery. There is also a national organisation called the Public Legal Education Association of Canada, as well as a national electronic bulletin board called Access to Justice Net.

The public legal education network in Canada is financially and politically supported by the Federal Department of Justice, provincial ministries of the Attorney General, other government ministries, and a variety of private foundations. In addition to the sole-purpose public legal education organisations like the People's Law School, many other entities such as branches of government, neighbourhood associations, women's groups, and organisations serving the immigrant population, now embrace the idea of public legal education as one of their important functions. For example, immigrant settlement agencies see the provision of information to immigrants on the legal aspects of housing, employment and parenting in their new country, as an important element of immigrant settlement. We work closely with these organisations in co-sponsoring public legal education activities in places where immigrants feel comfortable and, where possible, in the language of the immigrant group. A third of our staff, in fact, are drawn from immigrant communities and speak five important immigrant languages. In learning of our experience with the growth of public legal education programmes in Canada, elements may emerge that are transferable to the United Kingdom.

## Modest beginnings

The People's Law School began when a group of idealistic law students at the University of British Columbia decided that knowledge of the law should not be the monopoly of lawyers. They felt that the law – and its institutions – were, in fact, the property of the people. Knowledge about the law ought to be available to ordinary people. This was almost a quarter century ago. Some people thought that ideas such as these, along with televised parliamentary proceedings and uncooked vegetables, were radical innovations. Yet the idea was not really a new one. As early as 1894, Woodrow Wilson told the American Bar Association that 'every citizen should know what law is, how it came into existence . . . and how it gives to society its fibre and strength . . .' Even Viscount Hewart's much-quoted 1923 dictum about justice being seen to be done implies that those doing the seeing know enough about the principles of justice to make the conclusion that the needs of justice have been met. And so, with the enthusiasm of the day, our founding members created a tiny charitable organisation whose first office was the chairwoman's basement.

## Key elements of success

Many organisations never grow beyond the basement stage. Public legal education, however, was an idea whose time had come. But even timely ideas fail to take root unless people – through hard work and good will – create fertile conditions. For the People's Law School to flourish, we had to cultivate a number of key conditions. This turned out to be the case in other Canadian jurisdictions as well, and it may well also be true in the British context.

These elements, each of equal importance, were:

– a rationale for public legal education;
– support among the people, ie, a desire to learn about the laws affecting their lives, as well as support from community groups;

- the creation of an independent, credible public legal education organisation;
- support from local lawyers and their professional association, the Bar, as well as from the bench;
- financial assistance from government and foundations to fund the core costs of an independent legal education organisation; and
- demonstrated outcomes.

Each of these elements needs some elaboration.

## Rationale for public legal education

There are many – and sometimes conflicting – arguments in support of public legal education. Indeed, we in the Canadian public legal education movement have spent a good part of the last 25 years or so arguing about just what public legal education is, or should be, and whom it serves. It is an axiom of our respective justice systems that everybody is presumed to know the law. From this presumption flows another. People will conduct themselves in accordance with the law. If they do not, they face a strong possibility that they will find themselves involved in either a criminal or civil action, at considerable public expense and personal risk. The paradox is that we know that the primary axiom that everyone knows the law is false.

And yet, people *do* need to know the laws affecting their lives regarding a host of day-to-day activities. These include life in the family, schooling, the workplace, the marketplace and even what happens to their property and young children should they die. Simply put, people need to know their rights and responsibilities in order to function effectively in our legally complex society. Another axiom is that a fair justice system is one which provides equal access to justice for all people. Legal aid is one important way we ensure that those without money still have reasonable access to the justice system through the services of a lawyer. But it is also important that people have equal access to knowledge about their rights and responsibilities under the law. The same argument was advanced by the Legal Action Group in *A Strategy for Justice*.

Public legal education can also be seen – along with legal aid – as part of an overall package of legal services which enhance people's access to justice. In British Columbia, our legal aid plan has long recognised the need to provide legal education and information services alongside legal aid. Perhaps the most compelling reason for this is that a properly-informed person may be able to avoid or solve the problem without the need for costly legal representation. Effective public legal education, while representing a fraction of the costs of legal aid, may actually reduce legal aid costs. Also, unlike legal aid which is usually restricted to the relatively few qualified to receive it, public legal education benefits a far wider group of people. In a recent *Review of Legal Aid Services in British Columbia,*[1] the author concluded: 'A legal services system which does not suitably integrate effective information and education services into its client services strategy will inevitably waste expensive professional resources and will not provide clients with the most effective service possible.'

Accordingly, the provincial body responsible for legal aid, the Legal Services Society, has since the 1970s operated a public legal education programme as an adjunct to its legal aid activities. This consists of a law library and legal resource centre for the public, a publishing wing, and a grants programme to organisations like the People's Law School to operate community-based public legal education programmes. The Society has for years also operated a popular schools legal education programme. This is an important supplement to the high school law course offered by the Ministry of Education. A variety of organisations, such as the Law Courts Education Society, also produce additional law-related educational materials which are used by high school teachers of law, history, business and English as a second language (ESL). In a province like British Columbia, where immigrants constitute one in five of the population, the legal information needs of immigrants cannot be underestimated. We produce an extremely popular ESL introduction to the law. This booklet, now in its fourth edition, introduces ESL students to fundamental notions of our laws and legal system while they are learning English.

## Support among the people and community groups

Of course, all this activity would be quite academic unless there were a desire among the people to learn about the law. A host of academic studies performed in Canada, the United States and Australia, directly or indirectly, provides proof of public demand for public legal education. But such an approach would, indeed, be academic. We know far more concretely that British Columbians want knowledge about the law from the simple fact that many tens of thousands of them voluntarily attend our free law classes. Last year, for example, more than 22,000 people attended our free law classes and speaker placements. Indeed, we calculate that from the beginning to the middle of the 1990s, more than 100,000 people will have attended our classes. A further 50,000 will have attended our Justice Theatre dramatisations. Countless more will have read our pamphlets, heard our radio interviews and seen our video programmes. Why do so many people voluntarily give up their evenings to learn about often complex and difficult legal subjects?

Public legal education programmes need to address issues *as they arise in people's lives.* The vast majority of those people who access information about the law do so because they have a specific problem or concern in a given area of law, *not* because they have a general interest in the law. The preface to *A Strategy for Justice* observes that legal needs in civil law areas – such as family disputes, personal injury, debt and unemployment – tend to get overlooked in favour of the criminal justice area. We concur completely. In our experience, most people seek legal education and information in civil and administrative law areas such as family law issues, work-related problems, landlord and tenant law, consumer complaints, property law, bankruptcy and wills and estates. Only relatively few are interested in criminal law matters for the simple reason that only relatively few have a brush with the criminal law. Our experience is that people will take advantage of opportunities to learn about the law but only if those opportunities are perceived by people as meeting their own legal information needs. That is why it is of critical importance to work with community organisations in correctly assessing community needs. These needs differ from one community to the next.

At the People's Law School, we work with approximately 217 community organisations scattered throughout the province. These organisations are very diverse, and include public libraries, community colleges, neighbourhood houses, schools, women's centres, senior citizens' groups and immigrant settlement organisations. A rural community may be interested in learning about reforms to the gun control laws. Urban dwellers may be interested in landlord and tenant law. High school students about to enter the workforce will be interested in employment standards regarding minimum wages, statutory holidays and other work-related issues. The issue of date rape has recently emerged as one requiring urgent attention. Certain topics – such as family law, housing and wills and estates – appeal to all groups.

In order to be effective, a public legal education programme needs to be driven by the needs of the community. That is why we say that the People's Law School operates on a community-needs model. Community-driven public legal education ensures that programmes meet needs identified by the people in a community, and not some other agenda. This is very important. It is also important because it leads to community support in the most practical of ways. Our organisation, for example, has only one headquarters with a set of offices, a classroom and meeting rooms in downtown Vancouver. Yet 90 per cent of our events occur elsewhere, in libraries, churches and schools scattered across large distances. We need our community partners not only to target services, but also to provide on-the-ground practical assistance, such as locating a venue, arranging for local advertising, and to host the event itself, very often hundreds of miles from Vancouver.

Community-based legal education can provide specific communities with the knowledge they need to push for law reform. Much of public legal education, of course, only describes the law as it is. There is a tendency for public legal education to get stuck at merely describing and legitimising the status quo. We all know, however, that the law frequently needs a push in order to stay in tune with emerging needs and values in society. A vigorous public legal education movement can provide law reform with a healthy impetus. In part, this occurs by giving community members knowledge about the law as it affects their lives, and how it can be improved. But this approach also validates the community's knowledge about a given issue, rather than simply making its members passive consumers of knowledge about an all-powerful legal system.

Throughout the existence of the People's Law School, we have worked with several disadvantaged communities in our society, notably people with physical disabilities, senior citizens, assaulted women and people with AIDS/HIV. The effect of this is that these communities, armed not only with greater knowledge of the legal system but also with a stronger sense of their own expertise in the area, can now press for reforms in the law and policy which will alleviate their disadvantage. This has been called *community legal education*, a better description for much of what we do than *public legal education*.

Community legal education is exciting. It is interconnected with the driving social issues of our times. When seen as a factor in addressing issues like unemployment, poverty, poor education and family violence, it has a crime prevention component, since we know these conditions are associated with criminality. In Canada, concern about crime and its root causes has led us to point out to government that public legal education can be a factor in reducing the root causes of crime, and should be seen as a form of crime prevention in itself. This raises the very important question of who provides community or public legal education.

## An independent, credible organisation

We place considerable importance on the independence of the People's Law School. The organisation, a registered charity, is an independent body. Its board of directors consists of a judge, several lawyers, a chartered accountant, a social psychologist and a notary public. They are evenly divided between men and women, several have been recruited from cultural minorities. They are elected to the board on an annual basis by the Society's small membership.

While we value the good relations we have with various government ministries, we have never wanted or accepted a government representative on our board. This would undermine our independence. It is precisely our independence from government which permits us to aid and abet social activism which a government-dominated body would find difficult to countenance. And, again, it is our independence from government which gives us credibility in the eyes of the communities with whom we work.

Canadians are no longer inclined to believe what their government tells them. They tell us frequently that they are more inclined to believe an independent, non-profit organisation because we are not perceived to be in the government's service. Given our dependence on government support, it is sometimes difficult for us to live up to this perception. In reality, it is hundreds of volunteer lawyers – each with his or her own very individual views – who most often impart legal education and information to participants in our events. Their opinion on how the legal system operates with regard to any particular issue can range from conservative to radical. We believe this diversity of opinion is a further strength of our independence. No party line prevails; instead, each volunteer instructor brings forward his or her own views based on experience. Participants, for their part, are free to accept or reject the instructor's view, which they sometimes do volubly. The Legal Action Group has correctly called for the creation of an *independent* legal services commission whose purposes, among other things, would be to provide legal aid and education to the public.

Our reliance on volunteers from the legal profession is yet another reason why we must remain an independent, charitable organisation.

It is rare indeed that people will volunteer for government, or for a body perceived to be operating on behalf of the government. However, the tradition of volunteering for community organisations remains strong in Canada. Each of the 960 free law classes, speaker placements and training workshops on legal topics offered in 1994 was taught by a volunteer professional, mostly a lawyer. Depending on your view of lawyers, this may or may not seem astonishing. But it is true and one of the keys to our success. You can imagine how the involvement of so many volunteer professionals enhances the cost-efficiency of our programmes. We estimate that the in-kind support from these volunteers is worth about £500,000 per year.

## Support of the Bar and bench

In our experience, gaining the support of the legal profession in British Columbia was another critical element in the eventual success of the People's Law School. In the early days, there was the occasional grumble that public legal education was a threat to lawyers' livelihoods or that a little legal knowledge was dangerous thing.

In the main, however, young, progressive lawyers were quick to support us as volunteer instructors in our classes. It satisfied their social concern that access to the law be available to ordinary and often disadvantaged members of the public and did no harm to their practices to receive exposure in their communities as civic-minded volunteers.

As a volunteer, the lawyer has an opportunity not only to render a public service but also to overcome barriers of mistrust which might prevent a member of the public from taking his or her own problem to a lawyer. Ideally, public legal education can prevent legal problems. When they do occur, however, a responsible public legal education programme directs people to obtain qualified legal help from a lawyer. We have never advocated a do-it-yourself approach to serious legal problems.

Today, the People's Law School operates with a database of about 900 volunteer lawyers or about 12% of the 7,000 practising members of the British Columbia Bar. Our volunteer-based programmes could not survive a week without the continued goodwill of lawyers throughout the province. Early on, we obtained the formal endorsement of the Law Society of British Columbia and the BC Branch of the Canadian Bar Association for our programmes. Similarly, the judiciary has actively supported our efforts. Over the past decade, we have made it a practice to have a judge on our board of directors. Our chair for the past two years has been a provincial court judge.

## *Funding for independent public legal education groups*

Naturally, from the beginning, it has been a struggle to obtain funding for our organisation from governments and foundations. For the most part, we have been blessed in Canada with federal and provincial governments who have shared our views that public money should be spent on public legal education, and that independent, community-based public legal education organisations are in the best position to identify and meet local legal information needs.

In most Canadian jurisdictions, there is a law foundation which pools the interest income on lawyer's trust accounts. Most are mandated to fund public legal education efforts, as well as legal aid, law libraries, legal research and other law-related projects. We were lucky in British Columbia in that the first law foundation in North America came into being 25 years ago in 1969. Only a few years later, the British Columbia law foundation agreed to provide core funding to the People's Law School, and does so to this day. Around the same time – the fiscal year 1973–74 – the provincial Ministry of the Attorney General also agreed to provide core funding, which it has continued to do to this day, despite several changes of government.

Over the years, we have worked to create a diversified funding base. This currently consists of three federal ministries, four provincial ministries, two foundations and one legal services society. Our headquarters are located in rather palatial settings, far beyond our means, in the downtown core of Vancouver, courtesy of the City of Vancouver.

Keeping all these balls in the air requires constant attention and can distract us from programmes. On the other hand, a diversified funding base avoids the precariousness of putting all your eggs in one funding basket, however tempting a sole benefactor might appear. It can also be a useful argument against a single funder who wishes to call the shots.

It also represents our success in persuading ministries other than the obvious ones that it is their business to fund public legal education. We only receive funding from two obvious law-related ministries – the Federal Department of Justice and the provincial Ministry of the Attorney General – but we have also received funding from ministries responsible for immigration, women's equality, human rights and citizenship. Funding sources for public legal education are not, therefore, necessarily restricted to government branches concerned with law-making and law-enforcement. Here in Britain, you may also have to look to more than one funding source to achieve viability.

## Demonstrated outcomes

Funders will eventually look for demonstrated outcomes. However, like many services – especially those of a preventative nature – it is frequently hard to demonstrate the outcomes of public legal education. How can we prove, for example, that someone avoided a problem through legal education? How can we prove that someone managed their problem better as a result of learning the legal aspects of it?

There is, however, a body of research which indicates that public legal education has positive effects both for groups and individuals. Research has been conducted in several countries, including the United States, Canada and Australia. Two examples come from our own experience.

In 1980, the 12th year of our existence, the Federal Department of Justice conducted an external evaluation of our free law classes.[2] The survey produced some satisfying conclusions, including these: 83 per cent of class participants surveyed felt they had a better understanding about the role and function of the legal system in Canada; 92 per cent felt they knew more clearly when to consult a lawyer about a legal problem; and 92 per cent felt they had a better chance of avoiding future legal problems.

More recently, the Department of Justice and the Ministry of the Attorney General of British Columbia commissioned a research project in which bilingual interviewers conducted face-to-face interviews with 300 people from five immigrant communities.[3] This research project – more qualitative than quantitative in nature – found that immigrants are keen to learn about the laws of their new country but face barriers caused by language, lack of time due to family and work, and lack of information about where to seek legal information.

One of the research objectives was to measure the degree to which legal education and information programmes play a role in immigrant settlement and adaptation. Half of the respondents had participated in our public legal education programmes. The researchers discovered that participants not only found the experience helpful in gaining information about specific legal issues, but a number reported that their sense of isolation and alienation as immigrants was reduced by their increased knowledge of Canadian laws.

## Conclusion

If the desire is to build a public legal education network in the United Kingdom, there is already a large body of research on which to draw. I have briefly cited only two of many studies which suggest that public money spent on public legal education is money well spent. Similarly, in Canada, the United States and Australia, there is a wealth of experience upon which to draw. I have presented the experience of but one organisation in Vancouver. The British experience must be different, must be unique to that country. But some portion of our experience will, I trust, be useful in the United Kingdom.

## References

1　Tim Agg, 1992.
2　Dr Dale Rusnell, *An Evaluation of the Vancouver People's Law School Distance Delivery for Public Legal Education*, Department of Adult Education, UBC, 1980.
3　Dr Brian Burtch and Kerri Reid, *Discovering Barriers to Justice: First Generation Immigrants in Greater Vancouver*, 1994.

# CHAPTER 7

# The Citizenship Foundation and publicly funded legal education and information

JAN NEWTON

*Jan Newton is a former teacher and now the chief executive of the Citizenship Foundation. One of her major interests has always been to make young people, especially women, more aware of their potential to contribute effectively and to influence the wider society. Her particular responsibilities at the Foundation include developing schools' involvement with mock trial and youth parliament programmes, a project to establish links with newly democratic countries and work in Northern Ireland and Eire. She is a member of the Council of the Hansard Society for Parliamentary Government.*

Little is done involving others in our daily lives which is unaccompanied by consideration of legal rights and duties and yet no instruction in them is provided as a regular part of education.
*Final Report of the Royal Commission on Legal Services 1979*

The Citizenship Foundation celebrated its fifth birthday in October 1994. It was established by Andrew Phillips, a London solicitor, on the fifth anniversary of the setting up, also on his initiative, of the Law in Education project from which it grew. That imaginative and pioneering project, largely funded by the Law Society, had already developed a major resource to help schools to be more effective in preparing students to know and understand their rights and responsibilities as citizens.

But the evidence was that people, especially young people, had little sense of citizenship in that they felt increasingly unable or unwilling to be involved with their communities or society at large. There was a growing gap between citizens and law-makers and enforcers. The level of ignorance and apathy seemed to deepen as the law reached into more areas of daily life in a more complex    101 way. It was generally viewed as restrictive and threatening: rarely as enabling and protective.

## Law in Education

Addressing these issues through seeking to increase legal awareness had been the main purpose of the Law in Education project and its work demonstrated that law-related education in schools is one, potentially extremely effective, way of achieving it by not only knowing what the law says and when and how to use, or indeed not to use, it, but, crucially, trying to engender commitment to justice and the rule of law by developing a better understanding of the values underlying the law. Why is it necessary for a society to have laws? How do you judge if those laws are fair and just? If they are not, how do you change the law in a peaceful and democratic way?

The first publication from the Law in Education project, *Understand the Law*, for 14–16-year-olds, has been bought by a quarter of all secondary schools. It is now being revised and updated for a new edition in 1995. Teachers welcomed it as having a wide appeal across the ability range and for providing a stimulus for discussion and involvement, especially from students normally very reluctant to contribute. Its approaches appeared to combine useful knowledge with the kind of issues which pupils found helpful in clarifying their thoughts about difficult concepts like justice and society. What is more, they enjoyed learning about the law and found it 'real'.

## The Citizenship Foundation

So, in 1989, the same year as the publication of *Understand the Law*, the Citizenship Foundation was set up to build on this work. The organisation continues to grow steadily. It employs six full-time staff and one part-timer and plans to take on more staff in the immediate future. It also has some valuable voluntary help in running a number of projects. The Law Society, together with a modest trust, remains the core funder. Other funding is attached to the twenty or more projects currently running.

The Foundation's stated purpose is to enable people of all ages, but especially the young, to become more effective citizens by developing their capacity to understand social, moral and political issues and to make critical judgements based on a concern for democracy, justice and the rights of others. Over the past five years it has developed a range of projects directed to fulfilling this purpose. Increasing legal awareness, in the broad sense indicated, remains a central theme and a key route to achieving the wider aims. Being a 'legally competent' person should involve an appreciation of the values underpinning the law. In a pluralist society, the law must be seen as a compromise between differing viewpoints. Knowing your rights under the law should make you aware of your legal duty to respect the rights of others. It should also make very plain when the law is no help at all.

The Citizenship Foundation can perhaps claim the main credit for introducing law-related education to the curriculum and a share in the responsbility for the establishment of education for citizenship – certainly the recognition of its value and importance. In *Curriculum Guidance 8*, published in 1990, 'The Citizen and the Law' was one of the key sections to be covered by schools. The central concerns of citizenship education are the rights and responsibilities of citizenship and respect for values such as justice and the rule of law. It concerns people's relationships with each other and with small and large groups in society. Curriculum materials have now been produced for 11–14-year-olds, with funding from the Law Society and the National Curriculum Council, the body overseeing curriculum development at the time the project was set up. *Living with the Law* has three books covering issues such as offending behaviour, school rules, environmental protection, the role of the police, the duty of care, and compensation and damages.

*You, Me, Us!*, a primary school pack, has recently been developed with teachers, trainers and police school liaison officers with funding from an enlightened section of the Home Office. Several difficult issues of moral and social responsibility are tackled, some of which, such as theft, have a definite law-related dimension. Since its publication in May 1994, 6,000 schools have taken it and it is clear from the extremely positive response and specific requests for training that there is a huge unmet need in this area.

Materials for adults, *Can They Do That?*, are to be published in the spring of 1995. Included are sections on access to justice, dealing with professionals, citizenship rights and exclusion, and lobbying. They are intended to combine knowledge, understanding and potential for action and are designed to be used by a wide range of adults including those on access courses, those in basic education and possibly those in a less formal community setting. There are plans to adapt some of these materials for 16–19-year-olds, probably within some kind of accreditation framework. A project has already begun to produce classroom resources for the same age group, based on the European Convention on Human Rights and cases brought before the European Court of Human Rights.

We are also producing some law-related curriculum resources for secondary school students with special educational needs, both in mainstream and special schools. This is part of the overall aim to develop more resources in citizenship education for groups who are in the greatest need of building their self-confidence and self-esteem through an extension of their skills and understanding.

## Trial competitions

The effects of these curriculum initiatives on the level of legal awareness are difficult to measure and the foundation is proposing to undertake more detailed research. The evidence from teachers, however, is of a very positive response from students, with those using them showing a demonstrable increase in the skill and confidence required to make their own judgements about legal, moral and social issues. At a practical level, this can most obviously be seen in the Bar mock trial competition, now in its fourth year. Schools prepare a team of students to take on the role of barristers, witnesses, defendants, juries and court officials. Specially written cases are presented to 'real' judges in 16 Crown Court complexes around the country. Each of the schools taking part is assigned a barrister to help them prepare and to give them moral support on the day.

This is not designed to produce the lawyers of the future. It is intended to give school students, most of whom have never been in a court before, a proper feel of how and why the legal process operates in the way it does, at least at one level. In addition to the many lawyers who give up a Saturday to take part, judges of the final have included the Lord Chief Justice and the Lord Chancellor. This signals some awareness and concern about the need for the law to have a more human face. Follow-up questionnaires certainly illuminate the extent to which each group involved has a stereotyped view of the other. Judges are 'surprisingly human' and students 'unexpectedly skilful and courteous'.

An exciting, potentially enormous, and vastly important expansion is planned in the area of mock trials for younger students, using magistrates' courts and supported by the Magistrates' Association and the Lord Chancellor's Department (LCD). A successful pilot has been run for this junior mock trial competition for 11–14-year-olds.

Such trials will eventually be organised all over the country and involve magistrates, local solicitors and police officers. Students would be asked to hear cases and make decisions in discussion with an experienced magistrate. Familiarity with such courts would be more representative of the reality for most people of the contact they are likely to have with the law during their adult lives.

## Other initiatives

Some examples include those below.

### A young offender project

This programme is concerned with looking at the fast-growing problem of young people who have had direct experience of the criminal law and the courts. Negative feelings and attitudes towards the law are magnified many times in those young people who are caught breaking it. So far, the project has run some group discussions with young offenders using existing materials and some which have been specially developed. We hope that this will encourage greater moral awareness and help to correct what is often a distorted view of the law and society. In addition, by increasing the self-confidence and self-esteem of the offender they might engender a deeper understanding and empathy for those affected by the offending behaviour. The materials are being tried out by a number of probation services and intermediate treatment centres.

### Solicitors' twinning scheme

This is another attempt to bring practitioners and school students closer. It involves Linklaters & Paines, the City firm which funds the legal research assistant post. The project is in its early days but seems to have great potential for making skills and knowledge, particularly of trainee solicitors, available to teachers. The idea is definitely not to give careers advice but to help teachers use law-related materials, often our own, in a relevant and skilful way from a legal viewpoint.

### BUZZ

Outside the curriculum and the formal school setting, there are several other projects which are directly aimed at extending understanding of the process and substance of the law. To try to meet one of the clearest objectives of the Foundation, some of these programmes are aimed at those whose quality and experience of citizenship, especially in relation to the law, is particularly poor: the less academic who have been largely ignored in educational initiatives. The magazine *BUZZ*, which went to schools at a hugely subsidised price for five issues, covered some profound current issues in a popular way, making use of cartoons and design. This format and approach is one which could be used extensively if more resources were available.

## Youth parliament competition

Many schools also take part in the Motorola youth parliament competition to increase students' understanding of making and changing the law and to develop participative skills. They regularly involve 200 or more of their pupils across the whole ability range. Members of Parliament across the country take an interest in this and give practical help to schools.

## Northern Ireland

The Northern Ireland Citizenship Award Scheme was established two years ago to recognise and encourage young people who are trying to be aware of other people's rights as well as their own. Awards are made to individuals and groups in four categories, including one for 'those working to support groups such as the disabled, or from ethnic minorities, to improve the quality of their citizenship'. The awards will be on an all-Ireland basis from 1995 and will include a further category for work specifically aimed at increasing knowledge and understanding between the communities of the North and the South.

## Europe

On the broader scene, there are so many important and complex issues surrounding the law about which people are confused and powerless to affect. To begin to tackle this, the Foundation has produced information in the clearest and simplest way possible and then tried to ensure that it gets to the people who need it. An example is the Maastricht Treaty, potentially of enormous influence in the lives of most people, yet understood by only a handful. *Maastricht Made Simple*, a 50-page booklet produced in conjunction with the *European*, was sent free to every school – as was the follow-up video. (The booklet was also available through a number of newsagents.) Students were appreciative of the impartial and informative explanation offered, with the 'thumbnail' summaries of the arguments for and against each section of the treaty. Accompanying notes were produced for teachers.

There are plans to develop more accessible materials on the whole area of European law, especially leading up to 1996 and potential revision of Maastricht. This might take the form of a comic, or a video using the techniques normally associated with music promotion, something to engage the ordinary Euro-citizens of tomorrow.

## Young Citizen's Passport

Accessibility is also the key to the *Young Citizen's Passport*, published in December 1994. This is a passport-sized, practical, first reference guide to the law for school leavers. It covers all the vital topics including health, work, housing, money, family, the police and the courts. The booklet is lively in content and layout, and fully illustrated. It is also clear, straightforward and as succinct as it is possible to be, whilst giving accurate information about real-life law. It includes a comprehensive list of useful and relevant organisations with numbers to contact. Two free copies have been sent to every secondary school and local solicitors will be invited to donate a set of copies to the pupils who are leaving their neighbourhood school. The cover price will be low and the aim is to sell it through the most accessible outlets. It will be updated annually and we hope it will become an essential life-tool for every school leaver. Again this could be a blueprint for a wider programme of legal awareness.

## Radio and television

Radio and television have a major potential for spreading legal awareness and understanding and the Foundation has been involved in one or two projects. It provided a background booklet for two Channel 4 TV series on the law, 'Street Legal' and 'The Brief', as well as advising and producing classroom materials for some schools' programmes. This seems to be an underexploited resource in the UK, with a few notable exceptions, and at both local and regional level should form an important strand of any major programme to expand legal awareness.

## Central and Eastern Europe

The knowledge and understanding gained through all these projects is now being shared with some of the newly democratic countries of Central and Eastern Europe. For different reasons, their citizens feel distrust and disillusionment with the old system of law and government, but considerable apprehension about what is being put in its place. They also need to believe that justice and the rule of law can be a reality. With funding from the Law Society, the Foundation offered to get involved in supplying any of its materials which seemed likely to help, plus training in using them. This builds on general experience of running a wide variety of courses for teachers in the UK, including a human rights education summer school.

So far, the Foundation has worked with teachers and educators to adapt materials for schools and colleges in Bulgaria, Poland, Russia, Slovakia and Hungary. In many cases the law-related approach is welcomed, as in the UK, by teachers who see it as both highly practical and less contentious than 'education for democracy'. Some of the main people involved in developing the programmes in colleges and universities are themselves lawyers by training.

## Future plans

What does all this add up to in terms of the aims and objectives of the Citizenship Foundation? A beginning. The level of ignorance about the law remains profound and the number of people who, partly as a consequence, do not fulfil the responsibilities or enjoy the rights of citizenship is unacceptably high. This threatens social cohesion in a pluralist society as well as creating unhappiness and injustice for too many individuals. It is also wholly self-defeating for a society depending ever more on the artifice of law for its order and functioning.

The Foundation has various longer-term projects and ideas about how best to make a more dramatic impact on the problem. Some of these would require quite large public resources. Others would employ an approach which relied on volunteers and more limited local funding. All would depend on a definite commitment from the Lord Chancellor's Department and the government to the imperative of extending legal awareness and the translation of that into some form of funding for legal information and education.

A major concern has to be how to ensure that programmes reach the people with the greatest need. A necessary pre-condition, or an integral part, of any publicly funded legal education programme would therefore be to establish who is in the greatest need and where they are. This would not have to take forever or be on the scale of a Royal Commission. Much of the research has been done and some of the evidence is not hard to collect from existing agencies such as citizens' advice bureaux (CABs). Gathering it together would the first task of a publicly funded, independent legal awareness agency, whose overall brief would be the extension of legal awareness through education and other programmes.

The second task might be to draw up an extended legal equivalent of the citizen's charter. This could address such issues as the obligation on a government department to provide a plain person's guide to the law affecting the areas for which it has responsibility. Some departments have already established an excellent record in this respect, but others are sadly wanting. This, incidentally, would require reform of our law of copyright which restricts reproduction of printed legislation and reports of parliamentary proceedings.

By what other means could publicly funded legal education and information be delivered? There are a number of possibilities.

- a requirement on all law students that they undertake some kind of 'legal advice placement' (like the 'elective' or houseman's role for medical students). This could be done in a school or college, with a CAB, law centre or firm, in any institution where professional training takes place, in a prison – in the USA this is directed to helping prison officers understand their rights and responsibilities as much as prisoners – or within the regionally-based legal information centres recommended elsewhere;
- a requirement that legal awareness, in the terms set out in *Curriculum Guidance 8*, should be part of a new citizenship curriculum, alongside social and moral awareness. There are implications for teacher training courses and the provision of in service training. Such a requirement would help to target groups in greatest need such as ethnic minorities;
- the provision of equivalent courses within further and adult education institutions and wherever professional or vocational training is provided. In some cases these are already part of the basic training, but it is clearly absurd that plumbers and hairdressers should have no awareness of the duty of care or what is involved in a contract;
- readily available and easy-to-read guides to the legal aspects of everyday life should be published, where appropriate in additional languages to English. These would be for groups meeting certain criteria such as: major groups affecting most people like householders, parents, children, car owners; groups known to be particularly at risk due to ignorance of their rights, eg, the elderly, the homeless, workers in dangerous environments; and

groups where the public would have a major interest in raising awareness of rights or duties, eg, users of national parks, environmental polluters;

- provision could also be made for these guides to be used as the basis of informal, but organised, discussion and learning within a community setting. (There are excellent models for this in the kind of schemes administered by the People's Law School in British Columbia.) In this, as in several of the suggested initiatives, imaginative use could be made of local and community media;

- the provision of a series of regionally based information centres, possibly in central reference libraries which already have many of the necessary facilities. (Again there is a successful precedent for this in New South Wales, where libraries also house innovative technology for public access to legal information and advice.) These would have available easy-to-read summaries of the most important laws and would be staffed, at least part time, by law students on their placements or possibly a local authority officer with some paralegal training;

- more information should be made available about the increasingly important work of tribunals and what is involved in appearing before them;

- better support should be made available for CABs and law centres – many of these are doing excellent public information jobs and it is not necessary to re-invent them. However, the legal profession as a whole should be involved in this, possibly through a compulsory requirement on all trainee solicitors and Bar pupils to give some time.

Effecting even some of these could, in the longer term, reduce the cost of legal aid because people would have a clearer idea of when it is appropriate to use the law to bolster their rights and what their responsibilities are towards other citizens.

## Conclusion

Working with both branches of the legal profession and having established a singular relationship with schools throughout the country, the Citizenship Foundation is in an excellent position to play a major part in many of these suggested developments. It has several projects planned which could be linked into the kind of new structures outlined. One is to set up a a multi-cultural programme involving the development of materials and other initiatives. Another will look at the problematic area of young people's relationships with the police and the negative view of the law which this tends to reinforce.

The foundation has already drawn up a proposal to establish a national network of county co-ordinators who would be responsible for promoting better public understanding of the law in their areas. They would do this by identifying volunteers to cover particular groups with which to work, for example schools, youth groups, existing voluntary organisations, local solicitors. Schools would be linked together and would organise local 'law days' or 'law weeks' with help and involvement from police and lawyers. Co-ordinators would organise newsletters for everyone involved and bring representatives of the groups together on a regular basis for discussion and training. They would also join with bodies like CABs and representatives of local community groups to build up a clearer idea of where the greatest need is and to try to work out the best ways of meeting it. The exact role of the co-ordinator would depend on the local circumstances and resources. To develop a comprehensive national network would require some central funding from the LCD (or a new legal awareness body) to pay at least an honorarium to the co-ordinators. The Citizenship Foundation has already received some non-government funding to run a pilot scheme along these lines in one county.

Alongside this, the foundation would like to set up an affiliation scheme to link itself with schools and colleges, probably on some kind of subscription basis. As well as offering its own resources, it would provide a central source of information about all available resources in the field of legal awareness and citizenship education generally. It could offer a legal cuttings service and, in partnership with other organisations, investigate the possibility of providing a help line.

Making public resources available to translate some or all of these plans into a coherent and comprehensive programme to increase legal awareness will not create a population of more responsible and effective citizens overnight. But it would give a signal that those who can make a difference recognise how vital it is for the majority of ordinary people to have a stronger sense of ownership of their system of law and government.

Many words have been written and spoken about the causes and effects of anti-social and criminal behaviour, and the extent to which they both reflect and contribute to the breakdown in community. The restoration of community spirit and the rekindling of a sense of responsibility towards it is sometimes held out as the solution to society's problems. Though there is undoubted strength in this argument, it is also the case that people are more likely to feel greater commitment to community when they care about and believe in themselves. The language of rights is indeed the language of responsibilities: my right to walk about safely is mirrored by your responsibility not to harm me. All citizens need to understand and appreciate that.

Neither rhetoric nor any number of new methods of punishment appear to have made an impact on crime and the general lack of caring for others. This is because both are a reflection, in part at least, of too little knowledge and understanding and inadequate skills, giving rise to a wholly negative attitude to law, to government and ultimately to society itself. A programme promoting greater legal awareness which concentrated on increasing knowledge, extending understanding and developing skills could not fail to change attitudes in the citizens it involved. If, as a result, more people, especially young people, came to feel that they had a stake in society then the concepts of justice and the rule of law would seem more meaningful and worth upholding: for themselves and for others.

The challenge and the opportunities are clear. We need the means.

# CHAPTER 8

# Law centres' experience of information work

## JOHN RICHARDSON

*The author is publications and information worker at Leicester Rights Centre and a member of the executive committee of the Law Centres Federation.*[1]

The debate on the future of the provision of legal services in Britain is reaching a critical juncture. The changes in legal aid eligibility rules and the introduction of franchising have had an important impact. The experiment just beginning with franchises for non-solicitor agencies will have implications whether it is deemed to have succeeded or failed (see p34). These developments are the most public manifestations of government concern to address the problem of the rising cost of providing legal services.

It is in this context that the issue of information provision as part of a comprehensively funded service has emerged back onto the agenda. The Lord Chancellor's Advisory Committee's paper on the *Underlying Principles of Publicly Funded Legal Services* specifically cites provision of information as a duty of primary advisers. This follows recent explorations of the idea of block funding by the Legal Aid Board. These tentative steps would not constitute a radical new departure: they would represent development of current activity.

Law centres have long recognised the need to devote resources to information. We take it as self-evident that a better informed community can assert its rights more confidently and make better use of the system of justice.

## Information work in law centres

Law centres in the UK are now almost 25 years old. The first centres were started by radical lawyers dissatisfied with the quality of service provided to the public in general and the poor in particular. The 113 centres were characterised both by their accountability to their communities and clients as well as their utilisation of non-traditional methods to advance the interests of their clients. Information and community education work were important components of their approach.

The movement has grown from a small number of centres in London to the current 55 centres in England and Wales. Until recently, Northern Ireland and Scotland had only a single law centre each. As a movement, we have not managed to secure a funding base which allows law centres to be established in all the communities which need them. Until they are, it will be impossible to talk of a 'typical' law centre or to set down parameters for our work. From the beginning, however, there was recognition that much more needed to be done than simple casework – although there was a great deal of that.

Law centre activity other than casework has undergone many changes of terminology over the years. We currently use the following categories:

- publications and information;
- community and development;
- education work and training;
- campaigning;
- community resourcing.

These provide the headings that are used below. Law centres also do proactive and preventative work as well as policy, research and consultation.

## Publications and information

Most law centres produce publications of one kind or another. These range from simple leaflets, outlining the work and opening hours of the centre, to technical manuals on specific areas of law.

The first step to helping potential clients to articulate their problems can be simple explanations of what we do; where we are; and how to get in touch. Most service providers will have had experience of the irritation of clients who have been pushed from agency to agency, battling with the arcane opening hours and eligibility criteria of each one.

Leaflets and short pamphlets can also be very useful in outlining rights and duties in specific areas of law. The problems of a significant number of immigration and nationality clients arise, for instance, from misunderstanding their situation when interviewed by officials. Reliable information in accessible language can transform their experience. On the other hand, ill-drafted information can have the effect of mystifying a fairly straightforward process. There is a suspicion among many working in the field that a lot of leaflets designed to be self-help guides in fact have the effect of frightening the client into not taking on the issue him or herself. The availability of more resources would improve our self-help publications.

Practical guides are an important area of publications in which law centres could make an important contribution if resources were available. This is demonstrated by the example of our work in relation to the poll tax recounted below. The very expensive legal textbooks essential to the work of the specialist are far beyond the economic reach of most advice agencies. They may also not have access to the training and support necessary to advise at an advanced level. There are few equivalents to the excellent Child Poverty Action Group handbooks on social security in other areas of social welfare law. First-tier advisers are often left without reference materials other than the specialist advice magazines. These are excellent but, in practice, it requires great conscientiousness to ensure that they are read by all relevant staff.

Some law centres produce regular and successful periodicals. In the mid–1980s, Central London Law Centre helped to establish *Restora*, a magazine for the Bengali community. Thamesdown and Leicester Rights Centres also produce periodicals. In Leicester, we found that most readers have no access to other advice publications. As well as articles on developments in the law and case studies, we also run articles from local policy-makers. In the course of their publications work, law centres have also produced posters, tapes, videos, computer programmes, badges and postcards. Electronic mail and bulletin boards potentially provide an outlet for centres and others to use each others' publications more easily and develop new ways of working together.

## Community and development work

The provision and gathering of information are central to community and development work. The communities within which law centres operate suffer such general problems as housing disrepair and specific groups within those communities suffer specific problems such as racial harassment or discrimination on grounds of sex or disability.

Information work takes place in a number of different ways, depending on the context. It may be directed to preparing cases for the courts, as in the case of mass actions for tenants living on estates with chronic dampness problems. It may be directed to disseminating knowledge about the progress of test cases. This was, for instance, an important component of the activity of Humberside Law Centre in its pursuit of two Court of Appeal cases linked to a campaign for redundancy payments for the former workers in Hull's deep sea fishing fleet.[2]

In other situations, communities and individuals clearly need to be informed about the legal background in order to assess their most effective remedy. This is particularly the case where collective action is contemplated, such as judicial review against a public body.

## Education and training

Many law centres are increasingly involved in education and training. Historically, most advisers have looked to national bodies such as the Legal Action Group, Shelter or the Child Poverty Action Group to provide expert training. Increasingly, however, the cost is putting these sources beyond the reach of cash-strapped voluntary groups.

Law centres including Humberside, Leicester and Thamesdown have identified training as a central activity. They run schemes which provide updating on the law for those in voluntary agencies. Local training also has the advantage that local sources of information can be integrated into resources available. Training events have an important side-effect of forging links between people from, for instance, the local council and the advice community as well as providing a forum for discussion of local policy in addition to the national law.

At a different level, many law centres provide teaching for law courses at their local universities. This can add an invaluable element to the legal elements in a diverse range of courses, ranging from law degrees to courses on social work or housing.

## Campaigning and community resourcing

The availability of a law centre can be critical to the effectiveness of community campaigns. This is particularly the case as powers are being taken from elected bodies, such as the local council, and placed in the hands of non-elected institutions which may not have the same regard for public accountability. Access to information on developments in the law and the potential availability of a law centre to disseminate information can be critical to the success of a campaign.

Law centres play a key role in straightforward and non-contentious areas such as the provision of information packs on the constitutional frameworks for voluntary groups of various kinds.

## Law centres and housing

Housing provides a very good illustration of the successful integration of information work within law centres. Housing law as a specialist area of legal practice was first developed by law centres. Most of the leading practitioners, authors and editors have worked in, or been briefed by, law centres. Many of the leading cases originated with complaints from law centre clients.

Law centres' involvement with housing matters also exemplifies many aspects of successful information work. Early law centres quickly realised that many of the individual housing clients faced problems that were common to whole blocks, estates or neighbourhoods. By publicising their services and developing relationships with community organisations and tenants' groups, centres promoted group actions. The development of training courses in basic housing law for advice agencies and community groups allowed law centres' legal expertise to be used to empower communities. Many published tenants' handbooks and do-it-yourself manuals to enable tenants to pursue actions to get their housing conditions improved. Some local authorities involved law centres and their clients in research and policy formulation.

In Leicester, for instance, we have advised tenants during a decade-long struggle to improve the condition of their badly constructed houses. This has taken us and them through the myriad housing changes that were implemented during the 1980s. The case began with attempts to apportion responsibility for the original defects; then to get the council to act against the builder and, finally, to guide the tenants through a range of proposed solutions. These included a number of options as to how their estate might be transferred to a housing association or placed under some form of tenants' control. The amount of information work aimed at this local community and particular to its problems has been immense.

## Poll tax: a case study

The community charge or poll tax was developed in the mid–1980s as the government's response to what it saw as problems with the rates, a property tax. It caused chaos for advice agencies. The administrative burden overwhelmed local authorities. Enforcement action was taken in thousands of cases of deliberate and unintentional non-payment. Most defendants were unrepresented and the courts were flooded. Poll tax cases exposed serious problems with local authority policies and practices, the capacity of the magistrates' court to deal with civil debt cases and with the powers of bailiffs. It led to a significant number of successful judicial review cases.

The involvement of law centres and the Law Centres Federation (LCF) began with the projects designed to provide information. In 1989, two workshops on poll tax were organised at the LCF's annual conference. They were facilitated by a worker from Castlemilk Law Centre in Glasgow which had just begun to receive clients because the poll tax was implemented earlier in Scotland than England. English and Welsh centres were unclear as to how they were going to incorporate poll tax casework into their other activities. The highly political implications of working in this area were also evident. Some centres were already aware of direct threats made by local authorities to cut funds to agencies advising on the poll tax. Some management committees made similar decisions without external pressure through concern at the political context in which anything to do with poll tax was seen. These problems were national and widespread.

In the aftermath of the conference, a member of the management committee of Bradford Law Centre, who was a trained lawyer employed as a community worker on one of the estates in the city, put together a small working group. It included one of the lawyers at the law centre, another member of the management committee, who was a welfare rights worker, and the information worker from Leicester Rights Centre. The group decided that its immediate task was to produce a short booklet which people who would face financial problems as a result of the new tax could use to guide themselves through the various stages of the registration, collection and enforcement procedures. The process of analysing the legislation and attempting to render it into straightforward language exposed a number of problems with the legislation itself and with procedural matters such as the powers of bailiffs and the rights of unrepresented defendants in magistrates' court. It was decided to designate the first edition as a draft which would be revised after the tax's first year. (By the time the second edition was produced it was clear that the poll tax was going to be replaced, so no definitive version was ever written.)

The 50-page booklet was produced with the cost of printing being met by a charity. It was promoted through the LCF, the two centres' own networks and a small notice in *Legal Action*. This resulted in hundreds of requests for copies from individual citizens' advice bureaux, advice agencies, some local authorities, firms of solicitors and several anti-poll tax groups. A booklet initially produced as an information source and guide for people with poll tax cases became an unofficial handbook for lawyers and advisers. The sponsoring law centres also found themselves being consulted by agencies and individuals from all over the country. The *ad hoc* relationship between the two centres continued and an informal network developed of law centre workers concerned with poll tax and related issues. Workers from this group joined the Public Law Project working group which drew up guidelines for local authorities' use of bailiffs. They also provided a number of training courses through the LCF. These were modified for regional and local use. As experience grew, it became clear that as well as the problematic nature of the legislation itself, the fact that council bureaucracies were finding it hard to maintain efficiency in the face of a massive administrative burden was in itself being reflected in problems faced by clients.

In Leicester and Bradford, relationships were developed with officers and members of the local authorities. These have gone through periods of both intense hostility and close co-operation (sometimes both at the same time). Both centres have confronted the authorities' policies and procedures at the local magistrates' court and the High Court. One of Leicester's cases continued to the Court of Appeal with support from Liberty, the National Council for Civil Liberties. Both have also assisted clients with the preparation of complaints to the local government ombudsman. At the same time, both councils have established forums for discussion of poll tax policies and practices.

Bradford Law Centre established a duty representation scheme on committal days in local courts. As part of that scheme, it developed materials and techniques to facilitate the rapid collection and organisation of information from clients who may only have a few minutes of consultation before appearing in court. Training and support was provided for 'McKenzie friends', non-lawyer assistants to litigants in person, from advice agencies, the CABs and local groups. In Leicester, the city council agreed to promote the availability of independent advice on the back of bills and summonses. A city-wide information day was organised for anyone involved with advising on poll tax to provide both training and to allow discussion of local policies and lobbying for change.

Leicester Rights Centre and Bradford Law Centre used volunteers to research the procedures and decisions of the local magistrates. Both studies exposed the vulnerability of unrepresented clients; the wide divergence of decisions by different benches in similar cases; the confusion of both clerks and magistrates about the latter's role in civil matters and the fact that virtually all those coming before the courts were poor. Unfortunately, the approaches made to individual academics and university departments to develop the research further have not, as yet, been unsuccessful.

Many law centres continue to be heavily involved with poll tax problems in their casework and advising on the new council tax which replaced it. Law centres are still concerned with the wider issues that their poll tax work exposed, for example, the activities and powers of private bailiffs and firms serving warrants on behalf of local authorities, the vulnerability of unrepresented clients before tribunals and magistrates' courts and the unregulated way in which many local authorities carry out their duties.

The example of Bradford and Leicester's involvement in poll tax reveals many of the advantages of law centres in legal information work. These include the following.

– The entire project was a product of relationships established through the law centres network. The existence of the network bringing together people with similar concerns for joint work and support is invaluable.
– The law centres' management committees were able and willing to release staff time for the project. The two centres concerned were both fortunate in that their funding was sufficient to allow development and information work such as this to be carried out.
– Similarly, they were able to take on an informal resourcing and training role for other law centres and advice agencies. They were also able to devote staff time to involvement in the Public Law Project policy work and to support volunteers in carrying out local studies.
– They were able to represent in individual cases and provide proper support for McKenzie friends.

– They were able to use their long-standing relationships with the local authorities to press for changes in local policy and practices.

A growing list of ways in which justice is administered in Britain have been and are being challenged as a result of poll tax hearings, including the rights of defendants to have assistance in court; the powers of councils as prosecutors; the nature of evidence and the way it should be interpreted in civil cases in magistrates' courts; and the use of imprisonment for civil debt. In addition, there are a host of technical problems such as what constitutes residence in an area and the meaning of 'wilful refusal or culpable neglect' that are fundamental to the confused way in which local taxation is levied. Most of these points have emerged as a result of individuals being informed about legal procedures and their legal rights and of questioning decisions of councils or courts and seeking further advice. An informed community gives deserved headaches to high-handed officials and arbitrary courts.

Another important issue illustrated by this example is the difficulty of measuring 'efficiency' in statistical terms. A qualitative judgement has to be made. The poll tax also illustrates the integral link between information and individual casework. Legal aid was not available in poll tax cases. Many magistrates' courts acted in an arbitrary manner towards unrepresented defendants. The two types of activity complemented each other. Information work will never replace casework. Indeed, it may increase it.

The LCF and the Legal Aid Board have discussed, for some time, the possibility of block funding for non-casework activity such as information provision. Secure funding is one of the elements that is vital to ensuring proper attention is given to this work.

## Conclusion

To develop this side of their work to its greatest potential, law centres require the resolution of some long-standing problems and a new relationship between law centres and other institutions both locally and nationally. Some funding method is required to integrate information work into law centres. Whilst resources are insecure, the pressure to abandon information initiatives for casework will always be present. This is not simply a matter of salaries. The production and distribution of locally-developed materials needs to be under-written. The amount of funding available is clearly going to be a determining factor in the sort of work undertaken. City- or district-wide information campaigns would be costly.

One obvious solution would be to combine elements of national government and local authority funding, with central government paying for the staff and local authorities underwriting resources. The most obvious drawback to this system is the uneven distribution of finance. There are local authorities who take no responsibility for providing even the most basic advice services to their citizens; such authorities are unlikely to take a more liberal view towards funding information work.

Another element in the funding jigsaw could be local trusts. The Law Society has recently suggested the establishment of legal services trusts as part of the development of its *pro bono* work. A levy on law firms' incomes would certainly provide a regular and independent income. Paul Boateng MP, the Labour Party's legal services spokesperson, recently suggested that an incoming Labour administration may look to the private sector to fund some of their legal services proposals.

The strengths brought by law centres to information work are many. They are independent and able and willing to address politically controversial issues in a professional manner; they can take a multi-disciplinary approach; through the LCF they can draw on national experience; they have a broad set of national, regional and local contacts; they can draw on their casework base to refine and develop information strategies; they often have contacts with local academics, local authorities and legal professionals. We have demonstrated this in the past; we hope to continue to do so in the future.

# References

1  I have benefited in the preparation of this paper from the time and assistance of a number of workers at the Law Centres Federation, members of management committees and staff at various law centres and other advice projects as well as academics in the law department of Leicester's De Montfort University. I am grateful to all of them. This paper represents my own views, however, and all errors, misinterpretations and insults are my own. I have been struck in the preparation of this paper by the paucity of academic material on the work of law and advice centres. Our successes have not been properly celebrated, nor our failings adequately analysed. As we move into a new era this deficiency should be corrected.

2  See H Forrest, 'Fishermen fight for their rights' May 1994 *Legal Action* 6–7.

Part IV

# The organisation of publicly funded legal services

# The organisation of publicly funded legal services

The three chapters in Part IV describe the recent history of publicly funded legal services in two countries very different from each other and from our own. There are clearly enormous differences in the histories of the United States, South Africa and Great Britain. These will have affected the contrasting ways in which publicly funded legal services have developed. The extent of the difference should serve as a caution against drawing too easy lessons from the experience of other countries. Even so there are lessons for British developments within South African and US experience.

The historical analyses given by Gerry Singsen of the US and Geoff Budlender of South Africa underline how closely the public funding of legal services is bound up with politics and history. In the UK, legal aid was the product of the post-war welfare state. Its growth, at least until now, has largely been politically bipartisan. This may now change under the pressure of restricted resources. By contrast, in both South Africa and the United States, the development of legal aid or its equivalent has always been part of an intensely political struggle. Gerry Singsen describes how civil legal services developed as part of a Democratic president's 'war on poverty'. Those involved have held to the faith of being a political movement orientated towards the better achievement of social justice.

In South Africa, Geoff Budlender shows how legal aid, both criminal and civil, is still in its infancy. The new South African constitution gives protection to the right to publicly funded counsel in the case of at least some criminal defendants. Faced with very scarce resources, South Africa seems likely to decide that the best method of delivery of criminal services will be public defenders.

The form and extent of South Africa's civil legal services is much more open to doubt. The struggle against apartheid has left as a legacy a network of paralegals in community organisations. It is this theme which is taken up by Thandi Orleyn. Legal aid funding could further both the political purpose of maintaining this network and the legal purpose of delivering publicly funded civil legal services.

The common themes of the importance of politics and the consequences of limited resources provide the strongest links between US and South African experience and our domestic concerns. Many of the issues of debate are the same even if the context is completely different. For instance, the Legal Services Corporation's firm identification of its goal as 'equal justice' rather than 'equal access to justice' is a comment on the discussion in chapter 1 about the purpose of publicly funded legal services. The debate about paralegals in South Africa raises issues very relevant to the discussion in Britain of franchising advice agencies raised in chapter 3.

# CHAPTER 9

# The politics of legal aid in South Africa

GEOFF BUDLENDER

*Geoff Budlender has been an attorney with the Legal Resources Centre, a national law centre, in South Africa since it was founded in 1979. He is now its national director. He has been a participant in the CODESA (Convention for a Democratic South Africa) process which preceded the recent change of government. He was a member of the steering committee of the public defender project established by the Legal Aid Board in Johannesburg.*

The shape of legal aid in South Africa has always been heavily influenced by the wider political environment. As South Africa enters the democratic era, political decisions of a different kind will have a major impact on the shape, size and structure of the legal aid system.

## Background

The first attempt at a national programme for legal aid was the Legal Aid Scheme of 1962.[1] This was created by the Department of Justice in co-operation with the organised profession. The basis of the scheme was that attorneys (solicitors) and advocates (barristers) were asked to render services free of charge to people referred to them by officers of the scheme. Any person wanting legal aid would apply to a legal aid officer attached to the court, and would have to qualify in terms of a means test. It does not seem surprising that the system never really worked. Speaking at a conference 11 years later, a leading figure in the Association of Law Societies commented as follows, apparently without any intended irony: 'For one reason or another the legal profession lost interest in the scheme. It is probable that the absence of any remuneration was a factor . . .'[2]

The first really serious effort at providing the services of lawyers on a remunerative basis had a directly political origin. This was the Treason Trial Defence Fund, which was a special fund established to provide defence advocacy in the marathon treason trial which ran from 1956 to 1961. The fund raised money both locally and internationally, with most of its funds coming from outside the country.

In 1960, this became the South African Defence and Aid Fund, which provided representation to people prosecuted for political 'crimes'. Its task was very large: the early 1960s were a period of major political resistance to apartheid, and heavy repression. The banning in 1961 of the African National Congress and the Pan Africanist Congress, and the enactment of stringent 'security' laws, led to a large number of prosecutions. In 1966, the Defence and Aid Fund, too, was declared an unlawful organisation under the Suppression of Communism Act. The government insisted that it had no objection to the provision of defence in political trials, denying that in fact there was such an entity as a political trial. Prosecutions under the relevant 'security' laws were simply another genus of criminal prosecution, with no political content. However, its actions suggested otherwise. In 1971, the Anglican Dean of Johannesburg was prosecuted under the Terrorism Act, inter alia on the grounds that he had been providing funds for the defence of people charged with political offences, and 'this was likely to foster the morale of persons who were thinking of committing such offences and was therefore likely to encourage hostility towards the State'.[3] He was convicted in the Transvaal Provincial Division of the Supreme Court on this count and two others, and sentenced to the statutory minimum of five years' imprisonment. He was ultimately acquitted, in the Appellate Division of the Supreme Court.

In fact, the Defence and Aid Fund in South Africa had been succeeded by the International Defence and Aid Fund (IDAF), based in London. It carried on and expanded the work of the fund in South Africa. However, because of the political climate in South Africa, and the banning of the South African fund, it necessarily operated on a covert basis. It raised funds outside South Africa and then sent them to the lawyers in South Africa, using as conduits a firm of solicitors and a 'respectable' person outside South Africa who would pose as the true donor. Thus, for example, a year-long trial of student leaders in 1976 was supposedly funded by a Swiss professor with a great interest in academic freedom. It is difficult to believe that anyone was fooled by this subterfuge, but the lawyers and clients who were the recipients of the money learnt not to ask any questions, and the lawyers also learnt to direct any requests for support to a London firm of solicitors which apparently had an astonishing range of wealthy and philanthropic clients concerned about freedom in South Africa.

IDAF grew to be a major institution. By 1992, when it closed its overseas operations as a result of the 'unbanning' of political organisations in South Africa, it was raising and spending almost as much on legal services as the South African government legal aid system. Most of the funding came from foreign governments, either directly or through the United Nations Trust Fund for South Africa.

## Government-funded legal aid

In 1969, the first government-funded legal aid scheme was established by the Legal Aid Act 1969. It is difficult to avoid the inference that at least one reason for the establishment of the scheme was the criticism which had emerged after the banning of the Defence and Aid Fund. Introducing the Legal Aid Bill in parliament, the Minister of Justice (P C Pelser) immediately took steps to disabuse his listeners of any idea that he might be unduly 'soft on crime' or philanthropic:

> If legal aid is to give rise to the State having to guarantee to the skolly[4] element who loaf about, snatch handbags, steal purses and remove money from people's pockets, the additional security of being defended free of charge by legal practitioners provided by the authorities when they appear in court, I can say even at this early stage that the writing is on the wall. I want to put it very clearly that I shall never be a party to subsidising crime.[5]

The government's lukewarm attitude to legal aid is demonstrated by the fact that during the period March 1971 to February 1973, a total of 4,312 cases were handled. The majority of the cases were divorce actions by white people. Defence was provided in a grand total of 191 criminal cases. Of those represented in criminal defences, 39 were African.[6] 'Lukewarm' may be the wrong adjective: 'suspicious' may be more apt. This is demonstrated by the minister's remarks in introducing the Bill, and by the fact that both the government and the Legal Aid Board (established under the Act) refused to send representatives to a major conference on legal aid, held at a university in 1973. Since then, the Legal Aid Board has gradually expanded its activities. Over the last few years, the budget has been increased at a rate beyond that of inflation, but it still remains paltry. During the current 1994–95 financial year, the budget allocation for legal aid is R63 million (£11.5 million), or approximately R1.50 (less than 30p) per person per year.

Until recently, the state-funded legal aid system was run entirely on the judicare model, with private practitioners being appointed by the board on a case-by-case basis and paid according to a tariff which is significantly less than that usually charged by practitioners. Two years ago, in an unusual venture, the board and a range of non-governmental law-based organisations co-operated to establish a pilot public defender scheme in Johannesburg, funded by the board. The office employed ten lawyers on a full-time salaried basis, to take on criminal defences in the Johannesburg magistrates' court.

Generally, the project has been regarded as a success. It has also demonstrated that the cost of providing criminal defences in the magistrates' courts is substantially lower through a public defender system than through a judicare system. The average cost of a criminal defence through the judicare model (which continues to operate alongside the public defender office) is about £140. This figure excludes the fairly significant overhead involved in managing such a scheme. On the other hand, the cost of the public defender office has been calculated at approximately £75 per case. The result is that the board is keen to establish further public defender programmes, and has started to take steps in this direction.

The public defender scheme has met with some opposition, principally from lawyers who fear that it will compete with their own practices. For example, the criminal work committee of the Law Society of the Transvaal has reported to members of the Law Society that its views on the effect of a possible extension of the public defender project on the income structure of practitioners are in conflict wth those of the Legal Aid Board. With disarming frankness, the committee states as follows: 'The committee is inclined to place the interests of practitioners in this regard above the general public interest, as that is interpreted by the Legal Aid Board.'[7] The answer given by the board and the steering committee of the project, namely that the means test limit is so low that no-one qualifying for assistance could in any event afford the services of a private practitioner, is only partially valid. In the first place, some of those represented through the public defender office might have obtained legal aid through the judicare system – at twice the cost to the board. Secondly, it is common practice for family members to band together and raise the necessary funds for defence. The result is that some people who are undoubtedly indigent by any test nevertheless obtain the services of private practitioners on a fee-paying basis.

Thus far, the government (which ultimately provides the funds), the Legal Aid Board and the organised profession have not been particularly sympathetic to the objections to the public defender scheme, which are really a form of special pleading. However, if the scheme is introduced on a national basis, it will undoubtedly lead to increased resistance from parts of the profession, and corresponding pressure on government. Paradoxically, the paltry state allocation to legal aid has created one significant advantage for any attempts at reform or reconstruction of the system: the number of legal practitioners who receive a significant part of their income from legal aid, and therefore have a vested interest in the maintenance and expansion of the existing system, is very limited. However, it is clear that any attempt to cut back the judicare allocation – and probably also any attempt to fund legal advice and assistance through other channels, whether public defender offices or other institutions – will lead to some mobilisation of resistance, and an attempt to bring political pressure on the government to halt it.

## Starting again

In any attempt to build effective publicly funded legal services in South Africa, it would be wisest not to attempt to build on the foundations of a rather shaky system, but rather to start again. In starting again, the following basic facts have to be taken into account:[8]

- South Africa has a relatively small population of practising lawyers – approximately 13,000 for a total population of over 40 million people.
- The lawyers are heavily concentrated in the urban areas, and their professional training and practical experience have been heavily focused on the problems of those who can afford to pay for legal services. Effectively, most South Africans have no access to a lawyer.
- During 1992, 684,246 people appeared in the lower (magistrates' and regional) courts without a lawyer. Of these, about 113,584 were sentenced to imprisonment.[9]
- The legal profession has not grown significantly over the past two years.

- Because of the structure of the profession, which requires articles of clerkship or pupillage for admission as an attorney or an advocate, access to the profession is very limited. The law schools now produce almost twice as many graduates as can be admitted to the profession through existing routes. The gap is growing.
- The last ten years have seen the development of a very large number of community based advice offices spread around the country. They are run by paralegals, under the direction of local community groups. While precise numbers are not known, there are probably a few hundred such advice offices. It has been estimated that there are approximately 1,200 paralegals operating in 400 organisations and projects in South Africa.
- A number of non-governmental law based organisations provide training, assistance and back-up to the advice offices.
- Most of the advice offices were previously supported by 'anti-apartheid' money from outside the country. A great deal of this money has dried up, and the advice office movement is now facing a financial crisis.
- Fifteen of the universities now have a law clinic, but most of them are very rudimentary. Altogether, the 15 university law clinics employ a total of only 25 practitioners.
- The projected national legal aid budget for 1995–96 is £12.5 million. It would cost approximately that amount again to run a reasonably effective public defender system on a national basis. Inevitably, funding for legal aid has to compete with many other pressing priorities in the national Reconstruction and Development Programme.
- The Constitution, in the chapter on Fundamental Rights, provides that every accused person shall have the right to a fair trial, which shall include the right 'to be represented by a legal practitioner of his or her choice or, where substantial injustice would otherwise result, to be provided with legal representation at the State's expense'.

The following fairly obvious conclusions emerge from this bare statement of facts:

- There are not enough qualified legal practitioners to provide the services which are needed by the population, even assuming that the services could be paid for.
- The advice office movement is the only part of the system of advice and assistance which provides a reasonably national cover-

age. It is a rich but dwindling asset in the provision of advice and assistance.
- There is a large pool of law graduates ready and willing to provide services if they could find appropriate employment.
- Given the present structure of the legal profession, it would require a doubling of the present legal aid budget simply to meet the constitutional mandate of a fair trial including representation. This would not in any way address the need for civil legal services and advice.

Any attempt to design a new legal services system for South Africa will fail unless these facts are recognised and taken into account.

## Building a broad base of publicly funded advice and assistance

The emergence of a paralegal movement is part of a wider movement towards the increasing use of para-professionals. Particularly (but not only) in developing countries, it is recognised that the use of para-professionals offers a number of advantages. In relation to legal services, South Africa vividly demonstrates the truth of three propositions. First, where lawyers are not evenly distributed throughout the country, access can be improved by deploying paralegals. The reasons for the concentration of lawyers are primarily economic: there are not enough paying clients elsewhere to make setting up in practice economically viable. In addition, lawyers need staff and other infrastructure which are often not readily available in more remote parts of the country. Paralegals have much more modest needs in this regard. Second, cost can be reduced by the use of paralegals. This is not simply a matter of the ability of clients to pay the cost, although that is obviously a fundamental issue; in addition, in many instances the costs of a lawyer's services would outweigh the value of the service to the client. Social pensions, worker's compensation benefits and unemployment insurance claims are examples of this. Paralegals can therefore make it economically viable to attempt to recover benefits to which clients are entitled, and on which they are dependent. Third, it is often overlooked that in some areas, paralegals can provide a better quality service than lawyers. This is so for a variety of reasons: they can develop specialised skills in the areas in which they are frequently consulted; they often have a better 'connection' with the clients, as they tend to be less remote and more community-centred than lawyers; and they can afford to spend more time with clients.

Given these factors, it is not surprising that the paralegal movement in South Africa has grown and flourished over the past decade. When the Legal Resources Centre first started working with advice offices, the paralegals referred about 15 per cent of their cases to lawyers. Now that the paralegals have developed skills and experience, the figure is probably closer to 2 per cent. The advice offices have done this work as a voluntary movement, funded largely by grants from anti-apartheid sources, and with little institutional support. They are now in financial difficulties.

As we look forward, it seems that the paralegal movement must be the key to broadening the base of access to publicly-funded legal services. For just £2 million per year, substantial support could be given to 200 advice offices spread throughout the country. This seems to be the most effective and affordable method of providing access to basic advice and assistance throughout our society.

The existing advice offices are a valuable asset. The question we now face is how this asset can be turned to account in the development of publicly-funded legal services, without damaging it. The following are some of the important lessons we have learnt from our experience, for the development of an effective national paralegal service:

- It is a source of great strength if the service is community-based, in the sense that it is controlled and run by members of the community in which it is located. This helps to keep the service focused on problems of broad concern to that community, and makes the service a source of empowerment for the community.
- Independence from formal authority structures helps to ensure that the service is not afraid to challenge authority on behalf of clients.
- Paralegals need training – both before they undertake the work, and on a regular basis. At the moment, this training is provided by a range of non-governmental organisations, again on 'soft' grant money.
- The advice office needs to be organically connected to a legal service to which it can refer cases for litigation. If this is not the case, parties with which it comes into contact will soon recognise that any claim made on behalf of clients can simply be ignored.

These requirements raise a number of practical questions.

- If the service is locally-based, what steps can be taken to ensure that it is effectively available to all, and is not 'captured' by particular political or other groups within the community? A public funder needs to be assured of this.
- If it is publicly funded, which is necessarily the case, what is the most appropriate source and structure of that funding to ensure that independence is maintained, while at the same time ensuring accountability for the expenditure of public money?
- Who is to provide training, and is there to be either certification (a voluntary process) or licensing (a compulsory process) of paralegals?
- How is the provision of paralegal services to be integrated with other publicly-funded legal services?

There is also an underlying question: should paralegal services be provided only on a non-profit basis? What should the attitude be towards people who carry on these activities for a fee, for profit? In South Africa at least, there seems to be a fairly broad consensus that this work should be restricted to non-profit (and probably non-fee) services. There are two main reasons for this: the experience we have already had of exploitation and over-reaching by people who do this for reward; and a recognition of the likely massive opposition from the legal profession to any other answer. (As it is, there are already rumblings from parts of the profession about the growth of para-legal advice offices.)

## An integrated legal services system

With an advice office system in place as the base of the legal services system, what would the other components look like? It is necessary to look separately at criminal and civil services.

## *Representation in criminal cases*

The full extent of the constitutional mandate to provide publicly funded legal services in criminal cases is debatable, but its core content is unequivocal. At the barest minimum, at least 120,000 additional criminal defences must be provided each year. At existing levels of cost, this implies about an additional £18 million per year. Providing the same service through a public defender system would cost half of that.

An attempt to establish a national public defender scheme will undoubtedly evoke resistance from the legal profession, and particularly that part of it which is to some extent dependent on the existing legal aid scheme. Government will have to make a political choice about priorities in the allocation of resources. It is difficult to believe that the interests of a segment (even a relatively influential) segment of the legal profession will win the day; but stranger things have happened, and not only in South Africa. Whatever the decision in relation to a national public defender system, some elements of judicare will undoubtedly remain, particularly in areas where the volume of demand does not justify the employment of full-time lawyers.

Another controversial question will be whether paralegals should be permitted to represent clients in court. The new Minister of Justice has drawn attention to the fact that, by virtue of their experience, paralegals are capable of representing people and said the following: 'Whilst we want to see avenues being created to enable paralegals to intervene, especially in situations where people are unrepresented, we need to make sure that this does not lead to abuse and that there is some regulation.'[10]

There will obviously be vigorous debate on this issue. Many paralegals are anxious about the proposal: on the one hand, they would welcome increased rights and powers; on the other hand, they are concerned about the prospect of regulation which would surely follow. One can predict that much of the legal profession will not be enthusiastic about the proposal. A likely solution is a compromise: permitting licensed paralegals to appear in limited matters (for example, bail applications), and requiring licensing only for that purpose. A further possible limitation is to require the leave of the court for a paralegal to appear.[11]

## Civil representation

In relation to civil representation, a more fully mixed system seems likely to emerge. One can envisage a system which includes the following elements:

- Judicare or fee for service through the private profession: this is particularly attractive in geographical areas where demand is relatively limited, or in areas of work where the private profession has specialised expertise and there is a good prospect of recovery of substantial costs from the losing party. Motor accident personal injury cases are the obvious example of this.

- Staff lawyers in offices run and fully funded by the Legal Aid Board, on the same basis as the existing public defender pilot office.
- Salaried lawyers in law centres and university law clinics: here the board would contract with non-governmental organisations to do particular work.

In at least the second and third options, the increased use of paralegals seems likely and desirable.

If paralegals and advice offices are to form the base of the system of legal aid and advice, the system must also ensure that they receive adequate training, back-up and lawyer referral facilities. At the moment, all of this is done by non-governmental organisations. The Legal Aid Board would have to accept some responsibility.

## Providing access to the legal profession

The paradoxical over-supply of law graduates and under-supply of lawyers obviously requires attention. Unless this is done, there will not be enough lawyers to staff the system. Dealing with that problem is also one of the means of dealing with the unrepresentative character of the legal profession:[12] when jobs are in short supply, as they are now, it is predominantly black and female graduates who find themselves unable to enter the profession.

Towards the end of 1991, all the major role-players in the legal system held a conference known as the 'Access' Conference, at which the related problems of access to justice and access to the legal profession were discussed. Arising out of that conference and the work of a continuation committee, a committee was appointed to make proposals on the question of a 'ladder' system of entry into the legal profession.

The committee recommended[13] the institution of a three-year university law degree which will qualify graduates (after some practical training) to represent clients in criminal cases in the 'lower' courts (magistrates' courts and regional courts). This will accelerate and facilitate entry into the profession for very many graduates; provide a pool of practitioners for the envisaged national public defender scheme as well as private criminal law practitioners; and probably reduce fee levels by increasing supply substantially, and introducing a group of practitioners with significantly lower finan-cial investments and overheads. It is referred to as a 'ladder' system because the proposal is that lawyers with these qualifications should be able to obtain 'add-on' qualifications to enable them to undertake all other kinds of legal work.

The proposal is awaiting a response from the government. In the meantime, it has been welcomed by many participants in the legal system (attorneys, universities, non-governmental organisations, advice offices) with the notable exception of the Bar.

## Finding the money

Of course, none of this can be done unless the money is found. The present inadequate legal aid system can barely be sustained on the present budget, which comes from the annual Department of Justice vote by parliament.

Will the money be found? Again, this is partly a question of political will. Legal services have to compete with many other pressing national demands in the process of reconstruction and development. A solution may have to be found along the following lines.

In the first instance, the state will have to accept that it is now under a constitutional obligation to fund criminal defences in a substantial number of cases. If it wishes to hold down the cost of doing so, a public defender system seems to be the preferred route. If it fails to provide the necessary funding for this purpose, a few cases in the courts will no doubt provide the necessary corrective. In most societies, providing a defence for alleged criminals is not a popular cause; but it is a much more popular cause than the acquittal of convicted criminals on the 'technical' ground that they did not have a lawyer.

Second, international grant aid can provide very important bridging funds while the new government is in its early years. Already there are indications that some of the international funds which previously went to the international fight against apartheid may become available to government through bilateral aid arrangements, and some governments show a particular interest in the broad area of human rights and the administration of justice. This would bring new and dedicated finances into play.

Third, to the extent that funds are limited, priorities may have to be determined. This means focusing on particular areas of need, always a difficult matter; and it may also mean giving priority to cases which affect the interests of large numbers of people.

And finally, the time will surely come when the government will call upon the Fidelity Fund, into which is paid the interest on money which attorneys hold for clients in their trust accounts. The fund is controlled by the attorneys' profession, which reports to the minister. There is no public accounting, but the fund probably now stands at just under £30 million. It is used to provide clients with protection against theft by attorneys, to provide attorneys with professional indemnity insurance, and for a range of activities related to legal education. The attorneys' profession by and large regards this as its money, as a result of an extraordinary act of alchemy that converts interest on clients' money into the profession's money. Speaking to the Annual General Meeting of the Transvaal Law Society in October 1993, Nelson Mandela said the following in this regard:

> . . . is it not time to look again at how the monies in the Fidelity Fund are used, and who has responsibility for making decisions in this regard? The money in the fund, of course, comes from interest which is earned on monies in attorneys' trust accounts, in other words, on monies which belong to clients. It does not belong to the legal profession any more than it belongs to the individual attorneys who held the original capital in their trust accounts. It would surely be very appropriate to use some of this money to promote access to justice. And is there not a case to be made for some measure of public accountability in the spending of what is really public money?[14]

In many other jurisdictions, the interest on clients' money has been dealt with in a more seemly and appropriate manner, and that this is now the subject of a study being undertaken with the assistance of the Ford Foundation. The point is really this: if some or all of this money is used for legal services for the poor, it is the most painless form of redistribution (or to use a more polite word, cross-subsidisation) possible: those who can afford to pay for legal services contribute to the cost of services for those who cannot afford to pay – but they contribute money which they would in any event not have received. Surely this is an issue on which all concerned with legal services should be speaking loudly. Certainly, it would help us in South Africa.

## The decision-making structure

At present, state-funded legal aid is managed by the Legal Aid Board, a statutory body. Until fairly recently all the members of the board were state functionaries or appointed by the legal profession. The extent of government representation has now been sharply reduced.[15] The board now consists of a judge appointed by the Minister of Justice; five members appointed by the legal profession; two state functionaries; one member appointed by the minister; and three members nominated by the other members and appointed by the minister. Whatever the theoretical merits of such a structure, the result has been a board consisting entirely of lawyers, all but one being white, and all but one being male. While the membership of the board is significantly more independent of the state than was previously the case, it still largely reflects the 'old order', as does its staff.

Previously, those in the human rights community insisted on the need for an independent board rather than a state-dominated board. That is no doubt correct. There are too many examples from other parts of the world of the inclination of politicians to attempt to interfere with legal services programmes which support cases they do not like. However, we now have to face the issue of accountability – what is the appropriate structure for ensuring that public funds are spent in a publicly accountable manner? There is no doubt a great deal we could learn from others.

## Managing reform and transformation

There is a need for fundamental change in the South African legal system, and not least in relation to the provision of publicly-funded legal services. Of course, identifying the desired goals and structures is only the first part of that process. Changes then have to be implemented. The analysis in this chapter suggests that there will be resistance from at least parts of the legal profession to at least some of the steps which seem necessary. Once again, political choices will have to be made, this time principally about what interests are to receive priority.

A process which is now being adopted in South Africa may suggest a novel approach to the problem of systemic change in a society like ours, in which the formal structures of the legal system are not adequately representative of broader interests. During the last few months of the outgoing government, a body known as the Legal Forum was established. The body was intended to be broadly representative of 'role-players' in the legal system. These included the Ministry of Justice, the organised legal profession (law societies and bar councils), the Legal Aid Board, the South African Law Commission (a statutory law reform body), the university law teachers and clinics, and law-based organisations in the human rights field.[16] In the end, the Forum came to nothing, after a series of lawyerly meetings at which political issues masqueraded as procedural and definitional issues. The Minister of Justice made carefully friendly noises but kept his distance.

The new minister has indicated that he wishes to see the Legal Forum revived. He intends to use it as a major consultative body in respect of the transformation of the legal system. If this happens, vested interests will continue to be consulted – but they will be consulted in a context in which it becomes clearer that they are only one group of relevant interests. The balance of power is likely to shift significantly, as the human rights organisations see their constituency as being a wider constituency than lawyers, even though they remain law-based and lawyer-run.

## Conclusion

The provision of publicly-funded legal services in South Africa has to 'start over'. The answers to a series of political decisions will determine the extent to which we succeed in this. For the most part, these are decisions about two questions. To what extent are legal services perceived as a priority, given the many pressing demands on the national budget in the process of reconstruction and development? The omens so far are not promising. As in so many countries, the lawyers have not been able to present this as a compelling national need, and their client 'constituency' is not organised or vocal. To what extent are existing vested interests to be protected, where they are inhibiting the development of innovative and progressive systems for the provision of advice and assistance? Here, the omens seem more favourable, but it is still too early to be confident in this regard.

## References

1 I exclude from this description the *pro deo* system, through which persons accused in potential capital cases in the Supreme Court are provided with the services of counsel, usually the most junior and least experienced.
2 G Cook 'History of Legal Aid in South Africa' in A S Mathews et al (eds), *Legal Aid in South Africa* 1974, 32.
3 John Dugard, *Human Rights and the South African Legal Order* 1978, 245.
4 'Skolly' is a derogatory term for a petty criminal. The term generally carries a racial slur as well.
5 *Hansard* 25 col 1496 (26 February 1969). The statement is almost worthy of Otto, the dull-witted thug in *A Fish Called Wanda*, who, the closing titles tell us, became Minister of Justice in South Africa.
6 P Gross, 'A Legal Aid in South Africa' in Mathews et al *op cit* 45.

7 *Society News*, September 1994 p2: own translation from Afrikaans original.

8 Statistics drawn from N Steytler et al 'Report to the Access Continuation Committee on the Ladder System and Paralegals' 1974.

9 *Hansard* 6 Questions and Replies col 434 (10 March 1993).

10 A M Omar MP, interviewed in *De Rebus*, the official magazine of the attorneys profession, July 1994: 489–490.

11 See, for example, Legal Services Act, British Columbia s7.

12 About 10 per cent of the profession is black, and women occupy relatively few senior positions.

13 Steytler et al *op cit*.

14 *De Rebus* December 1993, 1040.

15 By the Legal Aid Amendment Acts 47 of 1989 and 1 of 1991.

16 This is the closest I can come to an umbrella term for the Black Lawyers Association, Lawyers for Human Rights, the Legal Resources Centre and the National Association of Democratic Lawyers.

# CHAPTER 10

# Paralegals in community advice centres and access to justice

N D B ORLEYN

*Thandi Orleyn is an attorney and director of the Johannesburg office of the Legal Resources Centre. She is a member of the Independent Mediation Service of South Africa and chair of Moleleki Community Trust, Katlehong and the National Consumers' Forum.*

For centuries black people felt alienated from the South African legal system, whose basis has been Roman Dutch law. Although this has always been applied to black people, most who stay in the rural areas and 'black homelands' have been subject to customary law. They have had little understanding of the South African legal system. Also, the fact that court proceedings in the past have been conducted in languages which black people do not understand has contributed to a sense of alienation from the system.

In addition to this sense of alienation, the present legal profession has failed to provide legal services for the population of South Africa. The hardest hit people have been those in rural areas, villages and townships, who are the poorest and most oppressed. Although the Black Sash and Citizen's Advice Bureau had been in existence since the 1950s, paralegals were unknown within the black community. Most black organisations were banned in the early 1960s. It took a decade for black people's groups and movements to re-establish themselves. The paralegal movement gathered impetus in the late 1970s and early 1980s, mainly as a result of oppression from the apartheid regime and the emergence of the trade union movement amongst black workers. Most of the activists who were involved in the 1976 uprisings found themselves banned, persecuted or unable to continue with formal education or find gainful employment. These frustrations led to self-help organisations within the communities. The 1980s also saw the mushrooming of democratic political organisations. People started taking up issues

143

like worker rights (unfair labour dismissals and retrenchments), forced removals, evictions, social welfare and other services aimed at responding to the needs of their communities.

The Legal Resources Centre (LRC), which was established in 1979, was also one of the organisations that responded to this need within communities. The LRC developed an advice centre project at the end of 1981. This project arose out of approaches made to the LRC by various community groups for assistance in setting up and operating local community advice centres.

## The definition of paralegal in the South African context

The term paralegal covers both those people who run community-based advice centres and those non-lawyers that service them. Most paralegals in South Africa have the defining characteristics set out below. They:

- have obtained their skills through training or work experience;
- are employed by non-governmental organisations;
- do not work, in most cases, under the direct supervision of a lawyer and are not accountable to a lawyer or lawyers;
- do not charge fees for their services.

One of the most striking aspects of this development was that the advice centres generally insisted on their independence from the law-based organisations which serviced them.

## The role of paralegals

In our experience at the LRC, we have found the role played by advice centres to be invaluable. We service about 100 advice centres countrywide, seeing about 10,000 of their clients a year. We estimate therefore that paralegals have fulfilled their role of assisting their communities. For example, statistics from the Industrial Aid Society[1], an advice centre situated in Johannesburg and handling labour related cases, indicate that it dealt with 7,059 cases during 1989.

Paralegals in community advice centres play three important roles:

- service;
- development and education; and
- human rights.

# Service

The majority of people in our communities are uneducated. One of the effects of apartheid was that black people could not question bureaucracies. People working for government institutions were very obstructive. Paralegals therefore filled the role of assisting the community in its day-to-day problems, for example helping people complete forms, taking them to government institutions, interpreting for them. In this role, paralegals also give people correct information and advice on matters ranging from legal to social welfare issues. They also act as counsellors and mediators, for example in marital problems and general family disputes. Where they have been unable to assist people, they have referred them to other and more specialised agencies, such as lawyers at the LRC and Lawyers for Human Rights. In fulfilling this role of enabling them to assist their communities paralegals have formed networking systems.

# Development and education

Paralegals have been able to build services and resources within their communities. For example, it was through the Industrial Aid Society, a paralegal organisation, that the Transvaal branches of the Metal and Allied Workers Union and the Transport and General Workers Union were formed. Paralegals have run community education programmes. With the assistance of organisations like the LRC, workshops have been run in the townships to inform people of their rights, for example, in labour, unemployment and other social services and consumer rights in general. Skills training for new paralegals and other communities has been run in conjunction with the LRC, Lawyers for Human Rights and other service organisations. Conferences have been run by paralegal organisations like the Black Sash.[2] These have resulted in a policy document submitted to the new government to help develop future policy on access to justice, social welfare and related issues.

# Human rights

Paralegals have helped within their communities to monitor and document political violence, the conduct of the police and other security forces. They ensured that such violations of human rights were publicised and brought to the attention of the broader human rights movements. They also worked closely with other human rights organisations in campaigns to improve conditions and services within their own communities. Paralegals also fulfilled the role of mediators and facilitators in disputes within their communities. In this way, paralegals have assisted in fostering a human rights culture in our society.

## Problems faced by paralegals in community advice centres

Problems are still faced by community advice centres. If the present Minister of Justice is serious about integrating advice centres and paralegals into the legal system, he will have to ensure that they are addressed. They include the following.

### Lack of funding

Most of the paralegals who initiated advice centres were volunteer workers who were not paid. Others were supported by churches or civic organisations in their communities. As community advice centres became more established, they received funding from the South African Council of Churches, foreign embassies and anti-apartheid movements. Many of these funders have now withdrawn or cut their funding. As a result, a number of advice centres have closed down. There is no government or local authority funding for community advice centres.

### Lack of resources

Even where some funding is available, paralegal work often suffers from shortage of resources. It can be hard to afford things like stationery, telephones, typewriters, accommodation and transport. In order to survive, some advice centres have asked communities to contribute towards the buying of such essentials for their work, but, of course, their ability to do this is limited.

### Lack of training/co-ordination of training

There is a lack of training or co-ordination of training where it is available because paralegals are not subject to a formal controlling body. Organisations like the LRC and Lawyers for Human Rights have their own training programmes. In some regions, for example, Orange Free State, paralegals have tried to co-ordinate the training. However, there is an ongoing debate as to whether paralegals should receive training at an institution like a university or technickon (polytechnic), and whether paralegals should receive certificates or diplomas. As the job of a paralegal is not secure, the turnover is very high. This means that new paralegals must be trained all the time. It is at present difficult to have a structured training programme because trainers generally need to focus on the basics.

### Lack of recognition and support

Many lawyers do not appreciate the role of paralegals in helping people to gain access to the law. Some regard it as an encroachment into their territory, which they guard jealously. This makes the work of paralegals very difficult, as their work is supportive of and complementary to that of lawyers.

As paralegals are a direct link to the community, they need to work closely with other professionals in their communities, for example, doctors, social workers, psychologists, architects, and town planners. However, in small towns these professionals do not want to work with paralegals, and state agencies and local authorities have refused to recognise the role of paralegals within communities. These bodies have even gone to the extent of closing down advice centres, thus hampering the work of paralegals.

## The future

There are some hopeful signs. The Minister of Justice acknowledged, on being asked about granting rights of audience to paralegals:

> What we have found in our experience throughout the country is that paralegals have played a very important role . . . and, in many instances . . . paralegals, by virtue of the experience that they have developed over the years, are quite capable of representing people.[3]

We must begin by looking at the experiences of the past and use them to build a more effective system. There are a number of ways in which existing paralegals and advice centres can be used. At present there is an investigation into paralegals and the 'ladder' system of legal education and practice (discussed by Geoff Budlender in the previous chapter, p137). This was undertaken by the sub-committee of the Access Continuation Committee.[4]

The Access Continuation Committee has made recommendations with regard to paralegals. These are:

– Legal advice offices, staffed by paralegals, should be seen as an important part of an integrated legal aid system in South Africa.

- The Legal Aid Board should be prepared to provide funding for legal advice offices.
- The legal profession should adopt a positive and supportive attitude towards the emergence of the community-based paralegal.
- The certification of paralegals should continue to develop on a voluntary basis, and at this stage there is no need for any form of licensing of paralegals.
- To the extent that paralegals provide legal services in the areas reserved for lawyers, the existing provisions of the Attorneys Act can be applied.
- At this stage of its development, paralegals should not be incorporated in the ladder system of legal practice. Any incorporation would imply licensing and that is presently not advisable.
- The training of paralegals may, however, be incorporated in a ladder system of legal education. Where law faculties have undertaken certification of paralegals, they may offer paralegals expedited entry into university and the recognition of appropriate courses.
- The technikons should continue with presentation and development of suitable courses for paralegals.

Implementation of these recommendations would go a long way towards clarifying the position of paralegals in our legal system. On the one hand, the grassroots nature of community advice centres will not be stifled, in that at present no educational qualifications will be enforced to enable one to be a paralegal. On the other, it will enable those who see paralegal work as a career to pursue it.

Acceptance by the government of these recommendations would alleviate the funding problems presently experienced by community advice centres. The recognition of paralegals will contribute significantly to alleviating the problem of the lack of legal representation within our communities. A mechanism can thereby be created where lawyers can work hand in hand with paralegals. Paralegals will therefore be the first point of access to justice and social welfare. The task of these paralegals would include: advice-giving, monitoring, mediating, community education, and referring cases to relevant agencies or law firms. The concept of paralegal services could also be introduced in state welfare organisations. Paralegals could be employed in magistrates' courts and state departments dealing with community affairs. Their duties would be similar to those of community advice centres. They could liaise with others employed by the state, for example, public defenders, social workers, legal aid officers, and with lawyers in the private sector. It will also be necessary for community advice centres to maintain their independence from lawyers and state organs.

## Training

If the problem of funding is resolved, it will then be easier to coordinate training. Paralegals will look upon their work as a career. They will be committed to advance themselves. Training can therefore be structured as follows: basic; advanced; specialised; in-service and refresher.

### Basic

This would be informally provided by non-government training organisations. The training could take place in the evenings and over weekends. The training would include general skills in office administration and training in regard to the type of work conducted in these offices. At the end of the course the paralegals could receive attendance certificates. They would not be expected to write exams.

### Advanced

Advanced training means a general paralegal training course including more developed skills training, such as counselling, bookkeeping, advanced mediating skills; more detailed content, for example dealing with advanced casework, criminal procedure or labour law; new skills training, including accessible writing and computer literacy. This training could happen formally at a technikon or university and run with the assistance of non-governmental organisations. The length of the course could be about six months and paralegals could be tested and thereafter presented with a diploma.

### Specialised

Specialised training means detailed skills and content training for a specific kind of work. It could also be undertaken at universities or technikons. It can take the form of longer training for, say, a year, after which a person can be tested and obtain a diploma, or a shorter period, attending short courses of, say, two to three weeks and thereafter receiving attendance certificates. Attendance at these could provide the mechanism by which a paralegal could move up the ladder system.

*Refresher*
This would allow paralegals to keep their skills and knowledge up to date.

## Conclusion

Rights of court audience raise vexed issues and will need to be debated extensively. In my view, paralegals should be able to appear on behalf of accused in minor offences in, for example, the traffic or labour courts and other tribunals. Paralegals should also be able to assist people to formulate small claims court actions. If the ladder system is introduced, paralegals can then progress with experience within that system.

We should remember that the use of 'barefoot' lawyers will not be a first in the world. The citizens' advice bureaux in Britain are an example of a system of lay people providing advice and assistance to members of the public. In parts of Latin America, Asia and Africa, the paralegal has sometimes been seen as the legal equivalent of the 'barefoot doctor' working mainly in the rural areas where there are few or no lawyers. In Zimbabwe, paralegals have been used to educate the people about their legal rights. In South Africa we have proved that the paralegal system is a necessity and that it can work. We only need to perfect it.

## References

1   Industrial Aid Society, Annual Report 1990, p2.
2   For example, the Legal Education Action Project and Black Sash Conference in July 1990 on 'Working for Justice: The Role of paralegals in South Africa'.
3   A M Omar MP, interviewed in *De Rebus*, the official magazine of the attorneys' profession, July 1994, pp489–490.
4   'An investigation into paralegals and the ladder system of legal education and practice' by the sub-committee of the Access Continuation Committee, April 1994.

# CHAPTER 11

# Reality bites: the US Legal Services Corporation

GERRY SINGSEN

*The author is currently Assistant to the President at the Legal Services Corporation, the national organisation funded by the United States Congress to receive and manage funds for civil legal services to people living below the federal poverty line. He was a lecturer in law at Harvard Law School from 1984 to 1993, directed Harvard's Program on the Legal Profession and was the Coordinator of the Inter-University Consortium on Poverty Law. He worked for a decade as a legal services attorney in New York; was Vice-President of the Legal Services Corporation from 1979 to 1982; and has written and lectured extensively on the provision of legal services to low and moderate income individuals.*

In late 1993, President Clinton appointed, and the Senate confirmed, a new board of directors for the Legal Services Corporation (LSC). These eleven individuals, with strong histories of support for the delivery of civil legal services to the poor, replaced holdover recess appointees of President Bush who had never been confirmed by the Senate and brought to an end a twelve-year history of hostility between the LSC board and the broad coalition of lawyers and politicians who have supported the federally funded corporation. The new board's most important initial responsibility was to mark the change in leadership by issuing a clear declaration that LSC was, once again, firmly committed to the pursuit of justice.

In December 1993, the board took several dramatic steps. First, it received the resignation of LSC's President (the chief executive officer) and a number of senior staff members, and appointed Alexander Forger as interim President. Then, in a clear departure from all of the corporation's history, the board passed a resolution firmly declaring its mission to be the pursuit of equal justice for people in poverty. This mirrored the language and commitment of a

151

trade association that represents corporation grantees, their clients, staff lawyers, paralegals and other staff members. Finally, in pursuit of that mission, and acting on a recommendation from the American Bar Association (ABA), the corporation's board decided to seek an appropriation of $848 million (about £560 million) for 1995, more than double what it was receiving for 1994.

These bold moves laid the groundwork for many important and exciting developments during 1994. Alex Forger has been installed as the permanent President; the corporation's operating behaviour has changed almost 180 degrees; grantee performance is being examined more effectively than ever before; and those running local pro-grammes are being encouraged to solve their internal problems and improve their client services.

But the last ten months have been very difficult for achieving the long-term goal of establishing a new sense of mission in civil legal services and building a base for the major increase in funding that will be needed if the United States is ever to approach the financial commitment to justice that is evident throughout much of Western Europe. There will be no easy road to change. The road to justice runs through territory occupied by doubtful politics, uninformed but firm opinions, and uncertain commitments to equal justice for people in poverty.

## A little history

Until the 1960s, legal assistance in civil or criminal matters was largely left to the charitable impulses of state and local governments and private organisations. Some states provided counsel to criminal defendants in most matters; others made little help available. In civil matters, almost no governmental funds were allocated to provision of legal aid. Instead, private non-profit legal aid societies, often affiliated with local Bar associations, made relatively meagre amounts of assistance available.

## *Criminal services*

During the 1960s there were major changes. Supreme Court opinions established a federal constitutional right to the assistance of legal counsel in state criminal matters which might result in incarceration. The financial burden of implementing this right fell on state and local governments, which responded by establishing assigned counsel systems using private lawyers or public defenders within city governments, or by entering into contracts with legal aid societies.

Thirty years later, the system is essentially unchanged. Funding for criminal defence services is approximately $2 billion (£1.3 billion) per year,[1] but there is no national co-ordinating body or authority. Each state, and often each city or county, maintains a separate and unique system for meeting criminal defence needs. About 40 per cent of these funds ($800 million or £530 million), accounting for about 30 per cent of the matters, are disbursed to attorneys in private law firms, either through contracts for predetermined volumes of cases or through an assigned counsel programme (the court assigns new cases to attorneys on a list of eligible lawyers). The other 60 per cent of the funds ($1.2 billion or £800 million) takes care of the other 70 per cent of the cases, through about 13,000 lawyers employed full time by private non-profit legal aid societies or by governmental public defenders.

The criminal defence system is in an increasing state of crisis in the 1990s. There has never been sufficient funding to provide equal resources for defence when compared with prosecution. But more than a decade of a war on drugs, of mandatory minimum sentencing, of the return of the death penalty and of increasing public fear of crime have produced massive infusions of funds for the police, new prisons and the prosecution, but very little counterbalance for the defence. Indeed, in an effort to hold down costs, a number of jurisdictions have shifted their criminal defence approach from a staffed system to a private attorney system. These shifts often produced deplorable declines in quality, in part because of 'low-ball', artificially low, bids and the assignment of inexperienced junior attorneys to fulfil the contracts. Staffed systems were consistently able to demonstrate a higher quality of services, perhaps because they routinely maintained supervisory control over cases. In fact, even the cost motive for shifting to private attorneys was generally unsuccessful, as contractors pushed second and third year prices well above the prior costs of public defenders or legal aid societies.

## Civil legal services

No comparable right to civil legal assistance has ever been established. Instead, under President Lyndon Johnson, the Office of Economic Opportunity (OEO) created an Office of Legal Services in 1965, to which was appropriated a relatively small amount of funding for the purpose of setting up civil legal services offices. In the four years between 1966 and 1969, legal services programmes were funded in most large cities, in the northeastern quarter of the country and on the West Coast.

The federally funded civil legal services programme is in the midst of its third opportunity for growth and change. The first chance lasted about four years (1966–1969) and the second lasted five (1976–1980) before President Reagan was elected.[2] The dark periods in between were longer; six years (1970–1975) and twelve years (1981–1992). The third period began in 1993,[3] and no one knows just how long it will last.[4]

The first period of development in civil legal services might be called the millennial period, driven by a vision of a transformed society. Because of its origin in OEO's 'War on Poverty', the express purpose of the Office of Legal Services was to use law as a tool in an all-out government effort to eradicate poverty. Legal services programmes were to engage in community legal education and organising, in law reform through test cases and legislative advocacy, and in economic development work for groups of low-income clients. Individual cases were, of course, still the bulk of the matters handled by the offices, but they were explicitly relegated to a lower rung on the priority ladder adopted in federal guidelines. Among its strategies to help the desired types of advocacy occur, OEO funded national support centres to explore cutting-edge substantive issues and consider the special needs of such portions of the eligible population as Indians, migrants, children and senior citizens. OEO also established a fellowship programme to recruit progressive and talented young lawyers into legal services, placing them in local programmes after putting them through a month of specialised training in social justice.[5]

About a year after President Nixon took office, he attacked the whole 'War on Poverty'. Many experiments from the sixties were laid aside, but not legal services. When bureaucratic attempts to sap legal services' energy failed, the president decided to try a different strategy. He agreed first to the concept, and then, after three years of negotiation with Congress, the reality of an independent LSC, outside the executive branch of the government. In July 1974, less than a month before he resigned, he signed the Legal Services Corporation Act.

During the full period of Nixon's presidency, the lawyers and leaders in legal services programmes maintained their commitment to the purposes of social justice that had drawn them to legal services in the 1960s. Moreover, President Nixon was himself a lawyer, and in at least this aspect of his presidency he showed some sympathy for the idea that the law should apply to everyone. President Gerald Ford appointed the Corporation's first Board of Directors, which took office in July 1975. This board, and its successor appointed by President Carter in 1977 and 1978, presided over the 'institutional' period in federal legal services. It is fair to say that the Nixon vision of an independent, relatively apolitical law firm serving the poor guided this era in legal services.

In five years, from 1976 to 1980, the federally funded legal services programmes expanded from about 2,000 to about 6,000 lawyers, from $79 million (£52 million) to $300 million (£200 million), and from a regionalised to a truly national programme with every county in the nation served, at least to some degree, by a legal services office. Almost all the corporation's energy and leadership was consumed by the growth taking place in this period. Many new local programmes were opened; massive training was provided to new lawyers and new managers; and a national network of technical advisors was hired to assist local office leadership. As the era came to a close, nearly every state had at least some funding for an ongoing state support effort to complement the sixteen national support centres.

While many programme managers and national leaders maintained a personal commitment to a social justice mission, this rapid growth was accompanied by, perhaps made possible as a result of, a new and less 'political' rhetorical lexicon. The express purpose for which funding was sought was to ensure that a local legal services programme would receive sufficient financial support to hire two lawyers and appropriate support staff for every 10,000 eligible persons in the programme's service area. This 'minimum access' approach was silent on the purpose of the lawyers' work, at most echoing the Legal Services Corporation Act's requirement of 'high quality, economical and effective' service.

Ronald Reagan was elected in November 1980. While some had hoped that a more bureaucratic, institutional legal services rhetoric would defuse the programme's political vulnerability, that hope was quickly dashed. Within a month of taking office and for seven years thereafter, President Reagan proposed that the LSC be defunded entirely. The reasons were not subtle. Legal services programmes encouraged people to sue the government, costing taxpayers money for defence and encouraging liberal judges to interpret the law in ways that conservatives did not approve. In one remarkable analysis, a transition paper, prepared on the eve of President Reagan's inauguration, concluded that there just were not enough conservative lawyers willing to work for the low wages paid by legal services programmes. Since the conservatives could not take the programme over, the paper argued for its elimination.

Despite effective control of both Houses of Congress in 1981 and 1982, President Reagan had only a very partial success. Provisions were added to annual appropriations bills that restricted some marginal types of advocacy and added administrative hurdles for others. Funding was reduced by 25 per cent for 1982 (and 1983), before it began to rise again in 1984. The Reagan administration obtained one further change: 60 per cent of the members of the local boards of directors for the 320 legal services programmes were henceforth to be appointed by local Bar associations.[6] Some thought this would be the most damning cut of all.

Many legal services programmes had been begun or expanded into areas in which the Bar was traditionally hostile toward legal services. Nowhere was this more apparent than in the rural southeastern United States, where race played a major role in the rejection of legal services funding during the 1960s. The Reagan strategy was to undercut social advocacy by turning programmes over to the hostile Bars in such areas. But two crucial miscalculations on his part turned this strategy into a key factor in the survival of the LSC during the 1980s. First, the LSC Board of Directors and the American Bar Association (ABA) had begun working together prior to the election to build a strong, national alliance between private lawyers and legal services. In August 1980, with corporation encouragement, the ABA adopted a resolution calling on the corporation to devote a substantial amount of its funds to involving private attorneys in the delivery of services to the poor. The election accelerated work on this alliance. Early in 1981, the LSC gave the ABA a grant for development of pro bono programmes around the country. When the 1981 appropriation incorporated a requirement for substantial private attorney involvement, the corporation adopted a local programme guideline requiring them to devote about 10 per cent of their resources to private attorney involvement. Early in 1982, the corporation and the ABA held a series of conferences to teach both legal services and Bar members around the country effective methods for using private attorneys to deliver services to the poor, with a strong emphasis on the pro bono methods that studies had suggested were often most cost-effective. Thus, at the very time when the Reagan administration was looking to the private Bar to put controls on local programmes, the same local Bars were joining with the local programmes to develop new, cooperative methods of delivering services.

The second miscalculation was more surprising. As Bar presidents began to appoint members to local boards of directors during late 1981 and 1982, the local boards of directors began to be part of the local Bar association's 'turf'. Rather than continuing to be the object of hostile attention, the programmes became the recipients of support and protection from their new patrons. The difference was psychological, not financial. Even with the 10 per cent guideline, very little money was moving from legal services programmes either to Bar associations or to private attorneys. Indeed, the private attorney involvement effort ended up creating about 800 local pro bono programmes through which more than 120,000 lawyers per year now contribute their time without compensation (and often at personal out-of-pocket expense).

Once the attempt to eliminate the LSC had failed, President Reagan retreated to a version of the strategy President Nixon had tried eleven years earlier; he appointed a group of people who mostly opposed legal services to be its board of directors. But here, again, he failed, although the costs of his enmity were borne on the backs of the poor and their legal services advocates throughout the decade. The first board appointed by President Reagan failed to obtain confirmation from the Senate, despite its Republican majority, and left office at the end of 1982. The second board, appointed more than a year later, was finally confirmed in 1985 and mounted an extremely aggressive and expensive attempt to prove that local legal services programmes were engaging in illegal activities. When their intemperance became clear, the United States Senate rebuffed them[7] by placing stringent riders on appropriations bills that made it nearly impossible for the LSC to abuse local lawyers. The board appointed by President Bush in 1989 was far more neutral in its approach to civil legal services, and supported increases in funding while seeking ways to pay at least some attention to improving services for clients.

One other development during this second dark age of legal services bears mentioning. Because Congressional leaders recognised that the corporation and the executive branch were opposed to the delivery of high-quality legal services to the poor, those leaders turned to the National Legal Aid and Defender Association and the Project Advisory Group for guidance on legal services policy during this period. These two trade associations developed strong ties with the ABA, among their local programme constituencies and within Congress, and were able effectively to recommend their drafts of statutes and reports between 1984 and 1993. Among their accomplishments was preserving the distribution of funds through the minimum-access approach during the entire 12-year period.

These two organisations also assumed central roles in efforts to review current legal assistance activity, defend programmes against the corporation's attacks, and initiate improvements in programme performance. For example, working with the ABA, they were able to develop standards for providers of civil legal assistance to the poor, and standards for monitoring provider performance. However, their activities suffered from a common problem for trade associations – they had some difficulty in being critical of individuals or organisations within their constituencies. As a result, some kinds of analysis and change were beyond their capacity to undertake. The challenge of initiating and implementing major improvements or revisions in the delivery system, or developing a new rhetoric with which to define the work of civil legal services, was beyond their reach. The absence of collaboration with a powerful funding source was too much of a problem.

## The current position

For 1994, the LSC received $400 million (£265 million), with which it funded about 4,500 lawyers and 2,000 paralegals to provide advice and either partial or full services to approximately 1.6 million clients whose families totalled perhaps five million people. Other sources of funds, primarily interest on lawyer's trust accounts, injected another $150 million (£100 million) into the delivery system, for a total of about $2.20 (£1.45) per person living in the United States. Thus, combined civil and defender funding was nearly $10 (£6.65) per head in 1994, or about $46 (£31) per poor person.[8] Almost all compensated providers of civil legal services are non-profit organisations that employ full-time lawyers, but a small percentage of the funds are used by non-profit organisations to compensate private attorneys on a reduced-fee basis (usually about 50 per cent of what the lawyers otherwise would charge), either through a closed-panel judicare system or on contract. The private attorneys are subject to close case review by the organisation, which often does the initial case interview and maintains a joint client-lawyer relationship along with the private attorney.

Each of the providers of civil legal services must make decisions about the work it will choose to do with its limited funds. These priority choices may be based on types of cases (refusing to do divorces, name changes or wills, for example) or types of services offered (paralegal help with social security disability or pro se advice clinics for uncontested divorces) or even on geography (by not locating offices where it would be particularly inefficient). No two local programmes are alike. Estimates vary, but it seems likely that only about one in five serious legal problems experienced by low-income individuals receive the help of a lawyer or paralegal.

The LSC board, president and staff, in consultation with the trade associations, the ABA and the local legal services programmes, must now consider and decide a number of fundamental policy questions during this opportunity. Moreover, they must reach their decisions in the circumstances suggested by the collage of images set out at the end of this chapter. Increased appropriations will be extremely difficult to obtain. The public attitude toward poor people, and programmes designed to help them, is relatively negative. The tenor of current political debate is obstructionist and harsh, with little credible seeking of the high ground on many issues. Commitments to constitutional purposes, to fundamental issues of justice and even to equality before the law are sometimes in doubt.

## A three-stage plan

The new board's exciting initial commitment to equal justice for people in poverty has fallen on barren soil in Congress. Reality has intervened. The commitment continues, but the method for moving forward has been clouded. Faced with these challenges, I think the corporation should develop a three-stage plan that will transform the debate about civil legal services delivery as the LSC it heads into the next century.[9]

The first stage of the plan should span 1995 and 1996, and build the base for the other two by redescribing equal justice as a practical, useful, cost-effective method of helping low income individuals become more productive and less expensive participants in the social contract. The short-term objectives would be to repair the damaged understanding of legal services advocacy for the poor and re-establish that the basic purpose of legal services work is to help poor individuals solve real problems by giving them high-quality legal advice and assistance.

In the second stage, from 1997 into 1999, an intellectual and operational analysis should be completed that demonstrates how true equal justice can be achieved at a cost that is commensurate with the measurable benefit to the society as a whole. Also in this period, the LSC must take the lead in developing public understanding of the importance of legal assistance for the poor in an overall strategy for improving society. Thus, the medium-term objective should be to create both the technical and the general understanding that will be required in order to accomplish equal justice for people in poverty. In the third stage, beginning in 1999 if all goes well, the long-term objective would be to put in place a legal services delivery system that can produce equal justice for all people living in poverty.

At the core of this plan is the belief that the LSC must maintain its commitment to a definition of high quality representation that includes advice and representation on the full range of client needs, using the full range of legal options. Artificially limiting the potential of legal assistance for the poor will, by definition, end any hope of fulfilling a vision of equal justice. At the same time, the plan accepts the reality of the current political debate in the United States; neither Congress nor state governments are enthusiastic about providing new funds for social programmes designed simply to provide goods and services to the poor. To justify growth, the LSC will have to demonstrate that the work of the lawyers it funds makes sense as part of our nation's larger effort to reduce dependence and increase the contribution of those who are currently poor to the social and economic well-being of the country. In a strange way, the LSC must return to its roots as an anti-poverty programme.

## *1995–1996*

Before the presidential election in the fall of 1996, the corporation's first priority is to demonstrate its accountability for funds from Congress and rebuild a stable infrastructure within which legal services programmes can operate effectively and improve their performance. Accountability has already been the watchword of the new board's first year in office. A $2.3 million (£1.50 million) deficit inherited from the previous board has been removed. A bankrupt corporation approach to monitoring the performance of grantees has been replaced with a multi-layered oversight system, working from self-certification through a 'desk review' and financial statement audit to on-site peer review in accord with performance standards that have now been developed and tested. Ideally, every programme will have been the object of a peer review visit and report by early

1997. In addition, the corporation is now in the process of employing experienced legal services advocates and managers to guide the programme review effort, conduct research and experimentation in programme improvement and provide technical assistance to local programmes.

A more stable environment will also result from changing the way that the programme is presented and understood. It is no longer persuasive simply to argue for new resources on the basis of unmet legal needs and the obvious inadequacy of current funding. The budget is too tight. Most social programmes are inadequately funded. Moreover, Congress has little interest in funding proposals that ultimately rest on a sense of entitlement or 'rights'. To make a change, the corporation must revise its approach by developing information that demonstrates how local programmes will actually use specific increases in funding. Will they serve additional people, will they achieve cost effective results that are of value in local communities, will they open new offices in underserved areas, will they develop new methods of delivering services that respond to important local needs?

Every local programme needs to participate in this change in the way that the value of legal services is described. It must become clear that the lawyer's role is producing just outcomes and that everyone, not only the poor, has an interest in seeing justice done. The perception must be overcome that lawyers clog the economic engine, that allowing the poor to be heard and to obtain justice hurts those who are less poor. Instead, we can show that practical benefits result to society when women are no longer beaten; when job programmes are available to all; when children are supported by their absent fathers; when racial bias does not stand in the way of employment; and when slum landlords put their excess profits into maintaining safe, decent and sanitary dwellings as required by law. This change in understanding will affect each lawyer and local programme. It will redefine the programme's responsiveness to its clients, perhaps making legal services even more 'consumer' oriented than they have been. It will increase local awareness that producing results defines success in work for the poor, not simply producing participation in process.

The corporation must at the same time reaffirm its historical commitment to high quality, effective and economical representation through staffed legal services programmes, particularly because this change will affect the workers' understanding of the role of legal services. It should not allow the emphasis on outcomes to mislead anyone into thinking it is adopting a preference for case counts over real results. The rhetoric of results must include a clear declaration that the results sought are consistent with the long-term purpose of equal justice. Without this clarity, the new description of the work may lead to greater understanding of legal services in Congress but also to a loss of commitment to the work among those engaged on the local programmes. For staff lawyers whose compensation is as much psychic as fiscal, the importance of a strong mission for justice can never be overlooked.

One of the ways that the equal justice purpose can be affirmed while the description of practical objectives is developed is through maintenance and improvement of the LSC's support infrastructure. The symbolic and practical meaning of that emphasis in funding policy will help to send a message to legal services workers that equal justice remains the long-term goal even while the LSC learns to make the immediate, practical effects of high quality representation better understood.

## 1997–1999

While establishing the basic, current value of an accountable pro-gramme of civil legal services, the LSC must also undertake a serious examination of the long-term value and cost of providing equal justice to low-income people. This examination should begin in 1995 and be designed for completion in 1998 or 1999, time enough to allow not only research and reflection but also some limited experimentation. Important allies in accomplishing this examina-tion will be teachers and scholars in law schools, who have been considering some of these questions for many years.

Many of the items on this possible research agenda will lend themselves to comparative law research as well as demonstration projects. For example, should eligibility for free services remain capped at 125 per cent of the federal poverty level? Should clients be asked to pay nominal fees at every income level, and increasing fees if services are extended to those above the current 125 per cent cap? Should the current prohibition on contingency fee damage actions be maintained either in order to protect struggling members of the private Bar or to avoid diluting the staffed programmes' sense of mission? Should the civil and defender delivery systems remain distinct and largely separate, or is there an advantage to joining them together? Can an equal justice system remain primarily reliant on full-time, salaried attorneys, even though that might mean as many as 40,000 staff attorneys? On the other hand, can a legal services system that relies primarily on private attorneys remain as inexpensive as the staff system, and can it maintain a commitment to a mission for equal justice in the broad sense? Perhaps a mixed system will be best, but how is the labour to be divided? What role will be appropriate for non-lawyers, whether as paralegals in staffed programmes or as independent legal technicians? Will there be a need for changes in the dispute resolution system in order to make a transition to equal justice possible? What will be the consequence of offering high quality representation, broadly defined, to all eligible persons in a community?

Developing public understanding about the positive effects of making legal assistance available to the poor seems a more daunting task, perhaps because it is so much harder to plan. The goal is simple enough. It should become common knowledge that a primary effect of good legal counsel is personal empowerment. A client not only solves a specific problem through resort to a lawyer but also learns a new way of relating to ongoing difficulties. Having received effective legal assistance, a client is often enabled to act more affirmatively and confidently in the future. Moreover, the resolution of one important problem can lead to the resolution of others and the removal of barriers to personal advancement. In addition, when the law is enforced regularly on behalf of the powerless, all members of society are encouraged to believe that it will be enforced again in the future, perhaps on their behalf. Respect for law increases; challenges to authority in the streets and schoolrooms decrease.

How can the LSC contribute to public education which conveys these truths? Are programmes in the high schools useful? Perhaps television drama is a better communicator. Can coalitions of political, social, professional and business leaders transmit this message effectively, or can it only be demonstrated through a million stories on the evening news? Will it be possible to convince people of moderate income, not now eligible for free services, that they have an interest in assuring that the poor can obtain help, or will it only transform consciousness if eligibility levels are increased first, so that the interest can be demonstrated directly? Is there any real hope that the LSC can make a significant impact on public consciousness at all, even with the support and active participation of many leaders throughout society? Or is current public cynicism and anger so great that education must fail and another dark age must arise for civil legal services before longer-term change is conceivable?

The possibility that the LSC may pass through another period of hostility requires mention of another task for the medium-term. Building on the base of accountability and the increase in stability already described, the LSC must constantly work to strengthen the ability of local programmes and their associations to maintain and improve themselves without LSC encouragement. Low-income individuals rely on legal services programmes for essential services. Even when the national political climate is less hospitable, local programmes must be able to examine themselves, obtain help from each other and watch out for their clients' interests. The experience of the last dozen years shows that this can be done, but that it is also possible to do it better. An ongoing responsibility of the LSC is to join with the ABA, other Bar associations, NLADA (National Legal Aid and Defender Association), PAG (Project Advisory Group) and local programmes to strengthen continuously their ability to function independently.

Finally, if a long-term research and education strategy is doomed to fail, should the LSC itself undertake a cynical change in direction and turn away from equal justice by offering Congress a legal services programme that concentrates on providing high volume, low impact legal advice and assistance in routine cases? Would such an offer be accepted, with a resulting dramatic increase in the availability of at least some assistance for a larger share of the eligible population? If it would, would obtaining new funds in that way represent a success or a failure?

## 1999 and beyond

The long-term objective of putting in place a system for delivering equal justice will undoubtedly be the most difficult objective to achieve but it is the easiest to describe from this distance. Using the base established in the short-term with the research and increased understanding achieved in the medium-term, the LSC should approach the Congress with a well-designed vision of an equal justice system and phase it into place over as many as five additional years. It seems inevitable that equal justice will involve a mixed delivery system, including pro bono, compensated private lawyer services for special legal problems and isolated populations, as well as a much larger staff attorney programme. Also likely, but less certain, is an increase in eligibility levels and the introduction of fees charged to at least the relatively less poor clients. Similarly, as part of a broader pattern of change in the legal system, the equal justice delivery system will probably involve more use of both staff and independent non-lawyers, and increased self-help by individuals who obtain some advice and counsel from the legal services programmes. Merger of civil and defender programmes on a broad scale seems a less likely development, however, given the strong preference in American politics for local rather than federal policy-making and control.

With all of these changes, the civil legal services programmes will edge closer to their Canadian and Northern European cousins. But the distinctly American focus on the social justice purpose of providing legal assistance, through a definition of high quality representation that encompasses a full range of advocacy on broadly conceived legal problems, will probably continue to be as unique as the federal programme's origins in the 'War on Poverty' in the 1960s.

## Sound bites from the legal services battleground

'Equal Justice' is a fundamental principle that our nation holds out to every person. It begins with the constitutional purpose 'to establish justice', and includes the explicit guarantees of due process and equal protection of the laws. It is the fundamental social contract of the Declaration of Independence that all are 'created equal' and entitled to the inalienable rights of 'life, liberty and the pursuit of happiness'. It is the enacted promise that our laws will be made and administered without bias, that disputes will be resolved without resort to violence or undue influence, and that people will be heard and considered as equals without regard to wealth, race, gender, age, disability, creed, sexual orientation or other personal characteristics.

It is the goal of the Legal Services Corporation to help bring equal justice to all people living in poverty.[10]
  – *The first words of the first Budget Request submitted to the Congress of the United States by the LSC Board of Directors appointed by President Clinton in 1993.*

The 1990 Census identified 13.1 per cent of the population as living below the federal poverty level. By 1993, census estimates placed the poverty level at 15.1 per cent, despite growth in the national economy. Since eligibility for civil legal services cuts off a little bit above the poverty line, the 1990 figures suggested that more than 50 million people were qualified by income for free services (about 20 per cent of the total population). The 1993 data suggest that at least six million more have become eligible in the early 1990s. LSC funding supported some assistance (more than 60 per cent is just advice or a phone call or letter) to about 1.6 million clients in 1993, which provided direct help to perhaps six million clients, family members and others closely affected. When all other sources of services are added, studies suggest that less than 20 per cent of the critical civil needs of the poor for legal assistance are addressed by even advice.

*– LSC Data*

When Helen J. comes to a legal services office seeking a divorce because her husband beats her, a proper interview by the lawyer not only obtains evidence of the beatings and probes Helen's desires regarding financial support and physical protection, but also discusses changing the locks, moving into a battered woman's shelter, whether Helen can support herself, needs help with public assistance, or is eligible for a job training programme. In addition, the lawyer may need to learn why her husband is violent, whether his union or his employer has a programme for substance abuse or knows he has been violent, and whether the husband would respond to importuning by his family, a friend or the family's minister. Moreover, the lawyer will determine whether a protective order has been previously issued against the husband's violence, and whether the police have been called and how they responded. If police response has been persistently inadequate in this and other cases, the lawyer may consider whether local legislation is needed to require better police performance in the future, or whether an injunctive or damages action against the police for failing to perform their duties is in order.

*– Sample of training lecture on proper interviewing of clients as part of providing high quality legal assistance.*

A federal court in California, ruling in a case brought on behalf of indigent clients by several legal services attorneys, decides that a certain piece of state welfare reform is illegal under federal law and orders the state to pay welfare benefits that the clients are entitled to.

Legal services attorneys in New Jersey file a federal class action that alleges that state welfare reform laws that refuse additional benefits for babies born to mothers already on welfare violate federal laws, should not have been approved by federal authorities and fail to provide help even when the birth results from the rape of a woman with religious scruples against abortion.

*– Spring 1994 news stories*

A community legal education pamphlet written by a legal services attorney accurately explains in passing that the law allows a welfare recipient, without any need even to see a lawyer, to expend rapidly lump sum damage awards they receive and then re-apply for welfare. A conservative newspaper describes the pamphlet as a blueprint for welfare fraud, and state legislators react by proposing criminal penalties for publication of similar pamphlets in the future and by seeking to eliminate millions of dollars of state funding for civil legal services. The legislation passes one house of the legislature, but fails by a small margin in the other.

*– Spring 1994 in Massachusetts*

But let us not use this good money for poor people to start suing the several States of America. That is really what is going to ruin Legal Services Corporation. I can guarantee it. . . . Anybody that says otherwise does not know what they are talking about, because I have worked this thing. I have defended the thing. I continue to defend it. I fight for increases. . . . I want to save that money for the poor. . . If you want to nullify a law, we are not going to give that money to Legal Services to get it nullified. Constitutional rights and privileges are fine business, but if there is a law – and particularly here we are talking about welfare reform – if you want to nullify that, do not use Legal Services. . . Under the Federal law, under the State Law, there are rights and, by cracky, use Legal Services Corporation. But when you want to attack and nullify the law itself, use the Attorney General, the Department of Health and Human Services.

*– Senator Ernest Hollings (Democrat from South Carolina), the*
*Chairman of the Senate Appropriations Subcommittee that deals*
*with appropriations for the LSC, speaking on 21 July 1994, in*
*support of an amendment offered by conservative Republican*
*Senator Phil Gramm of Texas, which would have barred the*
*use of LSC money to bring lawsuits challenging 'welfare reform'*
*legislation by state or federal governments.*

I do not know in advance how we can tie the hands of the Legal Services Corporation before any law is passed where there may be a matter of statutory interpretation which requires judicial action or there may be a matter of constitutional law which requires judicial action. . . There is no way, in my judgment, that we can anticipate whether or not there will be any valid contest to go to the court to challenge. . . It may be that when we pass a Welfare Reform Act, we are so confident at that stage there is no constitutional issue, maybe we ought to consider a prohibition at that time, as the Congress has the authority to limit the jurisdiction of the courts to take up statutory issues. . . But in advance of the passage of the law, it seems to me that this amendment is premature at best.

*– Senator Arlen Spector (Republican of Pennsylvania), speaking*
*against the Gramm amendment. The amendment failed 44–56.*

Performance Area One: Criterion 1: . . . The programme periodically makes effective and comprehensive assessments, analyses, and determinations of the most pressing unaddressed legal problems and needs of the low-income population in its service area . . .

Criterion 3: . . . [The programme] periodically sets explicit goals, priorities and specific objectives . . . expressed insofar as possible in terms of desired outcomes for the client community. . .

Performance Area Three: Criterion 1 – *Legal Representation.* The programme conducts its direct legal representation so that it comports with the relevant provisions of professional ethics, the ABA Standards for Providers of Civil Legal Services to the poor . . . Taken as a whole, the programme's legal representation achieves as much as is reasonably attainable for the client, given the client's objectives and all of the circumstances of the case, and also . . . the programme achieves as much as reasonably possible for other low-income people similarly situated, and for the target population as a whole . . .

*– Programme Improvement, Compliance, and Accountability*
*(PICA) Working Group, Performance Criteria Working Draft*
*– 25 June, 1994*


The United States Congress appropriates $415 million (£275 million) for LSC for 1995, a 3.75 per cent increase over 1994's $400 million (£265 million) and far less than the $500 million (£330 million) sought by President Clinton. (The corporation's February 1994 proposal of $848 million (£565 million), enough money to provide legal services for approximately a third of the serious legal problems experienced by the bottom 20 per cent of the population by income, was so far beyond what Congress would consider that it was revised in April to agree with the President's $500 million.)
*– August 1994*


In New York City, the Association of Legal Aid Attorneys, with about 900 members whose pay averages $45,000 (£30,000) per year, strikes for a 4.5 per cent wage increase over two years, equal to the raise just awarded to the management of the Legal Aid Society, a private non-profit organisation that provides most of the criminal defence services to the city's indigent defendants. The Mayor of New York cancels the city's contracts with Legal Aid and vows never to enter into another one unless the lawyers immediately return to work without a raise. He's trying to hold the line against any raises for municipal workers (even though the lawyers are not municipal workers). Under this pressure, Legal Aid management and union resolve the labour dispute overnight, agreeing on a 4 per cent raise over two years, and the attorneys go back to work. The mayor says the raise is unacceptable.
*– Synopsis of news stories, October 1994*

. . . The Corporation's Board of Directors will . . . [develop] a comprehensive budget justification which details the ways that investments in legal services in FY 1996 will result in practical benefits for the poor and improved administration of justice for the nation. We will develop firm estimates of the increased numbers of people this increase will allow our grantees to serve, the impact of the increase in services on client communities, the new offices we expect grantees to open and the new lawyers and paralegals who will go to work for the poor.

*– 14 October 1994 LSC letter to Hon. Alice Rivlin, Acting Director, Office of Management and Budget, Executive Office of the President. The letter urges President Clinton to propose a 1996 appropriation of $525 million (£350 million)*

# References

1 This translates into about $7.70 (£5.10) per year per person living in the United States. Eligibility levels vary state to state. Essentially, free services are available if the cost of hiring counsel would exceed the defendant's means; the more serious the matter, the higher the allowable income and assets.

2 One could argue that the second period extended through 1981, since President Reagan did not appoint his first LSC Board until New Year's Eve 1981. All of 1981 was so preoccupied with responses to the Reagan attack, however, that it seems unwarranted to describe it as part of a positive era of growth and change.

3 The Bush Board of Directors and staff made some significant efforts to improve the legal services system during their part of 1993 (through October), and they received a substantial increase in funding from the first year of President Clinton's Congress (from $357 to $400 million – £238 to £265 million).

4 The Board of Directors confirmed by the Senate in October 1993 is on staggered three-year terms, subject to reappointment in 1995 and 1996. If the members of the Board are renominated and reconfirmed in a timely fashion, a majority of the Board would serve until mid-1999.

5 The Reginald Heber Smith Community Lawyer Fellowship Program had a profound effect. In 1980, when President Reagan was elected and began his attempt to eliminate the Legal Services Corporation, seven of the top eight managers at the Corporation were former 'Reggies'.

6 Previously, the boards were composed of whatever accumulation of nominating bodies or appointing authorities the local legal services programme, perhaps influenced by local political and bar leaders, had selected. OEO and LSC regulations both required that one-third of the local board be com-

posed of individuals who were eligible to be programme clients at the time they were appointed. This requirement continues today.

7 By 1985, when this occurred, the Senate was back in Democratic hands, but the leader of the fight to protect local legal services programmes was Republican Warren Rudman of New Hampshire. Rudman's role during the 1980s cannot be overestimated. A former Attorney General of New Hampshire, a fiercely conservative state with the motto 'Live Free or Die', Rudman respected high quality advocacy wherever he found it, and had learned in New Hampshire that legal services attorneys did good work on valid issues for people with real needs. Again and again between 1981 and 1993, when he retired after two terms, Rudman stopped attempts by appointees of Presidents Reagan and Bush from damaging civil advocacy for low-income individuals.

8 $2,550,000,000 divided by the 56,000,000 estimated eligible for civil legal services = $46 per head.

9 Of course, the positions and conclusions presented here are simply my own and not the corporation's.

10 Legal Services Corporation, Budget Request for Fiscal Year 1995 (February 1994), p7. The same words appear in the same place in the Corporation's Revised Budget Request for Fiscal Year 1995 (April 1994).

# Public-interest and class litigation

# Public-interest and class litigation

This part contains three chapters. Indira Jaising considers the lessons to be learnt from the explosion of public-interest litigation in India since the ending of Mrs Ghandi's state of emergency. Martyn Day and Sally Moore, followed by George Pulman, deal with multi-party actions. In addition, a section of Carrie Menkel-Meadow's chapter in Part VI (p227–8) deals with class actions in the United States.

English law has reached a sort of half-way house in relation to public-interest cases. There are the beginnings of procedural recognition. Judicial review has been developed and, through advances such as those on legal standing, its scope broadened. Public-interest litigation against government, central or local, or public bodies is now easier, provided that a litigant with some form of tenuous connection with the case can be found.

The public interest is not, however, recognised in terms of legal aid, a point made by Martyn Day and Sally Moore. The Legal Aid Board labours away under rules based on the principle that litigation only takes place between consenting individuals concerned with their own measurable and individual interest. Nor, as Martyn Day and Sally Moore argue, is court procedure well adapted to identify the public interest elements in cases with large numbers of plaintiffs.

It is large multi-party or group actions rather than cases against the state which have raised this issue as a contemporary debate. The Legal Aid Board faces losses of around £35 million on a tranche of cases concerning the tranquilliser Benzodiazepene. Many of these were, individually, for relatively small amounts but, together, they constituted a major action that called forth the full resources of the defendants.

The two British contributions have different emphases. As plaintiffs' lawyers, Martyn Day and Sally Moore see courts as the proper venue for multi-party actions. George Pulman, a member of the Legal Aid Board as well as a practitioner, takes a more welcoming view of out-of-court determination. Both agree, however, that there might be some role for combining court and non-court processes.

The Indian legal system has adapted more flexibly to class actions. As Indira Jaising recounts, legislation has even constituted the Government of India as a representative plaintiff for the Bhopal victims. The burden of her account, however, concerns the new mechanisms developed to assist litigants against the state in cases which are recognised by the court as having a significant public interest. Some of these reforms, such as informal ways in which an action can be commenced, are probably not transferable to another context. More relevant, however, are the mechanisms which have been developed for enforcing court orders against the government or other official bodies, such as the appointment by the courts of commissions or commissioners to ensure that effect is given to their decisions.

# CHAPTER 12

# Public-interest litigation: the lessons from India

INDIRA JAISING, SA

*Indira Jaising is a Senior Advocate of the Supreme Court of India. She is also the editor of the monthly magazine, The Lawyers, on law and social justice. She has represented the pavement dwellers in Bombay and the victims of the Bhopal gas leak disaster. She is currently involved in challenging discriminatory provisions of Muslim and Hindu law which adversely affect women.*

India inherited a basically British legal system at independence at least in form, if not in content. But then, law is an area in which form almost dictates content and so the impact of this inheritance and its devastating consequences cannot be underestimated. To say that there is something incongruous about attempting to deliver justice or settle disputes using a sophisticated urbanised technique to administer local customs and native laws, would be to make an understatement. Yet that is what the system was: an adversarial mode of dispensing civil justice bound by technical rules of procedure and evidence – all drafted in English, administered by élite English-speaking judges, in a country where the vast majority of people were illiterate and incapable of enforcing their rights. The inappropriateness of the inherited legal system is apparent when you consider the differences between the two countries. One was a coloniser, the other was the colonised. One was the ruler, the other was the ruled. It was obvious that the transplanted legal system simply would not take root.

On independence, India became a republic with a written constitution, with guaranteed fundamental rights enforceable by the Supreme Court and the High Courts. The right to apply to the Supreme Court for enforcement of fundamental rights is itself a fundamental right (article 32). The Indian Supreme Court and High Courts can strike down not only arbitrary acts of adminis- 175 trative agencies but also parliamentary legislation. Indeed, the Supreme Court has asserted the power to strike down any constitutional amendment on the ground that it is opposed to the 'basic features' or 'basic structure' of the constitution.

Yet neither independence nor the guaranteed fundamental rights automatically put an end to a century-old inherited legal system. On the contrary, the system and all laws in force immediately before the commencement of the constitution continue, subject, of course, to the other provisions of the constitution. The Indian constitution is a post-second-world-war constitution and attempts to set up a welfare state. It includes directive principles of state policy. In pursuance of these directives, citizens' entitlements are enacted into law. But, as mentioned earlier, the system itself was slow to change, slow to respond to the needs of a basically impoverished people trying to get ahead of the poverty line.

The first 30 years of the new judicial system saw no change in its functioning. A glance at law reports of that period indicates that the only users of the High Court and the Supreme Court were the upper class. Cases mostly concerned disputes relating to taxation, property and corporate law. It would be no exaggeration to say that there is not a single decision of the Supreme Court on the rights of the dispossessed in that period.

Then came the Internal Emergency of 1975 imposed by the late Prime Minister Indira Gandhi, a period during which fundamental rights were suspended. It was during this period that the fundamental rights of citizens began to be eclipsed; the judiciary was either unable or unwilling to come to their aid. It appeared overawed by the late Mrs Gandhi's omnipresence. The Emergency was decisively rejected by the people in 1977, when Mrs Gandhi suffered a resounding electoral defeat. With the liberation of the people of India, the judiciary too seemed to be liberated and emerged from its own period of eclipse. The struggle that preceded the lifting of the emergency led to a heightened consciousness of civil rights among the people. The consciousness of civil rights was to have long-term beneficial effects for the legal system.

The era of what is known as social action or public interest litigation (PIL) is a post-Emergency phenomenon. The earliest cases in this category came to be filed in 1979. The two main institutions which played a role in the emergence of PIL were the media and the Supreme Court. In 1978, very graphic and well-researched reports appeared in the press on the plight of undertrials (people awaiting trial) who had been in prison as undertrials for terms longer than they would have received if they had been convicted. Based on these reports, journalists and lawyers filed petitions in the Supreme Court alleging violation of fundamental rights. Some of these petitions were filed in the name of the person aggrieved and others in the names of journalists or individual citizens or civil rights groups. The Supreme Court entertained all these petitions. Judges like Justice V R Krishna Iyer and Justice P N Bhagwati actively encouraged and entertained petitions on behalf of undertrials and prisoners complaining of torture in custody and police abuse of civil rights. Since the late 1970s and in the 1980s, the Supreme Court has entertained petitions on behalf of juveniles, women in distress, people in bonded labour, child labour, the mentally ill, homeless pavement dwellers and tribal people dispossessed as a result of development projects. Another major area of public interest litigation has been environmental litigations and mass disasters.

Thus, the origin of public interest litigation (PIL) in India lay in the active collaboration between organisations of the oppressed, a committed group of activist lawyers and an enthusiastic judiciary. Public interest litigation in India is directed mainly against the state and its agencies. It seeks to hold the state to its promise of social justice, to correct the imbalance between powerless groups and the state.

## What are the distinctive features of PIL?

Over the years, it was mainly Justice Bhagwati who was to spell out from case to case the identifying features of PIL and its rationale. He began by pointing out that the British adversarial system of civil litigation was based on what he called 'self-identification of injury and self-selection of remedy'. He then pointed out that the vast majority of the people of the country could not even recognise a legal injury and were not even aware of their legal rights. That being the position, there was no question of their being able to select an appropriate legal remedy; decide which lawyer to approach; in which court to sue and what relief to claim. If the rights of this group of people were to be protected, there would have to be a total departure from the adversarial system, with its insistence that only an aggrieved person would have a cause of action to sue. This led to the complete revolution of the doctrine of locus standi.

This is how Justice Bhagwati explained the need to liberalise the rules relating to standing:

If a person or determinate class of persons is, by reason of poverty, helplessness or disability or socially or economically disadvantaged position, unable to approach the court for relief, then any member of the public can maintain an application for an appropriate direction, order or writ in the High Court under article 226 and, in case of breach of any fundamental right of such person or determinate class of persons, in this court under article 32, seek judicial redress for the legal wrong or injury caused to such person or determinate class of persons.

Where the weaker sections of the community are concerned, such as under-trial prisoners languishing in jails without a trial, inmates of the protective home in Agra, or Harijan (untouchable) workers engaged in road construction in the district of Ajmer, who are living in poverty and destitution, who are barely eking out a miserable existence with their sweat and toil, who are helpless victims of an exploitative society and who do not have easy access to justice, this court will not insist on a regular writ petition to be filed by the public-spirited individual espousing their cause and seeking relief for them. This court will readily respond even to a letter addressed by such individual acting pro bono publico . . .

Today a vast revolution is taking place in the judicial process; the theatre of the law is changing fast and the problems of the poor are coming to the forefront. The court has to create new methods and devise new strategies for the purpose of providing access to justice to large masses of people who are denied their basic human rights and to whom freedom and liberty have no meaning. The only way in which this can be done is by entertaining writ petitions and even letters from public-spirited individuals seeking judicial redress for the benefit of persons who have suffered a legal wrong or a legal injury or whose constitutional or legal right has been violated, but who, by reason of their poverty or socially or economically disadvantaged position, are unable to approach the court for relief. It is in this spirit that the court has been entertaining letters for judicial redress and treating them as writ petitions and we hope and trust that the high courts of the country will also adopt this pro-active, goal-oriented approach.

But we must hasten to make it clear that the individual who moves the court for judicial redress in cases of this kind must be acting *bona fide* with a view to vindicating the cause of justice, and if he is acting for personal gain or private profit or out of political motivation or other oblique consideration, the court should not allow itself to be activised at the instance of such person and must reject his application at the threshold, whether it be in the form of a letter addressed to the court or even in the form of a regular writ petition filed in court.

We may also point out that as a matter of prudence and not as a rule of law, the court may confine this strategic exercise of jurisdiction to cases where legal wrong or legal injury is caused to a determinate class or group of persons or the constitutional or legal right of such a determinate class or group of persons is violated and, as far as possible, not entertain cases of individual wrong or injury at the instance of a third party, where there is an effective legal-aid organisation which can take care of such cases' rules relating to standing.

## The appointment of commissions

With the liberalisation of the requirements of locus standi came the liberalisation of the vast majority of the groups who were so far excluded from the justice process. Bonded labourers, the mentally ill, women abandoned in remand homes all found a voice and a space in the Supreme Court of India. Their problems began to be addressed at the national level. The next stage in the development of PIL was the appointment of commissioners for the purpose of fact-finding to bring the petition to a successful conclusion. In *Bandhua Mukti Morcha v UOI*,[1] an organisation devoted to the cause of release of workers from bonded labour addressed a letter to Justice Bhagwati alleging that a large number of labourers in Faridabad, only a few kilometres from the capital, were working in stone quarries under inhuman and intolerable conditions, that the provisions of the constitution were being violated and that the provisions of the Bonded Labour System Abolition Act 1976 were not being implemented. The court treated the letter as a petition and appointed a commission to inquire into its allegations. Explaining the role of the court, the judges said:

Public interest litigation is not in the nature of adversary litigation but is a challenge and an opportunity to the government and its officers to make basic human rights meaningful to the deprived and vulnerable sections of the community and to assure them social and economic justice which is the signature tune of our constitution. The government and its officers must welcome public interest litigation, because it would provide them with an occasion to examine whether the poor and the down-trodden are getting their social and economic entitlements, or whether they are continuing to remain victims of deception and exploitation at the hands of strong and powerful sections of the community and whether social and economic justice has become a meaningful reality for them or has remained merely a teasing illusion and a promise of unreality, so that in case the complaint in the public interest litigation is found to be true, they can, in discharge of their constitutional obligation, root out exploitation and injustice and ensure to the weaker sections their rights and entitlements.

When the court entertains public interest litigation, it does not do so in a cavilling spirit or in a confrontational mood or with a view to tilting at executive authority or seeking to usurp it, but its attempt is only to ensure observance of social and economic rescue programmes, legislative as well as executive, framed for the benefit of the have-nots and the handicapped and to protect them against violation of their basic human rights, which is also the constitutional obligation of the executive. The court is thus merely assisting in the realisation of the constitutional objectives.

Dealing with the procedure to be adopted in enforcing fundamental rights, the court said:

> It is not at all obligatory that an adversarial procedure, where each party produces his own evidence tested by cross-examination by the other side and the judge sits like an umpire and decides the case only on the basis of such material as may be produced before him by both the parties, must be followed in a proceeding under article 32 for enforcement of a fundamental right . . .
>
> Where one of the parties to a litigation belongs to a poor and deprived section of the community and does not possess adequate social and material resources, he is bound to be at a disadvantage as against a strong and powerful opponent under the adversary system of justice, because of his difficulty in getting competent legal representation and, more than anything else, his inability to produce relevant evidence before the court. Therefore, when the poor come before the court, particularly for enforcement of their fundamental rights, it is necessary to depart from the adversarial procedure and to evolve a new procedure which will make it possible for the poor and weak to bring the necessary material before the court for the purpose of securing enforcement of their fundamental rights. It must be remembered that the problems of the poor, which are now coming before the court, are qualitatively different from those which have hitherto occupied the attention of the court and they need a different kind of lawyering skill and a different kind of judicial approach. If we follow the adversarial procedure in their case blindly, they would never be able to enforce their fundamental rights and the result would be nothing but a mockery of the Constitution.
>
> We have, therefore, to abandon the laissez-faire approach in the judicial process, particularly where it involves a question of enforcement of fundamental rights and forge new tools, devise new methods and adopt new strategies for the purpose of making fundamental rights meaningful for the large masses of people . . . Now it is obvious that the poor and the disadvantaged cannot possibly produce relevant material before the court in support of their case and, equally, where an action is brought on their behalf by a citizen acting

pro bono publico, it would be almost impossible for him to gather the relevant material and place it before the court.

What is the Supreme Court to do in such a case? Would the Supreme Court not be failing in discharge of its constitutional duty of enforcing a fundamental right if it refuses to intervene because the petitioner belonging to the underprivileged segment of society or a public-spirited citizen espousing his cause is unable to produce the relevant material before the court? If the Supreme Court were to adopt a passive approach and decline to intervene in such a case because relevant material has not been produced before it by the party seeking its intervention, the fundamental rights would remain merely a teasing illusion as far as the poor and disadvantaged sections of the community are concerned.

It is for this reason that the Supreme Court has evolved the practice of appointing commissions for the purpose of gathering facts and data in regard to a complaint of breach of fundamental right made on behalf of the weaker sections of the society. The report of the commissioner would furnish prima facie evidence of the facts and data gathered by the commissioner and that is why the Supreme Court is careful to appoint a responsible person as commissioner to make an inquiry or investigation into the facts relating to the complaint. It is interesting to note that in the past the Supreme Court has appointed sometimes a district magistrate, sometimes a district judge, sometimes a professor of law, sometimes a journalist, sometimes an officer of the court and sometimes an advocate practising in the court, for the purpose of carrying out an inquiry or investigation and in making a report to the court, because the commissioner appointed by the court must be a responsible person who enjoys the confidence of the court and who is expected to carry out his assignment objectively and impartially without any predilection or prejudice.

Once the commissioner's report is received, copies of it would be supplied to the parties so that either party, if it wants to dispute any of the facts or data stated in the report, may do so by filing an affidavit and the court then considers the report and the affidavits which may have been filed and proceeds to adjudicate upon the issues arising in the writ petition. It would be entirely for the court to consider what weight to attach to the facts and data stated in the report of the commissioner and to what extent to act upon such facts and data. But it would not be correct to say that the report of the commissioner has no evidentiary value at all, since the statements made in it are not tested by cross-examination. To accept this contention would be to introduce the adversarial procedure in a proceeding where in the given situation, it is totally impossible.

With this judgment, the practice of appointing commissioners was firmly established. It represented a great leap forward for PIL, as the evidential hurdle was overcome.

The next question that the court was called upon to address was the nature of evidence sufficient to constitute proof. In the Bombay Pavement Dwellers case, the court was called upon to consider the question of massive and large-scale eviction of the pavement dwellers from the pavements of Bombay. In a letter, journalist Olga Tellis complained that the poorest of the poor who lived on pavements out of the sheer necessity and who were employed in the city doing manual work as cleaners and domestic help were being physically beaten up; their shacks pulled down; and they were being thrown out of the city on the ground that they were unlawfully squatting on the pavement. The petitioner relied on data available about the economic status of the pavement dwellers. She contended that if the pavement dwellers were evicted from the slums and pavements, they would be deprived of their livelihood and their right to life itself would be violated. This fact was incapable of proof in the conventional sense. This is the court's determination:[2]

> Turning to the factual situation, how far is it true to say that if the petitioners are evicted from their slum and pavement dwellings, they will be deprived of their means of livelihood? It is impossible in the very nature of things, to gather reliable data on this subject in regard to each individual petitioner and none has been furnished to us in that form. That the eviction of a person from a pavement or slum will inevitably lead to the deprivation of his means of livelihood, is a proposition which does not have to be established in each individual case. That is an inference which can be drawn from acceptable data.
>
> Issues of general public importance, which affect the lives of large sections of society, defy a just determination if consideration is limited to the evidence pertaining to specific individuals. In the resolution of such issues, there are no symbolic samples which can effectively project a true picture of the grim realities of life. The writ petitions before us undoubtedly involve a question relating to dwelling houses but they cannot be equated with a suit for the possession of a house by one private person against another. In a case of the latter kind, evidence has to be led to establish the cause of action and justify the claim.
>
> In a matter like the one before us, in which the future of half of the city's population is at stake, the court must consult authentic empirical data compiled by agencies, official and non-official. It is by that process that the core of the problem can be reached and a satisfactory solution found. It would be unrealistic on our part to reject the

petitions on the ground that the petitioners have not adduced evidence to show that they will be rendered jobless if they are evicted from the slums and pavements. Common sense, which is a cluster of life's experiences, is often more dependable than the rival facts presented by warring litigants.

This judgment represents a breakthrough in dealing with the cases of violations of fundamental rights. The nature of the violation being different, the nature of proof will necessarily also have to change in each case.

## Remedies

The next important and decisive difference between the British and Indian experience is in the nature of the remedies available to the group and the role of the court in monitoring the implementation of the relief. To remedy a structural wrong, the courts have provided structural remedies. Let us take a few examples. In a case which related to the complaint that orphans were being given for adoption abroad without any authority of law, the court directed the setting up by the Indian government of a central agency responsible for licensing civil and welfare organisations who were in turn authorised to place children in foreign adoption. The court imposed an obligation on all Indian Foreign Missions abroad to monitor the progress of children given in adoption to ensure that they were protected until they were legally adopted. The decision put an end to a long-standing problem which the legislators were unwilling or unable to address.

Several petitions were filed in the Supreme Court complaining of conditions within mental homes and complaining that, in utter disregard of the law, mentally ill patients were being locked up in jail as 'non-criminal lunatics'. The Supreme Court of India directed all states in India to identify all such people and release them immediately. Despite this order, not only were they not released but several states continued to admit such patients in jail. On an application made to court, the Supreme Court appointed a senior advocate to visit the jail, investigate the complaint, fix responsibility for the violation and personally ensure the release of all such non-criminal inmates from jail. As a consequence more than 400 inmates were released from prisons.

A technique adopted by the Supreme Court in dealing with a chronic abuse is to keep the petition pending over a period of years. Some petitions have been pending for the last ten years or more. This is not a question of delays in court but rather a question of the court retaining jurisdiction over a case so as to ensure that its orders are implemented. Thus, for example, a petition relating to a women's remand home has been coming up in the Supreme Court for hearing for the last ten years. The court has directed a new home be built for the inmates and periodic reports are submitted by the district judge to the court on the progress of the matter. The Supreme Court of India has thus defied the generally held notion that courts do not possess the power of the purse, a limitation that supposedly operates on them. Governments have been either persuaded or compelled to spend money and allocate budgets for remand homes and institutions for the mentally ill.

## Legistative responses

Developments in the judicial field have not left the legislature untouched. In 1987, the government of India passed the Legal Services Authorities Act 1987, taking note of a series of judgments of the Supreme Court that the right to legal aid was a fundamental right.

In 1980 Justice P N Bhagwati, in his capacity as chairman, had submitted a report *National judicare – equal justice, social justice.* Apart from recommending a national legal aid system, he proposed the setting up of a statutory corporation which would undertake legal research and conduct legal literacy programmes to spread awareness of legal rights and conduct public interest litigation. This report led to the passing of the Act. It sets up a central authority, state authorities and district authorities. The Chief Justice of India is the patron-in-chief of the National Legal Services Authority. The functions of the authority are to lay down policies and principles for legal services, frame schemes for legal services, take the necessary steps by way of social justice litigation with regard to consumer protection, environmental protection or any other matter of special concern to the weaker sections of society; give training to social workers in legal skills, organise legal aid camps in rural areas and slums, encourage the settlement of disputes through *Lok Adalats* (literally, people's courts), promote research in legal services for the poor, spread awareness of legal rights and enlist the support of voluntary organisations in their work. Each state is required to appoint its own legal services authority which will provide legal aid, organise *Lok Adalats* and undertake preventive legal aid programmes. The Act lays down the criteria for giving legal services. The following persons are entitled to legal services:

(a) a member of scheduled caste or tribe;
(b) victims of trafficking in human beings or beggars, as defined in article 23 of the Constitution;
(c) women and children;
(d) mentally ill and disabled people, victims of mass disaster, ethnic violence, caste atrocity, flood, drought, earthquake or industrial disaster;
(e) industrial workers;
(f) persons in custody, in protective homes, juvenile homes;
(g) a person whose annual income is less than Rs 9,000 (£180) in any court, and less than Rs 12,000 (£240) in the Supreme Court.

The authorities under the Act are authorised to organise local courts, *Lok Adalats*. A *Lok Adalat* has jurisdiction to determine and arrive at a compromise in a civil, criminal or revenue dispute. In any pending suit, if the parties make a joint application that they wish to compromise the matter, the presiding officer may refer the case to the *Lok Adalat* for settlement. If a settlement is arrived at after a joint reference, the award of the *Lok Adalat* operates as a decree.

The Act has several unique features. It institutionalises public interest litigation and attempts to consolidate its gains by giving it statutory sanction; creates a statutory machinery for spreading awareness of legal rights; it provides a right to legal aid without a means test to individuals who belong to the members of a given class; and facilitates settlement of disputes through *Lok Adalats*. Thus, Indian law has not developed the class action as in the US but has developed a distinctive form of 'social justice litigation' which enables the claims of large groups constituting a class to bring a petition for enforcement of their fundamental rights.

Tragically the Act, passed in 1987, has not yet been brought into force. It was criticised by some who felt that it eroded the autonomy of the judiciary and that the boundaries between executive and judiciary were not clear. Successive governments sought to amend the Act but never completed the task. This indicates that legal aid is low down on the agenda of all political parties. Nevertheless, the Act is in place and, hopefully, will be implemented shortly.

## Another imaginative response

Yet another imaginative response to a mass disaster claim was the passing of the Bhopal Gas Leak Disaster (Processing of Claims) Act 1985. December 1984 saw the world's worst industrial disaster. The escape of highly toxic gases from the facility of the Union Carbide Corporation (UCC) in Bhopal left more than 2,000 dead in a single night and more than 300,000 persons exposed to different degrees of injury. It would be impossible for each victim to have filed an individual suit against UCC in India or in the USA. The Indian government passed an Act authorising it to bring an action against UCC in the USA and then in India to recover damages on their behalf.

The suit was filed first in the USA and then in India with the Union of India as plaintiff. The Act set up a Claims Commission which would process claims and disburse amounts received from UCC. When the case was finally settled in 1991, the $470 million (£310 million) damages were deposited under the Act to the credit to the fund created under the Act. Since then, the amount has been disbursed to each individual claimant after verification of the injury. Though the Act is a one-time measure to meet a mass disaster, it sets a pattern of state intervention to protect the rights of the victims. The Supreme Court upheld the constitutional validity of the Act based on the doctrine of *parens patriae*, a doctrine which has the potential of being invoked in many different situations.

## Access to justice

Despite the innovation of social justice litigation, justice itself is still a distant dream for the vast majority of Indians. In 1986, Justice D A Desai, the chairman of the Law Commission, submitted a report recommending the setting up of Gram Nyayalaya (village courts). Such courts have traditionally existed in Indian villages. The suggested composition of the courts was one legally trained person assisted by a panel of two lay persons selected out of a group proposed by the district judge. The Nyayalaya would assemble in the village in which the dispute had arisen to hear the case. They would decide according to the justice and equity of the case after hearing the parties on the same day. They would have the powers to execute their decisions by directing the administrative officers to carry out their orders. Their jurisdiction would be both civil and criminal with pecuniary limits and limits on imposing fines. So far, the recommendations have not been accepted, a reflection once again of the low priority given to this area.

## Conclusion

The Indian PIL revolution is a unique response to a felt necessity. It has worked to make justice accessible to the masses, cutting across procedural and technical barriers. It has made fundamental rights a reality for the victims of undeserved deprivation. This is not to say that it has ushered in a social revolution. It has, however, made their problems visible in the national arena. Every judgment in this field addresses a structural problem and has been norm-setting. Public interest litigation has sought to hold the state to its promise of social justice spelt out in the constitution. It recognises that not just civil and political rights alone but economic and social rights are necessary for survival. Despite criticism that the judiciary is being activist, overstepping its judicial functions and entering into the legislative domain, judges of the Supreme Court of India and the high courts have not been deterred from protecting the economic rights of citizens. They have mandated the state to take affirmative action to put meaning and content into those rights and have prevented abuse of power by the police. The judiciary has participated in India in slowly unfolding social revolution – some might say too slowly. The gains of public interest litigation have outstripped those that might have been made by developing a class action – for the judgments of the Supreme Court in this sphere have shaped and moulded national policy.

# References

1   (1982) 2 SCR 67.
2   *Olga Tellis and Others v Bombay Municipal Corporation and Others* (1985) 3 SCC 545 at 574.

# CHAPTER 13

# Multi-party actions: a plaintiff's view

## MARTYN DAY AND SALLY MOORE

*The authors are solicitors and partners in the London firm of Leigh Day & Co, which has been involved in a number of multi-party actions. These have included litigation involving many environmental nuisance and disaster claims.*

Multi-party actions often raise issues of significant public interest. In particular, product liability actions invariably raise issues about public health and safety awareness. For instance, litigation vastly increased the amount of public information about asbestos and the Dalkon Shield. Cases relating to environmental questions perform the same function. As a result, state assistance should be available in cases which raise issues of public concern but where those affected may not meet usual legal aid criteria.

It is, admittedly, far from simple to separate out the public and private interest issues in multi-party actions. A case may concern the general public simply because of the large numbers of people pursuing individual cases. Conversely, there may be no public interest in a case which involves relatively few complainants. For example, the Sellafield litigation, involving allegations that a nuclear reprocessing plant was the source of a number of cases of leukemia, was confined to a specific area and affected relatively small numbers of people. Nevertheless, it raised matters of grave public concern both locally and nationally. This is often the case in environmental damage claims. Accordingly, there are strong grounds for 'public interest issue cases' to continue to be granted legal aid. The only viable alternative would require revision of the costs rules under which a losing party is liable for the costs of the victor, or some extension of conditional or contingency fees.

The root cause of the majority of existing problems in multi-party actions is the absence of adequate court procedures. The Legal Aid

Board's recent consultative paper on multi-party actions has been generated as a result of the problems associated with the Benzodiazepine litigation. At the outset of that case, the plaintiffs' lawyers requested the court to give directions on the generic issues involved. The board's experience of losing a considerable sum of money in this litigation is likely to have been different if the judge had agreed to take the generic issues first or if there had been practice rules setting out a presumption in favour of such a course.

The paper has been interpreted by the media as criticising plaintiffs for participating in multi-party cases. For all that there may be some opportunists, most people in this country do not go to law except as a last resort and when they have a genuine sense of grievance. Furthermore, the tactics of defendants have contributed to the failure of many multi-party cases. The range of court measures currently available is inadequate. There is an unjustifiable absence of any requirement on the judge to make directions for the manageable disposal of multi-party cases and to take control over the action so as to avoid incurring unnecessary costs on individual cases. This is particularly essential when more than one firm is running the litigation. To be effective, new practice rules need to be linked with judicial guidelines on how actually to manage the cases.

Consistency of approach is essential. Many practitioners consider that many judges simply do not know how to manage litigation.[1]

## Generic issues

Defendants argue that general or generic issues involved in a case cannot be investigated until they know the number of claimants and the strength of their cases. This makes multi-party actions problematic for all concerned – the Legal Aid Board as funder, the plaintiffs' solicitors and even, to a lesser extent, the defendants themselves. The defendants' arguments on this point are flawed. They know what their exposure is. They know how many of their products have been sold or, in environmental cases, the people likely to be affected by their acts. Almost invariably, they are aware of the hazards of their actions and will have considered these issues in deciding their commercial strategy.

Defendants oppose the generic issues approach for the simple reason that investigation of individual claims drives up costs. This is a classic defence tactic. It has been used successfully both here and in the United States. The generic issues approach would probably save the defendants' legal costs. However, these are insignificant when compared to the abandonment of the claims by the plaintiffs because of the cost to the plaintiff's lawyers of individual investigation. Defendants also know that they will be doomed to pay compensation if they lose on the generic issue. It is obviously in their interests to keep a court from deciding this for as long as possible – preferably forever. Paradoxically, an early decision on the generic issues in their favour would be the most effective and economical way of disposing of the litigation. It is puzzling that defendants who consistently and loudly assert that they are not liable are not more attracted to this approach.

The whole nature of a group action is a compromise over traditional procedures. It involves a fundamental conflict between two models of the civil process. All the different ways of handling them – whether they be representative actions, test cases, class actions, transfer to a single court under the American Multi-District Litigation Statute – represent, to a certain extent, a compromise for both parties. The generic issues approach is the only practical answer for the successful resolution of these cases.

The problem with prioritising the issues of individual plaintiffs in complex product liability and environmental cases is that determination of the strength of a case often takes substantial investigative work. The difficulties are exacerbated by the fact that there may be very little time in which to carry out the investigative procedures carefully so that lawyers, in order to protect themselves, are likely to give cases the benefit of the doubt when issuing proceedings. This may lead, at a later stage of the case, to large numbers of weak cases dropping out of the action.

The root of this problem lies in the insistence by courts and defendants that details of individual claims are supplied prior to investigation of generic issues. Should the generic issues ever be considered and fail, all the work done on the individual cases will be wasted and enormous amounts of public funds will have been lost. If there was no requirement to file individual cases prior to deciding generic issues on liability, causation and damage, this potential waste would be avoided.

## The purpose of public funding

The Legal Aid Board has expressly raised the question as to whether the public interest should be a factor in the refusal or grant of legal aid (see p36). It is not attracted to the idea.

The public interest should be a consideration. The board has listed the factors which might be relevant if the decision was to be broader-based. These include the nature of the claim; the board's previous experience of similar litigation; how claims are being generated; whether private clients are willing to join the action etc. Such a list might leave the decision too much in the board's control, without any objective basis against which it could be tested.

We would suggest the following as a test of whether a case is in the public interest: (a) the widespread use of the product/environmental exposure; or (b) the seriousness of the injury, even though numbers injured may be small; or (c) the issues raised in terms of the delivery of health care, consumer safety, or prevention of injury in the future.

The board is wrong to suggest that there are issues which are 'unlitigable' due to their complexity and the economic imbalance to the parties. The Sellafield childhood leukaemia trial was probably the most complicated case ever to be heard by the courts due to the complexity of the scientific evidence. The court was well able to cope with the issues. The economic imbalance of the parties did not prevent a fair and well balanced trial taking place. Nor is the fact that many people now fall outside the financial eligibility levels any reason to prevent legal aid being granted in cases of public importance where those who are still eligible are also involved.

## Alternative sources of funding

Whatever the position of the Legal Aid Board, the question needs to be raised as to whether there are alternative methods for funding multi-party claims. With conditional fee arrangements due to come into force in early 1995 for ordinary personal injury claims, by agreement with the insurers likely to extend to medical negligence claims, and with the Legal Aid Board likely eventually to dovetail their own arrangements with conditional fees, the one type of action which remains very much on its own is group actions. The key question is whether there are alternative ways of funding these claims. The primary way would be to adopt the American approach of some sort of contingency fee arrangement. There are two difficulties here, the first being the scale of the risk to the plaintiffs' solicitors and the second being the size of the costs if the group action is successful.

In the United States the standard contingency fee arrangements are for one-third of the damages to be paid to the plaintiffs' lawyers. For cases in the region of a few thousand dollars and even up to a hundred thousand dollars, that fee structure may well be entirely reasonable. However for claims that are worth very large sums and certainly those worth millions of dollars and those multi-party actions where each claim is worth a substantial sum, this can mean that the plaintiffs' lawyer stands to be paid an enormous fee and sometimes many millions of dollars if the claims are successful. Indeed in the United States, there are personal injury lawyers whose annual earnings are in the tens of million dollar bracket and who fly around in private jets. At the other extreme, the risk to the plaintiffs' lawyer in these actions is so great and the potential costs of defeat are so high that it may well be that those firms that are prepared to take on a group action under a contingency arrangement, would be bankrupted if the claim were lost. Indeed the reason there have only been a relatively few tobacco-related claims in the United States is largely because the tobacco industry have been prepared to fight the actions in an extremely aggressive way which has forced a number of firms to the very edge of bankruptcy before they have pulled the plug on the action, which has significantly discouraged others from following in their footsteps.

The problem, therefore, in basing a multi-party action on any sort of contingency arrangement is that for the lawyer there is either the prospect of bankruptcy or mega-wealth on the horizon. Whilst most lawyers would accept an element of 'putting their money where their mouths are', such extremes seem totally out of place in British society where one would be hard pressed to put forward any other work where anything like these extremes are the norm.

For contingency fees to work in any kind of realistic way, the indemnity cost rule that costs follow the event would have to be abolished for group actions. To the extent that the defendants primarily pick up the tab at the moment for their own costs and then also bear the risk of paying the plaintiffs' costs, it is unlikely that they would be greatly concerned at this prospect. It would, however, mean that for this one type of case the whole rules regarding costs would have to be changed. That this might well not be acceptable is another matter.

## Alternative dispute resolution

The board has suggested that some form of tribunal might be an alternative forum to decide multi-party cases. It is doubtful whether this would remove inequality between the parties, particularly if it entailed the absence of legal representation, or whether it would provide a suitable way of dealing with complex issues of law. Courts, however imperfect, are public institutions subject to constitutional restraints. Tribunals would find it difficult to meet the exacting standards of the courts. It is illogical to relegate the most complex area of litigation towards an alternative dispute resolution or arbitration procedure.

Furthermore, there is an important public interest in the private right to participate in the legal process. The party control approach of adversarial civil litigation is designed to further this. Research confirms that litigants prefer an adversarial system because of the sense of participation it offers.[2] Adjudication by a tribunal in the absence of litigant participation, as proposed by the board, would not satisfy this need.[3] Without a sense of participation, the parties are more likely to appeal the decision of any tribunal. As a result, there would be no net gain in terms either of cost and delay. An extra tier has been added to the civil justice system to little advantage.

Furthermore, informality of proceedings is not a benefit if it masks coercion and other threats to procedural rights. Thus, the proceedings would have to be formalised and this must include legal representation. Informal procedures that are permissible in mediation are not acceptable in any quasi-adjudicatory methods of dispute resolution such as arbitration and tribunals where a decision is imposed on the parties.

A point often overlooked is the need for legal precedents. Courts not only resolve private disputes but also give effect to the standards by which society has chosen to govern itself. This includes requiring public service providers and manufacturers of consumer goods to conform to such values as due process, equality and public safety regulations. Often, the public and private interests overlap. For example, both the parties and the public seek a full hearing as to what went wrong, and according to our arguments this is best served in public by a court.

The absence of an adversarial approach often means issues are less thoroughly investigated than they would be in a court system. For example, the Committee on Medical Aspects of Radiation in the Environment looked at environmental discharges of radiation from Sellafield. The court case revealed that there were a large number of relevant documents in the Public Record Office which the Committee had failed to investigate and which indicated that the levels of discharge were far higher than had previously been admitted.

Membership of any tribunal or board of inquiry is extremely important. History suggests that such bodies start off full of enthusiasm but after a few years become too friendly with the people over whom they are watching. It is often difficult for plaintiffs to locate experts who are unconnected with the multi-national industries being sued. The choice of tribunal members can be controversial. Members with other outside interests may be vulnerable to influence. This is particularly the case in the scientific community where the drug manufacturers wield enormous power in the terms of their ability to give or remove research grants.

A tribunal system would, in any event, need to encompass procedural rights such as those to information and of appeal. If these are to be accommodated, then it quickly reverts to a type of adversarial proceedings which erodes the desired cost savings. It could rapidly return to a court system, defeating the object of the exercise. The experience of industrial tribunals illustrates the type of problems the proposed tribunal system would face. They have become industrial courts where the absence of legal aid leads to the inevitable disadvantage of unrepresented plaintiffs against legally represented defendants.

Despite the above arguments, there may well be a role for tribunals after successful litigation on generic issues. For example, a tribunal might decide whether individuals fit within the criteria set out by the court to enable them to claim compensation. A tribunal might also assess compensation.

## Conclusion

The handling of multi-party actions by the Legal Aid Board and the courts needs to be reformed. Consideration of the public interest in deciding whether to grant assistance with legal costs is essential. Also important is that the courts prioritise trial of the generic issues of fact and law in the early stages of the action. Mechanisms should be developed so that large numbers of clients are not encouraged to come forward while the strength of the generic case is being tested. This might be done through a register of claimants or allowing the court to prolong any relevant limitation period. These three changes would greatly improve the capacity of the British legal system to handle multi-party actions.

## References

1   N Armstrong, 'Perspectives on Court Management', *New Law Journal*, 28 January 1994, p131.

2  Walker, Lind and Thibaut, 'The Relation between Procedural and Distributive Justice', 65 *Virginia L Rev* 1401 (1979).

3  See Tyler, 'A Psychological Perspective on the Settlement of Mass Tort Claims' 53 *Law and Contemporary Problems* 199 (1990).

CHAPTER 14

# Funding for multi-party actions

GEORGE PULMAN, QC

*The author chairs the multi-party action committee of the Legal Aid Board, of which he is a member. As a practising barrister, he has had wide experience of multi-party litigation. He acted as amicus curiae in the Opren litigation as well as for plaintiffs or defendants in a number of other cases, including litigation over the Zeebrugge ferry disaster.*

## Preliminary

Multi-party actions (MPAs) raise two conflicting principles: ordinary people should be able to pursue claims for damages against substantial organisations without fear of bankruptcy if they lose; and substantial organisations should not be faced with expensive, long running litigation for which (when they win) they have to pay.

Litigation on Opren in the USA is a good example of the first. The English litigants sought to bring proceedings in the USA, but the USA courts refused to accept jurisdiction because the English courts offered similar compensation in punitive or exemplary damages. The fact that nobody ever gets exemplary damages in a personal injury claim in the UK failed to impress the US court. But by then, all the costs had been incurred. These costs had to be set-off against any compensation ultimately recovered in English proceedings.

Big companies and state bodies will contest cases with vigour in order to win. They do this predominantly because they consider that they are not liable. It becomes a matter of principle to defend their researchers, their staff and their management. They also tend to believe in 'the floodgates argument'. If we concede on this case, they argue, where does it end? In the smoking-related disease cases the plaintiffs' advisers are publicly talking of closing down the tobacco industry when they win.

196

In the haemophilia/AIDS case, the government was advised that it would win on liability. The prime minister of the day (Mrs Thatcher) accepted that advice and the case continued. One of the first actions of the new prime minister (Mr Major) was to tell the Department of Health to settle. So decisions of such magnitude can be taken at the highest level contrary to legal advice given by experienced lawyers. There is a wider view of the 'justice' of the case.

## Management of cases

Multi-party actions must not be run for the benefit of lawyers. That does no good at all for litigants. Indeed, it does positive harm; yet it is what happened in the Benzodiazepine litigation. The Legal Aid Board spent about £2,000–£3,000 per plaintiff to prove that there was no case. The sole beneficiaries were lawyers and psychiatrists. The litigants, the sufferers hooked on the drug, got nothing: not even the sniff of a hearing for their case. It is right to observe that this was public money raised by taxation. The litigants, if offered the chance of '£2,000 now or a possibility of about £8,000 later' would, I think, say 'I'll take the £2,000 now'.

## Settlement of cases

Most personal injury cases are settled. The same is expected in most multi-party actions. Opren and the haemophilia/AIDS cases provide good illustrations. Settlement inevitably involves a discount from full valuation of the claim for the certainty of settling the case. If any case is to be settled, a defendant must know what he has to pay. He cannot say 'I'll pay £5,000 to each plaintiff' without knowing how many plaintiffs there are. In the smoking-related cases liability might extend to 10 per cent of the population: about six million people. And which tobacco company pays what is still going to be a difficult point.

The USA has different rules and different procedures. Its 'class action' allows a 'settlement' to be enforced by the court. The fund is set up, and everyone gets a share. This raises the problem of how you define 'everyone'. This existed in the Land Settlement Association litigation. After the case had been settled, previous LSA tenants continued to write to the Ministry of Agriculture, Fisheries and Food saying, 'Please can I have my share?' The answer was, 'No, you weren't in the case.'

A further problem is 'the global offer'. This is a persistent problem in multi-party actions where the defendant says, 'We offer £10 million plus costs to the plaintiffs'. The offer is not capable of being sub-divided (£10,000 for A, £20,000 for B and so on). It is for the plaintiffs to accept, or to reject. If one plaintiff rejects it, the whole offer lapses. Suppose one plaintiff is a patient suffering mental illness; another is bankrupt but seeking to get out of bankruptcy; and a third is obtuse but rational. How is their consent obtained? Can one obtuse litigant prevent all the others obtaining their compensation? Can one force all of them to go through all the litigation?

It has seemed to me that, in such cases (particularly 'commercial' multi-party actions) there should be a term in the agreement between the plaintiffs collectively to the effect that rejection of a reasonable offer excludes you from the group (so you are on your own as to costs); and what is a reasonable offer will be determined by written representations to an independent QC (ie, not one of the QCs conducting the case). This, too, arose in the LSA cases. My opponent undertook to 'secure' the agreement of the dissenting plaintiffs and he was able to do so in respect of all but, I think, three. The three were both obtuse and determined. Eventually the ministry settled with all but the three: and, ultimately, their legal aid had to be withdrawn. They soon fell into line.

## Costs

There are two possibilities: the present costs regime, where the loser is liable for the winner's costs; and the 'public inquiry' alternative.

The present costs regime requires that the loser pays the winner. It is, of course, not as simple as that. Winners never recover 100 per cent of their costs: perhaps 20 per cent will be taxed off. If the bill is £2 million and 20 per cent is taxed off, the loss is £400,000. If the damages total £10,000 for each of 40 plaintiffs, that is £400,000. The plaintiffs will get nothing unless the lawyers forego all the fees which have been taxed off (and that will mean paying some disbursements out of their own pockets).

Specific costs orders are sometimes made for specific parts of a case. If a specific issue is tried and the plaintiffs lose, the plaintiffs will be ordered to pay the costs incurred in trying that specific issue. This was a real point in Opren, where a substantial allegation of negligence was over the 'advertising' of the drug. The defendants expected to succeed in showing that advertising Opren was not a cause of the plaintiffs' suffering Opren-related disability. If the defendants were right, the plaintiffs would have had to pay the costs of that part of the hearing to the defendants. Could some plaintiffs say, 'Don't pursue advertising in my case?' Could that plaintiff thus secure a costs advantage for himself? There are various complications such as this which will arise.

## The public inquiry

There is a healthy and respected history of public inquiries in the UK. The parties appearing before the inquiry bear their own costs. This would be hopeless in any personal injury case: the costs would wipe out any damages ultimately assessed. Legal aid might be made available in something like its current form.

Such inquiries often have the power to provide for the costs of those who appear. It could be extended to those who say that they have suffered because of a tort. When the Legal Aid Board has granted a sufficient number of legal aid applications (perhaps 100), then the public inquiry mechanism could be triggered. Triggering the mechanism would involve an application to the Lord Chancellor's Department for the appointment of a chair to an inquiry on the specified issue. Thereafter, the inquiry would take over the running of the case, including the obtaining of a budget to run it. The inquiry has to have a budget and it has to have an accounting officer together with a staff. The inquiry also needs a timetable.

The public inquiry is a widely used aspect of our procedure. It is used in planning matters: to determine whether, for example, a particular site should be developed. The Boundary Commission holds inquiries to determine where the new line for a constituency should be. Anyone who has sufficient interest can put a case. This may be a limited point, such as retention of a small area of land because an unusual plant can be found there, or a wider point such as that Department of Transport figures for traffic are wrong. Public inquiries have been set up by private bodies. For example, the Church of England inquired about the life of churches in the countryside and about why the Church Commissioners seem to have lost most of the Church's money.

Such inquiries often have power to provide for the costs of those who appear in front of them. The usual rule is 'no costs': this means that each party bears its own costs. This would be quite hopeless for multi-party actions, because victims cannot possibly afford to represent themselves. Legal aid (as presently organised) could not be appropriate, because any damages assessed would be set off against the costs.

## Should the state pay the costs?

The fact that the state is also a party to the proceedings is no problem: it often is a party to proceedings, in judicial review, or in multi-party actions involving drugs (ie, the Committee on Safety of Medicines). It is often the defendant in a multi-party action: eg, radiation-induced injuries and deafness claims. Our jurisprudence is sufficiently sophisticated to be able to require the state to pay for an inquiry while at the same time a party to the inquiry is claiming damages against the state (albeit under another guise).

The important point is, however, this. There is no one else who can afford to pay such costs. No individual has sufficient funds to pay for such proceedings themselves. Legal fees insurers cannot, or will not, be able to afford such claims. Trade unions find that such proceedings are very expensive. In the deafness cases[1] the judge found that the defendants were liable for noise-induced deafness in respect of a modest period following the date of knowledge. The damages were therefore limited to hearing loss caused during that period. As a major part of deafness is caused during the first exposure to noise (where liability could not be established) damages were modest. The awards were all below the payments into court, so the trade unions had to pay the defendants' costs. An appeal was settled on unusual terms: no order as to costs of the trial; and scale agreement between the trade union and the employers to compensate all workers suffering from noise-induced deafness at about two-thirds or three-quarters of common law damages. It is, I believe, the only MPA that has gone to trial on all issues. The fact that the defendants effectively won is a point to be borne in mind.

If the state pays, then what sanctions are there on costs not being run up unnecessarily? Should potential defendants bear their own costs? If we get used to an interventionist approach, then this ceases to be a problem. The procedure of the inquiry will require that those to be represented have their costs provided for at an early stage. There will be 'counsel to the inquiry', a legal team for the 'victims', and a legal team for any possible defendants. The inquiry will determine who pays any costs at the end of the inquiry. The inquiry will take into account any offers to settle which have been made by any side. The report will include an appendix assessing damages for each victim; and determining which of several defendants should pay those damages. Subject to argument, the issue of costs will then be considered by the inquiry. Any party aggrieved by the result may appeal either by way of judicial review, or by a statutory appeal under the Tribunals and Inquiries Act.

## The public inquiry for multi-party actions

### Membership

The chair must be a respected legal figure. A senior QC would be satisfactory, but a judge is preferable. The chair must have sufficient status and respect to be able to control the proceedings robustly without riding roughshod through the material. Those appearing in front of him will be as senior: so the chair must command their respect. His purpose is to direct evidence and argument to issues; to reduce (not magnify) the paperwork; and to control the proceedings. The chair must have the powers of a judge to compel witnesses to attend to give evidence, and, possibly, to deal with contempt of the inquiry.

Other members should be experienced professionals in that area. In a drug case, the tribunal would be helped by pharmaceutical and business experience, so senior people from Zeneca (the demerged ICI drugs arm) and Boots would be useful in dealing with a case involving, say, Hoechst. In a defective consumer product case, you need similar personnel which could include, for example, people from a citizens advice bureau and/or the Consumers' Association.

### When is a public inquiry to be set up?

I suggest that when more than 100 people claim that one product has caused them loss then a public inquiry is appropriate. When the Legal Aid Board has received 100 legal aid applications, then the public inquiry mechanism should be triggered. Applications should then be made to the Lord Chancellor's Department for a chair; and on appointment the chair would take over the running of the case.

### Financial conduct of the inquiry

The inquiry has to have a budget and an accounting officer. The budget is the most revolutionary change which I propose, and goes to the root of the proposal. The 'fixed sum' is anathema to the conservative lawyer accustomed to 'hourly rate plus mark-up', which can be up to 100 per cent (and that is before conditional fees). The enlightened modern lawyer has, for some time, moved to fixed fees, quotations, 'beauty contests' and 'competitive tendering'. The Bar would say that the brief fee has always been within that category.

It is common experience that, when a budget is fixed, the work comes in within budget. In the Benzodiazepine case, the Legal Aid Board fixed a 'budget' figure for the psychiatrist's reports at £750. They all came in at £750 and they all came straight off the word processor at that price. The accounting officer is an important part of the process. He has to consider what sums are expended for what purposes. Applications to go over budget could be made to the accounting officer. If unsuccessful, they would be appealed to the chair of the inquiry.

### Sittings

In European courts, evidence is taken at different times by different people. In the UK, we require the personal attendance of each witness on oath, to give evidence and to be cross-examined, before the tribunal. We have only recently become used to statements standing as evidence in court.

Is there room for an 'informal' cross-examination? Two advocates would attempt to take evidence, and cross-examine a witness in private. His evidence would then be recorded. It would mean that the whole inquiry team did not have to hear every witness. The evidence, reduced to writing, would be available without the need for every single person to hear all the evidence orally. This happens, quite successfully, when evidence is taken on commission and thereafter read into the case in circumstances where the judge has no chance to see or hear the manner and demeanour of the witness.

Actual sittings can, at times, be suited to some of the parties, for example, in the evening, or at weekends. Sittings can be at different places. In the New Zealand inquiry into the Mount Erebus plane crash, Mahon J and counsel to the inquiry travelled to London to take evidence from one witness, without a complete circus in attendance.

### Issues, structure and evidence

The chair would specify the issues to be tried and would direct what evidence would be heard. Obviously this could only occur after s/he had heard argument from the parties about it. The submissions and argument for each party would be prepared in writing beforehand and handed in, as they now are in large cases. The inquiry would read those outside a hearing, before having a session when questions could be asked. In the European Court at Luxembourg advocates are limited to 15 minutes per speech: and that is quite long enough because everything has been said in the written case.

*Costs*

The inquiry would determine who would get what costs. That determination would be at the end of the inquiry. It would be subject to offers made, and counter-offers which may have been made. The funding of the litigation prior to that would be at the discretion of the inquiry. The essential difference between this and the present procedures is that the Legal Aid Board would not be assessing what was required. It would be the inquiry which assessed what was required. The area committee, charged with the responsibility for running a multi-party action, is told by the lead solicitors what they need to spend: but the area committee have little opportunity of checking this properly. The chair of the inquiry is far better placed to deal with this sort of thing. S/he has taken a grasp of the whole case right from the start, and will know what issues are relevant, what issues are not relevant, and whether money is being spent properly or not.

*Settlement*

It is important to remember that the people involved in the case want money: they do not want a long inquiry. Only the lawyers want a long inquiry, because that runs up their fees. There would have to be incentives built into the system to encourage settlement. The usual 'payment into court' terms would be effective; as would 'Calderbank' offers. This is a written offer which has an effect on costs. If the person to whom the offer is made gets less at trial than was offered, then from the date of the offer that person both has to pay the other side's costs *and* his own. It may be, for example, that other parties are represented before the inquiry, and they would like their costs paid. The inquiry should have power to deal with that.

## Conclusion

The public inquiry offers substantial advantages in large MPA cases. The inquiry has control of the litigation at the start. It also has control of the costs. At present even a designated judge has only a quasi-illusory control over the pace of the litigation; and he has absolutely no control over the expenditure of costs. It is my view that the public inquiry would ensure that the large number of victims of defective products or drugs produced by substantial companies have a much greater chance of getting compensation quickly and without a vast risk on costs.

## Reference

1   *Thompson v Smiths Ship Repairers* [1984] QB 405.

# Part VI

# The future of civil litigation

# The future of civil litigation

These five chapters assess current developments and potential future directions of civil justice. Cyril Glasser and Carrie Menkel-Meadow provide contrasting overviews of developments in the United Kingdom and the United States. Suzanne Burn and Martin Partington examine aspects of alternative dispute resolution, the former providing another overview and the latter concentrating on lessons from tribunals. Finally, Gillian McAllister and Terry Purcell indicate, in a very practical way, the value of more independent research on the workings of the system.

The question of civil adjudication is particularly topical because of the forthcoming report of Lord Woolf. It is with this that Cyril Glasser engages, warning of the problems that come from skimping on research.

The contributions share a number of themes. Chief among them is the need for better information, more research and broader debate. Gillian McAllister and Terry Purcell describe in detail what can be done by a research institution dedicated to consideration of civil justice issues. Cyril Glasser calls for a wide-ranging commission to keep civil justice under continual review. Carrie Menkel-Meadow reports that something like this already exists in a number of US jurisdictions. Such an impetus to continuing analysis of performance must be desirable.

Another common issue is the role of what is usually called 'alternative dispute resolution' but for which Carrie Menkel-Meadow deploys the better term, 'appropriate dispute resolution'. She gives a very balanced assessment of its success and failures, its advantages and disadvantages. The interaction of legal aid, generally only available in courts and not in other forms of dispute resolution, makes a domestic judgment on the value of ADR even harder in the UK. Suzanne Burn explores this difficult conundrum. 207

Tribunals are the great forgotten institution of the British dispute resolution process. Yet, since the mid-1980s, a part of the tribunal system has undergone dramatic change. Supplementary benefit appeal tribunals, as once they were, entered the 1980s as little better than a laughing-stock. Their performance was often amateur; their chairs were often bigoted; their members held to the myths of the deserving and undeserving claimant; claimants showed their confidence in their objectivity by very low attendance rates at hearings. Martin Partington describes some part of their transformation and argues that they may have evolved an organisational form from which the judiciary could learn significant lessons.

# CHAPTER 15

# Civil procedure – a time for change[1]

CYRIL GLASSER

*Cyril Glasser is a solicitor and managing partner of Sheridan's, a firm in central London. He is also visiting professor of law at University College, London. During the 1970s, he was special consultant to the Lord Chancellor's Advisory Committee on Legal Aid.*

Over the last 30 years there has been an enormous expansion in court case loads, together with a large growth in the funding of state-subsidised legal services. This has been in large part the result of extensive notions of rights in the modern state. The judiciary now plays a growing role as a mediating influence between individual litigants, commercial enterprises and government and administrative agencies. The perception of what constitutes the civil process has been enlarged beyond consideration only of courts and tribunals. Civil decision-making is often not the result of any dispute but may arise from the use of discretionary powers or regulatory decision-making. There has been a inexorable rise of public law and other specialised jurisdictions. Simple contract disputes, debt actions, personal injury cases and family jurisdictions have now to compete for time in the courts with large-scale international commercial litigation and disaster actions. A common core of procedure has proved unable to provide an adequate framework for processing the many types of litigation which now exist. The ability to litigate is now much more important than when a 1920s legal aid inquiry concluded that it was in the interest of the state that its citizens should be healthy but not that they should be litigious.

Two other relevant situations need to be kept in mind. The first arises from the existence of settlement processes where there is bargaining for gain, in Mnookin's phrase 'in the shadow of the law', and by reference to what the parties realise will ensue if their discussions turn into court disputes. The atypical 'trouble cases' which end up within the court system are only a tiny proportion of those which settle every day. The second arises because of the increasing centrality of a search for information on which claims may be based or settlements achieved. In the common law system this search may often be for material to found a cause of action. In Britain, the extent of pre-action discovery is slowly being widened, for example, in personal injury, race and sex discrimination cases. In an ever more secretive world, access to material held by government departments, drug companies or fraudulent traders has become a fundamental part of an on-going process. Subject to suitable safeguards, we need to expand, not restrict, the situations where pre-trial discovery is permitted.

## Government, the courts and the legal profession

The role of central government has become more and more critical. The state must provide an institutional framework for formal dispute resolution which can be effectively accessed by its citizens; it must establish and maintain a judiciary and a court establishment; it must prescribe procedures for courts and tribunals; it must fund a legal aid system; and it must supervise the activities of the legal profession. The state is no longer the 'hinge' or passive spectator in a dispute between private persons. It has become an active participant, as a funding agent and a provider of resources. It has a real and vital interest in the way litigation is conducted.

A litigation 'crisis' is a common feature in many countries in the western world, a consequence of the slowdown in the rate of economic growth which has been unable to keep pace with the increase in demand-led case-loads and legal aid payments. Statistics from English experience (see p22) illustrate the scale of the problem. By 1993–94, £350 million was being spent on civil proceedings. This is expected to rise to £685 million by 1996–97. During the period 1983–94, the retail prices index rose by an annual rate of 5 per cent, while the cost of legal aid rose by a yearly rate of 18 per cent. Little wonder that the government has moved drastically to reduce and control the legal aid budget. As a result of some of these measures, it has been estimated that the proportion of households eligible for legal aid on income grounds dropped from 81 per cent in 1979 to 41 per cent by 1993. The Lord Chancellor has recently announced a number of other measures to contain and reduce the high rate of growth on a year-by-year basis, and more are expected to follow shortly.

The legal profession has been a major beneficiary of an enhanced legal system. The numbers of both barristers and solicitors has grown considerably over the last two decades. In 1966, over two thirds of solicitors' gross income was derived from domestic conveyancing and other non-contentious business. In 1992, it has been estimated that solicitors were earning 40 per cent of their gross income from litigation. If only 25 per cent of this total were related to non-matrimonial civil cases, this would amount to a gross fee income of £1.5 billion, a staggering increase of nineteen times in twenty years. In 1974, the Law Society contested the suggestion that most London firms of solicitors were charging for litigation at the rate of £25 per hour. A leading directory has estimated that average hourly charges in 1994 were nearly ten times that figure, although the retail prices index had increased only four times and average earnings just over six times over the period concerned. Britain is said to have the highest hourly legal charges in the world. It is hardly surprising that a wide spectrum of public and private litigants have come to the conclusion that civil litigation is simply too expensive, too slow and too complex to meet their needs.

The government is faced with an acute dilemma. It must simultaneously limit public spending as far as possible, yet provide a framework for public legal services which citizens and commercial litigants can afford. It is not surprising that the problem has been referred to a Law Lord noted for his independence and radical views. With a polarisation in attitudes between the Lord Chancellor, consumer organisations and the legal profession, it is members of the higher judiciary who have been amongst the most active in seeking solutions for problems which threaten the integrity of the legal process. There is no doubt that the government genuinely wishes to find a way out of its dilemma. Hence the appointment of Lord Woolf.

## Procedure

There is an argument that procedural reforms, as such, can achieve very little in cheapening or speeding up court processes. The cost of civil proceedings is largely the cost of the lawyers who work the system and overall savings in this regard may be difficult to find. It is sometimes said that only the diversion of whole classes of case from the courts to some other cheaper forum will achieve any noticeable benefits. Yet any savings, even very limited ones, which help to restrain the overall rise in expenditure, must be worth having. The more difficult question is to attempt to analyse areas of cost, delay and complexity in a way which will suggest effective solutions. We know that very little research has been done on the litigation process. A number of parliamentary committees over the last eight years have criticised the Lord Chancellor's Department for not being able to say exactly why the cost of legal aid cases has risen and why delays are lengthening. The whole subject would benefit from thorough research, for example, on the effects of the indemnity rule and the payment-in scheme provided by Order 22 of the Rules of the Supreme Court. The operation of these rules is amongst the most potent factors in keeping litigants away from the court and they often produce settlements which outsiders consider to be unfair. We might benefit, for example, from a relaxation of the indemnity rule in particular types of situation. Ought we to introduce, as a matter of urgency, the Canadian rule which permits plaintiffs to make formal offers of settlement which have an effect in costs? Changes of this sort may have a dramatic effect far beyond any procedural tinkerings that we might otherwise contemplate.

In the absence of hard evidence, we are thrown back on lawyers' anecdotes, war stories and bar room chatter. The evidence of many previous enquiries suggests that lawyers are poor in analysing the system in which they work and in suggesting solutions which actually have an effect on cost or delay. Of course we all look at these issues from our own narrow perspective. Barristers and judges tend to concentrate on issues in which they are heavily involved such as pleadings, evidence and proceedings at trial. The position may change, for we now have a group of younger, more street-wise judges in the High Court and concerned judges at a higher level who see the integrity of the system being put into question by recent cut-backs and who wish to secure real changes in order to enable access to the courts to be increased.

There is a danger that a wholly misinformed consensus will emerge from the current debate, giving substance to misleading myths. Recently a number of senior judges have pointed to the perceived evils of excessive discovery. But where is the evidence that this is a major problem? Such discovery can be a problem in a minority of large, complex cases where case management by the court would be a considerable advantage; but material on this subject is thin. Similar assertions were made in recent years in the United States which have not been substantiated. Sometimes widely supported remedies have caused more difficulties than the evils they are said to be replacing. A good example is the conclusions of the

Civil Justice Review which recommended the introduction of the pre-trial exchange of witness statements to increase the 'cards on the table' principle. The review claimed that the change would achieve three main objectives: it would provide earlier, better informed settlements; it would improve pre-trial preparation; and it would shorten trials by helping to identify issues and reduce the need to take oral evidence. We appear to have no evidence that any of these objectives has been achieved. Indeed, the front-loading of cases which would have settled anyway may have materially increased overall costs throughout the system. The introduction of time limits is another example where things may go badly wrong. By trying to speed things up we may be putting ourselves into the hands of the big firms and their expensive cost structures, because they will be the only agencies with the staff who can be utilised at short notice to do the urgent work that may be required by court-imposed timetables.

## Court control

The issue of increased court control of civil litigation has been at the heart of professional and academic thinking over the last thirty years, especially since the publication of Professor Maurice Rosenberg's seminal research on the pre-trial process,[2] and it is important and welcome that this debate will now be the subject of wider public scrutiny and discussion. But a note of caution is necessary, for the phrase 'court control' can encompass a wide variety of differing concepts. These may range from mild court direction by way of timetable-setting in an otherwise party-presentation system, where the parties are left to get on with things on their own by an otherwise passive court, to one where there is not only rigid control on how the parties prepare but also active intervention to encourage settlement, instruct expert witnesses or cut down the issues to be determined at trial. There is general agreement that the efficacy of the civil court process would be enhanced by a greater degree of court direction, but there may be argument about the degree of interventionism which Lord Woolf has appeared recently to endorse. He appears to envisage judicial control of the allocative process to a large degree, so that a case will be dealt with at the right level of court and by the right level of judge from the very beginning. While it can be accepted that the judiciary ought to have an important part to play in the allocation of cases, it should be understood that this would involve a significant movement from the judicial function of deciding cases to one where the judiciary assumes a political role in the administrative process. In the 1960s, the then government put considerable emphasis on priority being given in the Queen's Bench Division to the disposal of personal injury cases. Now these cases are being largely relegated to the county courts, the result chiefly of new jurisdictional limits imposed by political decision-making within the Lord Chancellor's Department.

Before supporting any proposed changes of this kind, we should be satisfied that the judiciary is properly accountable for its decision-making and that machinery exists for a continuing discussion (not simply confined to lawyers) about the choices being made. The work of the High Court may soon be largely confined to specialised jurisdictions like the Divisional Court, with its general jurisdiction restricted to large class-action type cases with a public interest element. It may not be too fanciful to imagine some form of privatisation between individual parties of civil litigation which does not contain a public element so that these cases are removed to extra-court arbitral and settlement procedures.

The notion of procedural judges raises many conceptual and practical difficulties. The experience of some other jurisdictions is that it is the interlocutory supervision of the judge who will preside at trial which is the important factor. There must be doubts about recruiting a number of retired city solicitors, as suggested by Lord Woolf, for such a task. A back of the envelope calculation raises the question as to how much time could be given to each case by procedural judges and at precisely what stage of the case they would begin to intervene. There may be some confusion in the discussion which has taken place so far in distinguishing between a process of greater direction by the court to encourage parties to prepare their cases as cheaply and expeditiously as possible, and a system with the court responsible for even the collection of evidence and the instruction of expert witnesses. There is a danger that too great a degree of control will not only unnecessarily reduce the role of the parties but will also make the administrative machinery too costly to contemplate. The current state of the county courts, with their high turnover of unqualified staff, suggests we should be aiming at more moderate targets and should be trying to steer a middle course between the extremes. Extensive court management may only be needed in a relatively small number of complex and difficult cases.

A reduction in the degree of orality in the English process must surely be welcomed and will surely occur with the introduction of a wider class of advocate in the higher courts. But here again appearances can be deceptive. The costs of American proceedings, where the time allowed for submissions may be shorter, can be greater than under the English system, the result of the generation of a huge amount of affidavit evidence and written briefs forcing the judge to do a large amount of initial preparation aided by his law clerk. If the extent of orality in the civil courts is to be reduced, we need to ensure that the costs saved are not transferred to some more written system, spread in the too-early preparation of cases which would have settled anyway. There must also be an argument for deciding many more cases on paper or, at least, with minimal oral evidence, perhaps presented on video.

## Legal services and the courts

A further issue is the suggestion, again made by Lord Woolf, that savings resulting from reforms could be used to improve legal services and possibly lead to an increase in eligibility for legal aid. As much as there must be the hope that savings will occur as a result of the Woolf Inquiry and that further funds will be made available for these purposes, this does not appear to be a practical proposition.

There will clearly be additional expenditure resulting from any proposals which Lord Woolf makes which will have to be paid for before any savings accrue. If the courts are made more attractive to litigants, more cases may come in and thus increase overall costs. But these are subsidiary points. There is no method by which savings to the public purse from procedural innovations can presently be calculated. Even if such a method could be constructed, it is difficult to envisage that the Treasury would be much interested in it. Its concern is not simply the amount of public money which is being spent on civil cases but the rate by which that amount increases each year above the rate of inflation. The combination of costs per case and volume increase in the number of cases is a fatal cocktail which requires an ever-increasing amount of detoxification. The Woolf report may say very little or nothing about this major issue, nor about Treasury demands for additional savings on the civil side, however economically this work is conducted, to compensate for the higher and higher costs of criminal legal aid. Unless an enormous amount of financial planning is carried out on any reforms, it can paradoxically be the case that if there are savings in costs and time in processing individual civil cases the overall costs of legal aid may actually rise substantially. This is because there may be a once-and-for-all acceleration of the costs of cases which would have come in for payment at a later stage under the previous system. It should be emphasised, however, that if continual savings are not made, then the overall increase per year may continue to be unacceptably high.

So far as hopes for increased eligibility for legal aid are concerned, the Rushcliffe scheme created in 1949 has been largely dismantled and the principles which underlay it are being abandoned. Eligibility is becoming a subsidiary issue, as the Lord Chancellor has made clear recently. The notion of payment on a case-by-case basis is being replaced by block funding provided to franchised outlets which can offer the type of quality assurance which the Legal Aid Board now demands. Additional funds will only be provided for new ideas which fit this approach. We will have to wait and see whether the Woolf proposals will affect this strategy.

## An agenda for change

A more positive approach to the future needs to be considered and the means by which we can construct a civil system which will be adequate for the next century. Lord Woolf has clearly identified the major problems which have to be solved. Litigation is too inaccessible, too slow and too costly. A Rolls Royce system is a wonderful thing for those who are able to pay for it but for the majority of the population a cheaper model is a necessity. The possibility of choosing a type of car in which they will travel might be nice as well.

An agenda for change must be a wider one than that suggested by mere amendment of the rules of court. Even if there is general agreement that the proposals which will be put forward by Lord Woolf are exactly right and can be implemented immediately without alteration or criticism, it may not be long before they become out of date or need changing simply because events have overtaken them. We need to ensure that not only do we implement solutions for our problems but we also provide a permanent mechanism by which decisions can be considered and made in the future.

A first choice, therefore, must be for a continuous arrangement – it need not necessarily be a single commission – which co-ordinates a medium-term financial and institutional policy. Such a policy would integrate research, legal services and planning for the courts as well as alternative dispute resolution. At the moment such responsibility is fragmented through too many parts of the system to be effective and is the subject of too secretive a process. Contrast the position between the open nature of Lord Woolf's work and the very restricted exposure of the fundamental review of expenditure currently being conducted by the Lord Chancellor's Department.

The establishment of such a body may be seen as a rather evasive response and as an excuse for not producing concrete answers for difficult questions. But it is difficult to see how intermittent, one-off and short-term enquiries, however eminent their membership and however thorough their work, can possibly be satisfactory in modern conditions.

Over the last 20 years or so, a number of commissions and committees have been asked to look at these issues, often appointed as a matter of urgency and with a remit to produce a coherent, costed set of proposals within a short time-scale. The results of these have been very similar. A report is presented within the allotted time with ideas, sometimes sensible in themselves, sometimes not. The Lord Chancellor and his political machine proclaim them as the greatest thing since sliced bread. Some proposals may actually be implemented. Within a short time, however, we are back where we started with another instant inquiry. Consider, for example, the newspaper headlines only six years ago for the much-heralded Civil Justice Review, which produced some sensible ideas but which Lord Woolf has recently fairly criticised for not doing much in relation to cost or delay: 'Revolution in the Courts' (*Evening Standard*); 'Committee Recommends a Legal Revolution' (*Times*); 'Most Radical Shake-up for Civil Court Procedures Proposed for over a Century' (*Guardian*). A note of alarm sounded when the *Observer* recently described the Woolf Inquiry as amounting to, 'The biggest shake-up since the Act of Settlement 1701'. It is true that Lord Woolf does have a very different kind of agenda than the inquiries mentioned above. The question still remains, however, whether he can achieve the very radical objectives which he has set for himself.

## A chance for reform

These are grounds for considerable optimism about the outcome of the Woolf inquiry. The team is clearly prepared to consider far-reaching proposals. Given the scale of the problems, Lord Woolf ought certainly to be able to persuade the Lord Chancellor to implement any necessary changes. Faced with the existing position, many lawyers are now prepared to consider and adopt a range of solutions. There is a general feeling that the time for effective reforms is at hand.

How can we achieve these aims? We could start by looking at our indemnity and settlement rules, both inside and outside the court process. We ought also to be examining different types of litigation to see whether we can provide simple types of adjudication which can fit the issues involved and which are both expeditious and cheap. We need to get as far away as possible from the 'trial by ambush' system and to extend 'the cards on the table' approach in order to have an appropriate, fair and early exchange of information between the parties. There needs to be a reduction in the oral process, without front-loading the general run of disputed cases with the costs of too-early preparation. We must try to have trial dates fixed as soon as possible. We might provide for decision-making on paper submissions only. We certainly need to construct a viable system of alternative dispute resolution. Some of this may have to be provided through voluntary effort by the legal profession.

There also needs to be an attempt to allocate judicial resources on a consistent basis. We may be moving towards systems where we distinguish sharply between the maintenance of a central court system, concerned with litigation involving a 'public interest' element on the one hand, and arbitral systems, with minimum state funding and involvement, concerned largely with 'private' disputes on the other. Such an arbitral system might consist of a bundle of ADR methods and be funded by private insurance or in some other way. The allocation of judge-power by way of a resources plan would be an essential part of any such overall scheme. We will never be able to have as many senior judges as we would like. The present unsatisfactory method of trying quite important cases by the use of deputies already has a permanent air about it.

The formal adjudicative process ought to offer a choice, not just of remedies but of methods of disputing. Such a notice requires procedural innovation. The current situation is the result of monopoly arrangements. Why should litigants not be free to choose, sometimes with help or direction, the type of decision-making which they require? An appropriate process may allow legal representation or bar it. It might include swift adjudication on paper only or call for a particular type of judge. It might provide for structured settlement or diversion to other forms of resolution outside the courts. There might be particular resolution packages at a set price for litigants in person. The provision of a legal supermarket would encourage choice and help restrain cost and delay.

Next, there ought to be a greater variety in procedures. We need to examine cases on a 'type' basis in order to devise appropriate procedures for settlement and resolution. Such an examination would enable us to devise the appropriate procedural 'hurdles' to access or in-court settlement arrangements. These procedures would plan for common-form time limits for step-taking and the fair exchange of information at each stage of the process. They would also make provision for the extent of judicial interventionism during the progress of the dispute itself. The 'common core' procedural systems which are a feature of many court arrangements need to be abandoned for tailored rules.

A final preference is for a more careful and interconnected approach to advice and representation services of all kinds, and not simply those provided by the legal profession. We need to demystify court procedures. The role of non-lawyers in the disputing process is often under-valued and we ought to encourage a greater use of lesser skilled court professionals, perhaps with the assistance of new technology. It is difficult to see how a discussion of methods of allocating civil disputes can be divorced, either financially or organisationally, from this subject.

Alongside all this, we have to change the culture which pervades the way in which lawyers think and in their approach to disputing. There is no doubt that there are many disputes which are irreconcilable and in respect of which full-blown hearings will be necessary. But we must do more to identify those that can be resolved at a much earlier stage. A strategy which can try to look at these issues in the round is the better able to make informed choices about the resources available and to integrate the arrangements which result. If we are to democratise the system, then the private government of public money in this field must be made more accountable.

## References

1  This is a revised version of a speech delivered at a LAG conference on 12 November 1994. An earlier version appeared in the first edition of *The Litigator*, published by Sweet and Maxwell in 1995.
2  N Rosenburg, *The Pretrial Conference and Effective Justice*, Columbia University Press, 1964.

# CHAPTER 16

# Dream or nightmare?
# Lessons from the American experience

CARRIE MENKEL-MEADOW

*Carrie Menkel-Meadow is Professor of Law at University of California at Los Angeles. In 1994 she was Visiting Professor of Law at Georgetown Law Center, Washington DC. She served as a legal services attorney in Philadelphia in the 1970s, specialising in welfare rights, employment cases, domestic relations and public benefits litigation. She left to organise the Penn Legal Assistance Office. She was one of the founders of the 'alternative dispute resolution' movement in the United States and has received awards for both her teaching and writing.*

'It was the best of times; it was the worst of times', said Charles Dickens at the opening of *A Tale of Two Cities*. In a sense, this famous literary line captures the essence of what is currently happening in American litigation and what it might foretell for other common-law-based legal systems. Like Dickens' descriptions of Paris and London, there are a variety of perspectives that can be used to view developments and the future of civil litigation.

There is class (disparate effects of litigation developments for the endowed and disadvantaged), the relationship of the criminal caseload to the civil (there may soon be no civil trials in court in some American jurisdictions). There is the story of attempted innovations and changes (specifically, the promise of alternative dispute resolution and the 'multi-door courthouse'[1] and efforts to reduce the adversarialism and gamesmanship of litigation in compulsory disclosure rules and sanctions for 'bad behaviour'[2]) that have been co-opted and assimilated within the confines of the traditional adversary system[3] and the related tale of the increased privatisation of civil litigation.[4]

There is the complex issue of how the courts should respond to multi-party actions[5] (as they are termed in the UK) and class actions (as they are called in the US) with the interesting twist[6] of mass-tort class action settlements in the US,[7] representing tensions between individual and aggregate justice. Finally, there is the use of technology in the courts, representing the possibility of greater access and accessibility to legal services, with the danger of big brother surveillance. At a political and policy level, there are important questions about who will frame and control changes in civil litigation – who will write the rules, change the practices and influence how changes and innovations will be incorporated into the system? In a system as large as the United States', the question is also whether there will be uniformity (at least in the federal courts) or whether local experimentation (at federal district court level as well as state level) will be permitted. Will it be possible to involve procedural reforms in civil litigation transsubstantively or will such reforms produce greater variations in the handling of particular types of cases? Also at stake, as modern civil litigation is transformed, is the role of the judiciary. In the United States, judges, practitioners and academics argue about whether judges should remain passive 'neutral umpires' or whether they should become 'social justice bureaucrats' as they become more active in managing cases and facilitating the settlement of mass justice cases.[8]

This chapter reviews some of these developments and possibilities for radical transformation of civil litigation, looking both to the dream-like hopes of improved access to and quality of justice and to the possible dangers of deformed or co-opted change. As is always a problem in comparative legal studies, I cannot say which of these developments are directly relevant in the UK.

## The challenges to civil litigation

As we enter a new century, there are a variety of challenges facing civil litigation in adversary cultures – some produced by courts, some by parties, some by lawyers and most by modern life. In the United States there is much debate and dissension, both about what the challenges are and what the solutions should be. For example, a robust scholarly debate has been pursued for almost a decade about whether or not there really is a 'litigation explosion'; whether Americans are more litigious; and whether the assumed massive increase in our civil caseload can be managed.[9] Similarly, practitioners, scholars and judges have argued about whether there is too much gamesmanship, strategic play and 'overkill' in the way information is exchanged and litigation is actually conducted.[10]

There is now a debate about whether class action litigation, designed to promote efficiency and justice for groups of victims of various legal wrongs, has instead become a lucrative business or auction for plaintiffs' lawyers to finance great fortunes through settlements and fees.[11]

As the costs of litigation begin to climb (not through official court fees, but in the necessary discovery costs of paper interrogatories and in-person depositions, along with escalating attorneys' fees in non-contingent or statutory fee matters)[12] and as doctrinal developments (issues about legal standing, ripeness of legal controversies and other jurisdictional gatekeeping issues) have moved in more restrictive and conservative directions, questions about access to courts for the economically disadvantaged continue to be raised. With a deflation in the dollars assigned to free legal services (through the Legal Services Corporation), access to justice remains a very live issue. Finally, even for those who litigate public interest, law reform and poverty law cases, there remains an ongoing debate about whether litigation is an effective way to achieve legal, as well as social, change and justice, or whether legislative or more direct collective action would be more effective.[13]

## Reforms, responses and reactions

These issues or challenges to civil litigation in the United States have sparked a variety of legal reforms and activities in recent years, the end results of which we will not be able to evaluate fully for some years to come. I will focus primarily on my own areas of expertise: the use of alternative dispute resolution devices to deal with some of these issues; procedural reform; and the effects of mass torts case treatment on the legal system as a whole and on other types of cases; while briefly touching on the other issues suggested above. As suggested by my title, any of these developments can be explored through the dreamy lens of optimism or the nightmarish cloud of doom.

There have been two major formal legal developments affecting civil litigation in recent years. The first is the passage of the Civil Justice Reform Act,[14] which requires all federal district courts (the 94 federal trial courts in the United States) to develop and implement cost and delay-reduction plans, and report back to Congress on their progress. These plans are to be developed by local advisory groups consisting of judges, lawyers, parties and some public representation from each district. The Act encourages the development of alternative dispute resolution plans and also suggests case management devices to be used by judges and court administrators. Many state courts are far more advanced in their use of and experimentation with ADR, including compulsory assignments to mediation or arbitration in some states.[15] The second formal development is the amendment of the formal rules of civil procedure to require automatic disclosure of basic discovery information following the filing of pleadings and increased sanctions for lawyers who fail to litigate fairly or 'appropriately'.

There has been much controversy, among academics, the judiciary, the profession and most notably, within Congress, on a wide variety of issues implicated in these changes. For example, trial lawyers have lobbied actively to prevent mandatory ADR in the form of court-mandated arbitration (even the American Bar Association took a formal position against mandatory arbitration in 1994). Both plaintiff and defence lawyers have decried the new discovery rules, arguing that a reform intended to decrease costs and speed the process will lead to more litigation and squabbling between parties and lawyers. Many have argued that a serious breach of the separation of powers has occurred: the national legislative body has displaced the judiciary's right to control its own functioning.[16] While any and all of these issues could occupy the field, I prefer to concentrate on the possibilities for radical transformation of the civil justice system from these developments, while paying some attention to the underside or 'worst' possibilities of these reforms.

First, we must consider purpose. In any transformation of the civil justice system, the issue will be what we are trying to reform and for what reason – those who seek to reduce caseloads through ADR (the quantitative 'efficiency' maximisers) will have different objectives and implementation devices from those who are attempting to use alternative methods to increase access to justice or to improve the quality of justice (the qualitative or 'fairness' maximisers). In my own work on ADR, I have long been associated with the latter – using methods of mediation, some forms of facilitated negotiation and some of the hybrid forms of ADR[17] to increase access to justice by providing other methods of dispute resolution and to improve the quality of dispute resolution by providing solutions and results which would not be possible in a bi-polar (win/lose) situation. Further, in a visionary paper, which in many ways began the ADR movement in the United States, Frank Sander argued for a 'multi-door' courthouse in which disputes would be analysed, screened and assigned to the appropriate 'treatment' for that case (using such factors as long-term versus one-shot relationships, the need for speed, privacy and precedent by the parties),[18] a futurist plan for courts that has become a reality in several state and a few federal-level courts today.[19]

In my view, the variations of alternative dispute resolution currently being explored in a myriad of civil litigation settings can transform civil justice by offering both greater access to justice (through serving more litigants in different ways) and the potential of a greater quality of justice (through a greater variety of 'solutions' to legal problems, crafted by the parties, by experts and by involving more of the parties who are actually implicated in a particular dispute, including, in appropriate cases, governmental and legislative bodies). This is not to say that there are not also some risks and dangers to justice posed by such 'transformations'.

The use of ADR in civil litigation comes in a variety of forms. At the beginning, with government funding of 'neighborhood justice centers' many felt that only 'minor' (defined as low-amount or community) disputes were being shuttled to an inferior form of justice, just as poor clients, civil rights litigants, women and minorities were gaining access to the courts through new forms of legislation in the 1960s and 1970s.[20]

The story is more complex. The principal users of ADR were a group of large corporations and their in-house and outside counsel who signed a pledge, created and administered by the Center for Public Resources, a private non-profit organisation, to pursue private forms of ADR with each other.[21] ADR, in the form of privately conducted mediations, mini-trials (shortened presentations, usually without witnesses, to corporate executives and a third party neutral for the purpose of facilitating a negotiated settlement), arbitrations and summary jury trials (a slightly more formal form of the mini-trial, occurring in a public court with a panel of advisory jurors), was preferred to in-court litigation in cases where costs could be cut; principal actors could be gathered to focus on the problem; cases could be resolved more quickly or with the secrecy of a private setting and parties could choose an expert decision-maker, fact-finder or facilitator. Thus, those who could afford it realised that private ADR offered a way out of the congestion, expense and arbitrariness of the formal court system and it was the wealthy, rather than the dispossessed, who used ADR more often.

Indeed, where ADR was used in compulsory court settings or in domestic relations settings, many advocates for the poor were more likely to oppose than to utilise alternative processes for fear that power imbalances would operate to prevent the weaker party from achieving justice in a relatively informal environment.[22] More recently, sophisticated advocates for the poor (as well as advocates for any litigants) have realised that ADR is many things and must always be compared to the 'baseline' measure of what else might happen to the case – a private negotiated settlement or a trial.[23]

Some forms of ADR may be better (and others worse) for some forms of cases, regardless of the economic situation of the litigants (with the few caveats indicated below). First, long-term relationship cases (including domestic relations and parenting, landlord-tenant, some employer-employee cases, some consumer cases and even some social welfare and government benefits cases) do better with mediative or conciliative type processes. Second, in some cases, parties might desire more participatory input in the decision. In the United States, this has recently come to include complex cases with many parties, including the government, such as in administrative regulation negotiation,[24] environmental disputes, mass tort cases and public policy setting. Third, parties might seek a solution that is different from what a court would order. As I have argued elsewhere, our laws give courts a mandatory 'limited remedial imagination', because they are empowered to award only money damages or injunctive relief. Sometimes parties might want something else (such as some rules for future conduct, apologies, damages paid in kind in goods, future promises and commitments, options and opportunities). Fourth, enforcement of a 'solution' may be more effective if the parties agree to it. Fifth, people (as well as corporations) may desire secrecy in some matters (such as in resolution of defamation cases, employment termination suits and the like) and many also prefer finality (the avoidance of *Bleak House*-like continuation for decades of appeals and further orders). Sixth, in some cases parties may prefer to make their own rules of decision or fairness, rather than be guided by general rules that do not apply to their situation.[25] Seventh, for some, litigation is an opportunity for catharsis, and a mediation hearing which allows a relatively free opportunity to talk and be listened to may actually provide a fuller and fairer hearing than the stylised ritual of a court hearing.[26] Thus, even with the danger of power imbalances (which can sometimes be corrected with representation, third party neutrals with legal knowledge, or public advice and information), individual clients (and even disadvantaged people) might prefer different processes *in some cases*. The key to appropriate use of ADR is that parties should not be coerced to accept settlements they do not want. This is different from requiring them (or using the official court process) to attend an ADR proceeding. Courts debating policy in the US are now focusing on this question of voluntary versus mandatory ADR referral.[27]

With the advent of the Civil Justice Reform Act (CJRA), issues of transformation of the civil justice system have raised these concerns along several fronts. What may work in the private sector, where the parties choose ADR, either by writing it into contracts[28] or once the dispute has ripened, may not work in the public sector where parties expect certain public rules and rituals and judicial resolution of their problems. But the CJRA has now 'forced' some parties to try ADR, even if they do not really want it. In what comes closest to a scientific experimental design, the Western District of Missouri federal court has divided its caseload into thirds: the first third is automatically assigned to an early 'neutral' assessment, by a full-time court administrator, leading to ADR recommendations; the second third of litigants are given a choice about whether to use ADR or litigate conventionally; and the final third, the control group, is given the 'usual' treatment. Early empirical evaluation has suggested that not only are cases disposed of faster in the first two-thirds (an average of 100 days earlier), but settlement intervention and case-planning and discovery limits appear to be working earlier and earlier in these cases.[29] A recent new programme in Delaware grants special ADR treatment and limited discovery to high-stakes cases (cases involving more than one million dollars) with expedited appeal guaranteed to the Delaware Supreme Court in certain high-profile corporate take-over battles.[30]

Those who, like myself, see the transformative potential of the 'multi-door' courthouse offering parties an opportunity to craft their own processes to fit their disputes, see the courts as becoming more accessible to the people and offering what some have called 'appropriate' (not alternative) dispute resolution. If cases are processed faster and with different types of 'resolvers', there will be an opportunity to serve more.[31] Recently, several federal judges have seen this as an opportunity to be 'public problem-solvers', helping people to develop and choose appropriate processes for their disputes and then facilitating appropriate solutions and legal remedies.[32] In some 'futuristic' courts, electronic programmes describe these processes to litigants and let them choose how to file their actions and what process to use.[33]

The use of ADR inside the courts has raised several significant policy questions that can only be touched on here. First, who should the providers be and how should they be compensated? As we see in both the UK and US, in some areas a separate professionalism has already developed around the use of mediation, particularly in the sphere of domestic relations. Turf battles have been – and will continue to be – waged about whether lawyers, social workers or psychologists should control this work and how they should be trained, evaluated, accredited and chosen. In the US, accountants have recently entered the fray, arguing that they are best suited to mediate or arbitrate complex financial matters (not unlike the battles over conveyancing monopolies in the UK). This raises the issue of how economic and market forces may transform the legal system, with or without regulation.[34] Most federal and state courts depend on volunteer attorneys who trade on the prestige of being chosen as a court mediator or arbitrator. This may give them special access to judges and other court personnel that may present some ethical problems.[35]

New issues are developing over whether court-sanctioned ADR programmes are privatising justice by referring parties to private dispute professionals rather than publicly chosen and confirmed judges and whether parties are using ADR to prevent disclosure of their settlements. This has become a major issue in mass tort cases where corporate defendants seek confidential settlements and protective orders, and often demand that plaintiffs' lawyers restrict access to the information they obtained in seeking settlement to prevent sharing of information with other litigants.[36]

Recently, a number of large class action (multi-party) lawsuits in the United States have been 'settled' with a mix of public-private interventions – judges meeting with parties and counsel; private or special masters or magistrates appointed by courts; aggregation of claims in 'multi-district litigation' or in the bankruptcy court, with committees of lawyers negotiating with each other. Most controversially, settlements have been arranged before litigation is filed and the courts are then 'used' to certify and approve such settlements.[37]

These developments have raised enormous outcries from protestors but in many ways demonstrate the new possibilities of a more complex civil justice system. At issue is the basic concern of whether our legal system is designed to deliver individual justice in every case, at whatever price, or whether it is appropriate for courts and judges to consider broader issues involved in big disputes (such as the equitable division of limited funds);[38] and whether such social policy-making should be left to the legislature. Thus, the role of judges is very contested at this moment. Judges themselves do not share a common vision of what they should be doing or even whether they should have sole control over their decision-making responsibilities. Some activist judges believe it is essential for judges to aggregate claims and 'broker' and facilitate settlements when the legislature has failed to act, as in the case of asbestos-industrial illness or environmental clean-up superfund cases, in order to prevent the lottery of winnings attributable to particularly aggressive plaintiffs' lawyers.[39] Others see the federal judiciary as inevitably tied up in these issues as bureaucratic monitoring and rationalisation comes to affect this third branch of government.[40] Still others cling to the traditional notion of the passive judge in an adversarial system who hears only what the advocate puts before him. All of this, of course, is further complicated in the administrative area, where tribunals as well as the courts often both make regulations and adjudicate claims.[41]

In my view, the greatest challenge for the transformation of the civil justice system is not *whether* it should be engaged in these 'alternative' ways of doling out justice, but *how*. If the courts do not adapt and use some of these methods, the private sector will most certainly take over, as some have argued has already happened in such places as California, where statutes authorise 'rent-a-judges' (private, usually retired, judges) to hear cases with the full force of law and authority behind them. Then the class justice issue will become one in which those who can afford to do so will exit the system to purchase the types of decision-makers and forms of justice they want, while criminal dockets escalate[42] and 'smaller' civil cases will linger in the court for years without room or bodies for resolution. For those who seek to transform civil justice to make it more accessible and fair to litigants, the challenge is how to harness these new forms to concerns for fairness and ways of monitoring whether 'justice' is being delivered. The Civil Justice Reform Act provides for two independent research studies (one by the Federal Judicial Center and the other by the RAND Corporation) to assess and evaluate the success of ADR and case management innovations in a variety of federal district courts.

## The future

Some American courts have approached these dilemmas by organising and planning for the future – establishing commissions to study the justice system of the future. In several ambitious 'futurist' studies, both at the federal and state level, committees of judges, lawyers, government and business officials and public representatives have attempted to anticipate the future[43] and set a blueprint for change.[44] Commonly urged reforms include 'user-oriented justice' with 'multi-option justice' (involving decentralised community justice centres with a variety of process choices and types of legal 'helpers');[45] use of technology for access to legal information and courts and agencies from home and other remote places; 'unified' courts that treat the 'whole' rather than part of the problem (such as in the intersection of family law and social welfare law), responsiveness of legal providers to increasingly diverse populations (including translators, paralegals, and advice-givers, as well as lawyers, who service a variety of communities and promote understanding across differences, as well as guarantee some form of representation to all who have civil legal matters); responsiveness of the legal system to increasingly complex disputes (recognising that technical and other disputes will have more than two parties and will need to be handled in other than conventional adversarial ways), including using new fora and new methods for hearing either complex matters (using experts) or mass routine matters (such as victims of mass disasters or users of defective products); and responsiveness of the justice system to the public, as well as to constitutional and other principles of justice (recommending not just judicial and governmental oversight of justice functions, but monitoring and evaluation, with public surveys, research and satisfaction studies).

The key question in all these ambitious proposals, of course, is *financing* the justice system, both in terms of access for particular individuals with legal problems and financing the institutional changes demanded by a changing world. The private corporate sector and wealthy individuals will be able to pay for the justice they think is most 'appropriate' for their cases. The issue facing economically disadvantaged people in a civil justice system is whether they will have enough control over the choices and alternatives offered them or whether they will wind up with 'second class' or residual justice institutions. Many of the innovations suggested above are currently being exploited by private entrepreneurial justice providers, including private judges, private courtrooms and all the indicia of a civil justice system. In order to maintain equality and equitable access, public funding will have to be provided to assure access and quality of justice delivered to those who can't pay.[46]

All actors in the legal system are not created equal.[47] And not all legal actions are created equal either.[48] Thus, choices have to be made about what processes are appropriate for what kinds of cases[49] and what kind of representation or legal service is appropriate for which process – for example, when can clients represent themselves and when will they need specialised legal assistance? What kinds of monitoring, training, evaluation and quality assessments can be made of providers of dispute resolution services to maximise their usefulness and effectiveness?

## Lessons from comparative study

Both the US and the UK have a great deal to learn from each other. This chapter has raised some issues by focusing primarily on the American experience. By comparing, not London and Paris, as Dickens did, but London and Washington DC, we can address ourselves to the following questions.

1.  How can civil litigation best be handled? In court? Outside court? Can/should all cases be handled the same way?
    a) Who should the providers of dispute resolution services be, both 'facilitators' and 'deciders', as well as advocates?
    b) Who will pay for alternative dispute resolution services?
       (i)    the government – at what level?
       (ii)   user fees?
       (iii)  what are the effects of fee shifts and cost shifts? (Who is a 'prevailing' party in an ADR proceeding?)
    c) How will ADR be monitored, and evaluated?
    d) How can justice be made more 'accessible' as well as 'fairer' in less formal arenas?
    e) How do advice centres or other more local, decentralised bodies fit into the administration of justice?
    f) Who should make the rules and policies about uses of ADR – judges, lawyers, interest groups, etc? What will the role of the judiciary be in creating/adapting to change?

2.  What impact do non-civil matters have on civil litigation?
    a) What is the relation of criminal and administrative tribunal matters to the civil justice system?
    b) How does the divided Bar affect how civil litigation is conducted?

3.  How do changing types of disputes affect the civil justice system? (What do aggregate/mass/multi-party actions do to the functioning of the rest of the system?) Does a just legal system require

uniformity of treatment or are varieties of process also just and fair?

4. How might new private innovations be adapted to public institutions? (What are the benefits and risks of entrepreneurial and technological developments from the private sector being used in the public sector?) Who will pay for them?

## Conclusion

Whether new developments will be used to create greater access to justice for the disadvantaged or whether they will result in a solidifying of the class divisions in our justice system remains to be seen. In part, it depends on much control we try to exert on 'our times'.

## References

1 Frank Sander, 'Varieties of Dispute Processing', 70 FRD 111 (1977).
2 See recent rule changes in Federal Rules of Civil Procedure, requiring disclosure of key facts and experts (r26(a)), changes to rules for sanctioning lawyer and party behaviour (r11), and rules providing for assessment of costs for failing to accept a settlement (r68). See generally the symposium 'Reinventing Civil Litigation: Evaluating Proposals for Change', 59 *Brooklyn L Rev* 655 (1993).
3 See C Menkel-Meadow, 'Pursuing Settlement in an Adversary Culture: A Tale of Innovation Co-opted or the Law of ADR', 19 *Florida St L Rev* 1 (1991).
4 See Bryant Garth, 'Privatization and the New Market for Disputes: A Framework for Analysis and a Preliminary Assessment', 12 *Stud in L Pol and Society* 367 (1992).
5 See *Issues Arising for the Legal Aid Board and the Lord Chancellor's Department from Multi-Party Actions*, May 1994.
6 Excuse the Dickensian pun.
7 See the recent cases of *Georgine v Amchem Products*, CA 93-0125 (ED Pa) and *In Re Silicone Gel Breast Implants Products Liability Litigation* (MDL–926) (ND Ala, Aug 31, 1994).
8 See, eg, Resnik, 'Managerial Judges', 96 *Harvard L Rev* 376 (1982); Robert Peckham, 'A Judicial Response to the Cost of Litigation: Two-Stage Discovery Planning and Alternative Dispute Resolution', 37 *Rutgers L Rev* 253 (1985); John Coffee, 'The Corruption of Class Action', *Wall Street Journal*, 7 Sept 1994 at A15; Jack Weinstein, 'Procedural Reform as a Surrogate for Substantive Law Reform', 59 *Brooklyn L Rev* 827 (1993).

9 See, eg, Galanter, 'The Day After the Litigation Explosion', 46 *Maryland L Rev* 3 (1986); Idem, 'Reading the Landscape of Disputes: What we know and don't know (and think we know) about our allegedly contentious and litigious society', 31 *UCLA L Rev* 4 (1983); Idem, 'The Life and Times of the Big Six: or, the Federal Courts Since the Good Old Days', 1988 *Wisc L Rev* 921.

10 See William Schwarzer, 'Slaying the Monsters of Cost and Delay: Would Disclosure be more Effective than Discovery?' *Judicature*, Dec-Jan 1990 at 178; Wayne Brazil, 'The Adversary Character of Civil Discovery: A Critique and Proposals for Change', 31 *Vanderbilt L Rev* 1295 (1978).

11 John Coffee, 'Understanding the Plaintiff's Attorney: The Implications of Economic Theory for Private Enforcement of Law through Class and Derivative Actions', 86 *Columbia L Rev* 669 (1986); Idem, 'The Regulation of Entrepreneurial Litigation: Balancing Fairness and Efficiency in the Large Class Action', 5 *U Chi L Rev* 877 (1987). See also argument that cases are settled for 'nuisance' and other values (for attorney's fees) rather than on the basis of the merits of the case (including the legal principles at stake) in Janet Cooper Alexander, 'Do the Merits Matter? A Study of Settlements in Securities Class Actions', 3 *Stan L Rev* 497 (1991).

12 See, eg, Milo Geyelin, 'Going First Class, Soaring Legal Expense: Motorola Bemoans it but runs a Big Tab', *Wall Street Journal*, 5 October 1994 (describing the exorbitant costs of defending an environmental suit, with audits and declinations of coverage by defendant's insurance company).

13 See Gerald N Rosenberg, *The Hollow Hope: Can Courts Bring about Social Change?* (1991); Steve Bachman, 'Lawyers, Law and Social Change', 13 *NYU Rev L & Soc Change* 1; Idem, book review: 'Can Courts Bring About Social Change?' 19 *NYU Rev L & Soc Change* 391 (1991–2).

14 (1990) 28 USC Chap 471 (Supp II 1992).

15 The states of Florida, Texas and California have been most active in this field.

16 See, eg, Linda Mullinex, 'The Counter-Reformation in Procedural Justice', 77 *Minn L Rev* 375 (1992). Others see this as an opportunity for some form of 'local control and experimentation' with rule-making and civil justice; see Lauren Robel, 'Grass Roots Procedure: Local Advisory Groups and the Civil Justice Reform Act of 1990', 59 *Brooklyn L Rev* 879 (1993); Carl Tobias, 'Silver Linings in Civil Justice Reform', 59 *Brooklyn L Rev* 857 (1993) (suggesting that this statute has led to increased planning, local group participation in rule-making and court procedures, evaluation, dialogue, policy considerations of the role of courts and judges, oversight by Congress and independent research agencies and politicisation and discussion of the needs of litigants, courts and the policy for justice).

17 See C Menkel-Meadow, 'Toward Another View of Legal Negotiation: The Structure of Problem Solving', 31 *UCLA L Rev* 754 (1984); Idem, 'Lawyer

Negotiations: Theories and Realities – What we Learn from Mediation', 56 *Mod L Rev* 361 (1993).

18 For the most recent and sophisticated attempt to typologise which cases would benefit from which process, see Sander and Goldberg, 'Fitting the Forum to the Fuss: A User-Friendly Guide to Selecting an ADR Procedure', 10 *Negotiation J* 49 (1994).

19 Local courts in Washington DC and Massachusetts have implemented 'multi-door' courthouse plans and are currently being evaluated.

20 For a compilation of these critiques and others, see Richard Abel (ed), *The Politics of Informal Justice* (1982); and Christine Harrington, *Shadow Justice: The Ideology and Institutionalisation of Alternatives to Court* (1985).

21 See Center for Public Resources, *Corporate Dispute Management*, 1992.

22 See Linda Singer, Michael Lewis, Alan Houseman, Elizabeth Singer, 'Alternative Dispute Resolution and the Poor – Part I: What ADR Processes Exist and why Advocates Should Become Involved,' 26 *Clearing House Review* 2 (May/June 1992); Idem, 'Part II: Dealing with Problems in using ADR and Choosing a Process'; Trina Grillo, 'Mediation: Process Dangers for Women', 100 *Yale L J* 1545 (1991); Richard Delgado et al, 'Fairness and Formality: Minimising the Risk of Prejudice in Alternative Dispute Resolution,' 1985 *Wisc L Rev* 1359.

23 Many critics of ADR make two analytic errors: first, they lump all forms of ADR together, when in fact different processes are quite different, both in terms of what process is provided and what outcomes are possible. Second, many critics engage in what I have called 'litigation romanticism', assuming that the full panoply of adversary rights and courtroom fairness will be applied if the case is tried. Here the fallacies are evident if one watches what actually occurs in many courtrooms (ie, family, criminal or small claims courts in major metropolitan areas) and when one realises that the actual baseline for over 90% of all civil cases is private settlement, not trial by judge or jury.

24 See Stephen Goldberg, 'Reflections on Negotiated Rule-Making,' *The Washington Lawyer* 42 (Sept/Oct 1994).

25 This raises serious jurisprudential concerns about when it is appropriate for parties to make their own rules and contract out of the general, uniform rules which are intended to apply to an entire society. For a critique of ADR on this basis (and others) see Owen Fiss, 'Against Settlement,' 93 *Yale L J* 1073 (1984). Fiss is also concerned that too much settlement will not produce enough precedents with which to 'create' the common law.

26 This has been my experience as an arbitrator in the mass tort Dalkon Shield litigation in the United States, where parties who have very private details to talk about (such as their reproductive and sexual histories) want to tell their stories and blame the perceived evil corporate wrongdoer, but want to do it

in private. Some litigants would prefer the 'collective' experience of class action justice – others want individualised opportunities to be heard. For empirical studies of what people want from the process, see Tom Tyler, *The Social Psychology of Procedural Justice* (1988). See also Deborah Hensler and Mark Peterson, 'Understanding Mass Personal Injury Litigation: A Socio-legal Analysis,' 59 *Brooklyn L Rev* 961 (1993) and G Vairo, 'Reinventing Civil Procedure: Will the New Procedural Regime Help Resolve Mass Torts?' 59 *Brooklyn L Rev* 1065 (1993).

27  Lucy V Katz, 'Compulsory Alternative Dispute Resolution and Voluntarism: Two-headed Monster or Two Sides of the Coin?' 1993 *J Disp Res* 1.

28  An increasingly popular way to opt out of the costly litigation system is to place compulsory arbitration clauses in contracts of various kinds. Such clauses have, for the time being, been sustained both by the US Supreme Court, see *Gilmer v Interstate/Johnson Lane Corp* 111 S Ct 1647 (1991), and state courts, see *Badie v Bank of America*, 944916, Calif Superior Ct at B-1. Issues remain about how voluntary or 'consented to' these clauses really are, especially in cases of contracting between individuals and large organisations (like banks and major manufacturers). The Clinton Health Care Plan would have statutorily imposed some forms of mandatory ADR in medical malpractice cases.

29  See 'Early Assessment in Missouri Saves Times and Wins Fans,' 12 *Alternatives to the High Costs of Litigation* 110 (Sept 1994).

30  This is the first programme I am aware of that sets a high minimum value on ADR cases (big cases) rather than doing the opposite, sending 'lower value' cases to ADR ('lower' meaning cases worth less than $150,000 (about £100,000) in some federal courts and less than $25,000 (£16,650) in some state courts). Thus, ADR appears to speak to all economic levels of disputes. This is an example of the wealthy and powerful being able to create a system of ADR for quick and efficient resolution of matters involving multi-million dollars.

31  In an interesting argument, Professor George Priest has suggested that there will be a natural equilibrium in court filings and delays. As courts become more efficient, he argues, more cases will be filed, thus adding to the processing time. When cases take too long, filings will be down – thus an equilibrium will be reached. See Priest, 'Private Litigants and the Court Congestion Problem,' 69 *BUL Rev* 527 (1989).

32  See remarks of Judge Brock Hornby, National ADR Institute for Federal Judges, Harvard Law School, November 12–13, 1993.

33  See demonstrations at American Bar Association 'Just Solutions' Conference on Innovations in Justice, May 3–4, 1994, Leesburg, Virginia.

34  In recent rhetoric used by the American Bar Association, the Bar has begun to use market language, seeking to make the legal system more 'consumer-

friendly'. See Stephen P Johnson, *Just Solutions: Seeking Innovation and Change in the American Justice System* (ABA, 1994) at 33.

35 See Menkel-Meadow, 'Professional Responsibility for Third-Party Neutrals,' 11 *Alternatives* 129 (September 1993); Idem, 'Ex Parte Talks with Neutrals: ADR Hazards,' 12 *Alternatives* 109 (1994).

36 See Menkel-Meadow, 'Public Access to Private Settlements: Conflicting Legal Policies,' 11 *Alternatives* 85 (June 1993).

37 Raising issues about whether there has been 'collusion' or the absence of a 'case' or controversy'. These issues are currently on appeal. These are cases involving mass torts concerning Agent Orange, toxic waste siting, defoliant and environmental pollutants, breast implant litigation, Dalkon Shield product liability and asbestos cases.

38 See, eg, Peter Shuck, 'The Worst Should Go First: Deferral Registries in Asbestos Litigation,' 15 *Harv J of Law and Public Policy* 541 (1992).

39 See Jack Weinstein, 'Ethical Dilemmas in Mass Tort Litigation,' 88 *New L Rev* 469 (1994).

40 See Heydebrand and Seron, *Rationalising Justice: The Political Economy of the Federal Courts* (1990); William Schwarzer and Russell Wheeler, 'On the Federalisation of the Administration of Civil and Criminal Justice', 23 *Stetson L Rev* 651 (1994).

41 ADR is currently making its way, at differential rates, through the American bureaucracy as well. One might be surprised to know that the US Army, particularly in contract and procurement disputes, was among the first federal agencies to use various forms of ADR to resolve disputes efficiently and continue relationships with on-going suppliers.

42 A recent report indicated that when the 'three strikes and you're out' laws (after three felony convictions, offenders will have life, without possibility of parole sentences) take effect at both the state and federal level, there will be virtually no room or time for civil cases.

43 There have also been state and federal court task forces on gender and racial bias in the courts, seeking to study and evaluate claims of bias in the operation of courts and then to suggest and implement reforms. See, eg, Ninth Circuit Gender Bias Task Force Report (1993).

44 Representative publications include American Bar Association, *Just Solutions: A Program Guide to Innovative Justice System Improvements* (1994); *Justice in the Balance: 2020*, Report of the Commission on the Future of the California Courts (1993); and *Reinventing Justice: 2022*, Report of the Chief Justice's Commission on the Future of the Courts, Massachusetts 1992.

45 These proposals raise important questions about whether certain forms of ADR work better in local communities with shared community values or whether it is possible to impose national or uniform standards on an increasingly diverse population. Some have argued that as society diversi-

fies and shares fewer and fewer values, formal rules of law and procedure and commitment to our adversary system are some of the few shared values remaining and should not be disturbed. In the US, with increased immigration from nations with corrupt justice systems, we are actually finding less commitment to formal institutions of justice.

46 There are some success stories. With a relatively small yearly fee, the elderly can join the American Association of Retired Persons and have access to a relatively high quality 'elderlaw' telephone hotline that dispenses legal advice.

47 One commentator has suggested that mass torts should not be equated with civil rights and other 'disadvantaged' class action type disputes, since the victims of certain consumer products and securities frauds do have access to lawyers (especially with the American contingent fee doctrine) and will have greater claims (in the form of both increased special and general damages). Issues of transformation of the civil justice system must be linked to the difficult issues of how lawyers are paid and the economic incentives for bringing and pursuing litigation. (This of course implies the complex policy issues of fee shifting and cost shifting, issues on which the UK and the US have taken totally different routes.)

48 For example, in the UK much attention has been focused on rights of audience for solicitors and on rights of legally aided representation in administrative tribunals. In the US, where free legal services are provided, clients have had lawyers and paralegals represent them in administrative and social welfare hearings both before and since the landmark procedural due process case of *Goldberg v Kelly*, 397 US 254 (1970). We still hope to gain recognition of a constitutional right to counsel in all civil matters which thus far has not occurred. See *Lassiter v Department of Social Services*, 453 US (1981). Recent empirical research demonstrates that in some kinds of cases, paralegals are as effective as lawyers (ie, unemployment compensation cases) and in others, a lawyer's expertise does make a difference to the result and its quality.

49 An important policy issue here is determining who decides where cases belong. Certain kinds of processes, such as compulsory arbitration, clearly benefit certain kinds of parties, like large corporations in disputes with individuals, which is why banks and manufacturers are seeking to use them. If we do not monitor these reforms, we will see replication of the deformation of reform such as occurred when small claims courts, initially intended to create increased access for consumers, became courts of debt collection and default judgments against individuals, brought by large corporate plaintiffs.

# CHAPTER 17

# Alternative dispute resolution in the UK

SUZANNE BURN

*Suzanne Burn is the secretary to the Civil Litigation Committee of the Law Society and is the society's adviser on civil litigation issues. She worked in central and local government and as a senior employee of the Local Government Ombudsman before qualifying as a solicitor in 1989. She then spent a period in private practice and took up her current post in June 1994. The views expressed in this article are her own and not necessarily those of the Law Society.*

> Lawyers are in a bind when it comes to managing their clients' disputes if they are locked into the courts. Litigation has not kept up with modern fast-moving society. . . Compared to modern business, the civil courts have changed very little . . . ADR gives lawyers an opportunity to use new processes, encourages a problem-solving attitude and an openness to compromise.
> Robert Coulson, president of the American Arbitration Association

## Dispute resolution

Disputes can be resolved in a number of different ways but primarily by negotiation (with the parties and their representatives talking through a solution); mediation (with the parties and their representatives helped, by an independent neutral, to agree a solution) or by adjudication (when an independent person appointed either by the parties, as in arbitration, or by the courts, as in litigation, hears the evidence and makes a binding decision).

In the UK at present, most substantial disputes are resolved by negotiation, adjudication or a combination of the two. Mediation, as an appropriate method of dispute resolution, has been slow to gain a foothold. This chapter attempts to explore the reasons why and to suggest that in some types of case it may be a time and cost-effective way of resolving disputes. The multi-door court-house, with parties choosing or being guided towards different methods of resolving their

237

disputes appropriate to the particular case, is an interesting American concept discussed on p223. It may have a lot to offer in the UK. We must look at options other than, or combined with, litigation.

Traditionally, our civil justice system has been much admired. It has formed the model for many, particularly former Commonwealth, countries. Parties with a choice of forum, as in some commercial disputes, often opt for the UK because of the quality of the procedures and the product.

However, because of high cost, using the courts to resolve a dispute is increasingly becoming the province of the ever more poor, with the progressive reduction in the availability of legal aid, and of the very affluent. Our adversarial system is designed to highlight differences and conflicts between the parties. The process is designed to culminate in a trial based on oral evidence before an independent judge with no or limited knowledge of the case prior to the hearing. With costs following the event, the end product is 'win or lose' with commensurate high risks.

Many disputes are not straightforward: yet a very high percentage settle before they reach court. However, there is, at present, no built-in settlement machinery or little incentive except defendants paying costs into court and the sanction of liability for the other side's costs in the event of failure, a provision which generally does not apply to a legally aided party.

Trials can also be particularly stressful for the participants, partly because they are open to the public and because they are often planned to focus on the talents of the advocates. Lawyers have little incentive to shorten proceedings because they, like other experts, are generally paid by the hour for their time. No one can benefit from a system that is oriented to procedure that appears to have originated in a pre-paper, let alone pre-technology, era.

## Mediation

Currently about 95 per cent of disputes in which proceedings are issued in the UK settle without a full trial. Methods which promote earlier settlement, both within and outside litigation, should save both time and costs. They also increase the parties' satisfaction. Many litigants simply want their problem solved as soon as possible. Only rarely does a dispute require an adjudicated answer from a court. Litigation is frequently driven by lawyers, whereas mediation can offer the parties an opportunity to be more directly involved in the process, giving them greater control.

Mediation is flexible, adaptable and can be creative. It may introduce non-legalistic solutions to meet the needs, interests and concerns of the parties. Mediation usually takes place in a less formal setting than a court. Its emphasis on seeking a solution tends also to make it more forward-looking. It is less stressful. Some parties much prefer the privacy and confidentiality. Communication and such problems as lack of trust and 'emotional blocks' can be more easily overcome.

Even if mediation does not produce an immediate 'success', it can narrow down the issues and, therefore, speed up a resolution because it tests the strength and weaknesses of the parties' cases.

Some types of case are clearly more suitable for mediation than others. The most important criterion is that both parties have a genuine desire to settle. Another is that the parties have a wish or need to preserve an on-going relationship, for example between businesses, families, partners and shareholders, landlords and tenants, neighbours or employer and employee. Mediation may also be desirable where privacy and confidentiality are important to one or more of the parties. It is best suited for cases which are not too complex and do not have a large number of parties, unless the mediator is very skilled or the mediation is seen as a step in the process rather than a solution of itself. Mediation will also be attractive where the 'price' of court adjudication, whether in terms of time, costs or stress, is seen as too high.

Conversely, mediation may not be suitable for cases where at least one of the parties is unwilling to signal that he or she is ready to compromise or has other reasons for pursuing the dispute slowly. It is unlikely to be effective with disputes that involve new areas of law; raise issues of legal principle; are actions against the state; are group actions; or are cases in which public vindication or humiliation is sought. It may not be appropriate where an immediately enforceable court order is required, for example an injunction, or where there is a serious imbalance of power between the parties. The latter is difficult to overcome, especially where the party with the greater power is deliberately seeking a private settlement which may not be in the other party's, or even in the public, interest.

The appropriate time to mediate will vary with the case. There is an argument for beginning mediation before formal proceedings are issued. This is often before attitudes have become entrenched or feelings have escalated. However, sometimes a 'cooling-off' period is needed by the parties. Furthermore, issues may not be very clear at an early stage. If mediation is attempted during the litigation progress, an appropriate time might be either after close of pleadings or after discovery and service of witness statements. By then, the parties will have disclosed most of their case. The right timing is important, because mediation attempted too close to the date of the trial may lead to insufficiently small savings in costs to justify it, particularly in smaller cases.

There is little evaluated research in the UK, so we have to look at the results of mediation in other jurisdictions for some indications of the types of action where mediation works best. As a result, there is a limited literature on domestic alternative dispute resolution (ADR) developments. A partial bibliography is given in the appendix. The New South Wales 'Settlement Weeks' instituted in 1991 and 1992 have been well documented. The incentive was a backlog of cases waiting for trial. The scheme was annexed to the court, which provided lists of cases and sent out letters to the parties in target cases. The Legal Aid Commission paid the legally aided parties' share of the mediation fee. In 1991, 235 cases were mediated, with a success rate of 70 per cent. This rose to 80 per cent in road traffic personal injury cases. In 1992, 415 cases were mediated, with a success rate of 65 per cent. The evaluation suggested that the most suitable cases were those where legal costs were high but the value of the claim relatively low; liability not contested or very complex to decide; and, in personal injury cases, when the plaintiff's side had evaluated the potential damages. Estimated average costs savings per case were $95,000 (about £44,400) plus savings in court time, a significant amount.

## UK developments

This paper does not consider methods of arbitration. They are arguably closer to mediation than a formal court-based adjudication system. However, it is relevant to note that the county court small claims procedure is really a hybrid between mediation and arbitration. The National Audit Office is currently carrying out a survey of the small claims arbitration system, the results of which should be available soon. This may suggest that there are lessons for disputes other than small claims from the type of procedures adopted in the county court by district judges.

Generally, mediation of disputes, particularly those litigated in the civil courts, is still in its infancy. Exceptions are industrial disputes, where the Advisory, Conciliation and Arbitration Service (ACAS) has long played a major role, and family disputes, where mediation and conciliation have for some time been supported and encouraged locally by district judges as part of divorce procedures. This led to a number of mediation services being established in the 1980s. The Lord Chancellor has issued a green paper suggesting that substantial amounts of legal aid could be diverted to such matrimonial mediation.

Two main organisations exist which offer mediation services in civil disputes. IDR Europe Ltd/ADR Net was established in 1989 by lawyers, businessmen and mediators, and currently has more than 25 firms as members with more than 120 trained lawyer mediators. Cases are referred by insurers, industries, accountants and solicitors. A settlement rate of 92 per cent is claimed. Costs of £85 per party per hour (varying to a degree with the type of case) compare very favourably with solicitors' fees. CEDR, the Centre for Dispute Resolution, was established in 1990 by a group of individuals from the business, banking, insurance and professional worlds. It now has over 300 members and more than 400 trained mediators. By the autumn of 1994, a wide variety of about 500 disputes had been mediated. These were mostly business cases and have included some international and multi-party actions with values of up to £20 million. Again a high success rate is claimed, over 95 per cent. Mediation fees vary between £350 to £1,000 per party per day. The estimated average cost savings are £40,000 per case.

Anecdotal evidence suggests that some judges have informally encouraged parties litigating disputes to mediate and, to a degree, even assisted settlement discussions. A 1993 commercial court practice direction was, however, the first official court document encouraging court-annexed mediation. Judges are not involved directly in the mediation and at present there is no monitoring of the response to the direction.

There are other recent signs of an active interest in mediation in other fields. A City Disputes Panel has been established for financial service disputes. The Latham review of disputes in the construction industry advocated ADR. CEDR and the Chartered Institute of Arbitrators have begun to introduce hybrid procedures including combinations of mediation and arbitration, mini-trials and other supervised settlements.

## Slow progress

Solicitors have played a role in mediation, though mainly limited to family work. The Law Society has actively supported mediation experiments since the 1980s. In 1991, it recommended a five-year plan for the development of mediation services. In 1993, a joint Law Society/Bar Council report specifically recommended court-annexed voluntary pilot schemes. In 1994, the society actively supported a Bristol Law Society pilot scheme which uses the services of IDR Europe and CEDR. Currently, two working parties are considering mediation. One is looking at the scope for court-annexed mediation in civil disputes; the other at the need for accreditation and training facilities for mediators.

It has to be admitted that the legal profession, as a whole, remains cautious. The pressure for mediation currently comes more from clients than their advisers. There could be a number of reasons for this. Until recently, lawyers' training was oriented towards litigation procedure. Negotiation skills and methods of dispute resolution were not high on the agenda. Also, as previously discussed, court rules for litigation provide too few incentives to settle. Legal aid is not available for mediators' fees and the general lack of exposure of most solicitors to mediation understandably makes them unwilling to experiment at their clients' possible expense.

While the professions may have been cautious, the Lord Chancellor's Department and the judiciary have moved even more slowly. In a speech in 1990, the Lord Chancellor indicated some support for ADR in principle. The following year a Lord Chancellor's Department working group produced an interim report on ADR but made no specific proposals. In 1992, the Lord Chancellor's Advisory Committee on Legal Aid recommended pilot studies but in response the Lord Chancellor indicated caution. He saw a need to preserve judicial impartiality. He also wanted to concentrate on his on-going programme of reforms in the civil court system. Prolonged discussions about an early version of the Bristol Law Society pilot scheme with the Lord Chancellor's Department in the early 1990s did not result in any official approval to enable it to be court-annexed. The commercial court, however, began encouraging mediation in 1993.

In December 1993, the Lord Chancellor said in a Hamlyn lecture entitled 'The Administration of Justice: Alternative Dispute Resolution':

> We must first remind ourselves of what it is we want from our civil justice system. I start from the proposition that it is a primary responsibility of good government to provide a civil justice system which maintains and advances the rule of law and furnishes the means to secure legal rights and enforce legal duties. Those means must

operate impartially and must deliver compulsion, finality in the individual dispute on which judgment is given and, by association, the potential for certainty in the countless other disputes that are resolved by agreement in the shadow of decisions handed down by the courts.

In March 1994 Sir Thomas Bingham, the Master of the Rolls, in 'The Price of Justice' lecture to the Holdsworth Club of the University of Birmingham displayed his own caution:

Resolving disputes between citizen and citizen is a cardinal function of the State. It is a function which cannot properly be privatised so as to preclude access by those who wish to avail themselves of it.

## Caution and concern

It is no function of this chapter to argue against the continuing need for a public forum for resolving disputes. There are many reasons why the courts should remain the bedrock of the civil justice system, not least because many primarily private disputes directly or indirectly raise public-interest issues. It should always be a function of the State and the courts to provide a civil justice system which is accessible to citizens who need to use it or whose disputes have a strong public interest element.

It is perhaps not surprising, therefore, that there are a number of voices in the UK expressing concern about the promotion and advance of ADR, particularly for such disputes as judicial review, group actions and some personal injury claims, in the light of experience in other jurisdictions. This disquiet would be merited if mediation, or other forms of ADR, were to be substituted for litigation, especially compulsorily. But, in my view, that concern is misplaced when over 90 per cent of litigated disputes are resolved by negotiation and settlement, without adjudication by a court. This frequently means that there is no public dissemination of the outcome.

The lack of funding for mediation in legally aided cases is a real difficulty in getting mediation off the ground as part of a litigation strategy. The Legal Aid Board takes the view that mediation is not part of 'legal proceedings' and so cannot be funded under a legal aid certificate. This does not seem logical when negotiations between the parties are funded. Mediation should not just be available to the privately funded litigant. People who are legally aided should not be deprived of an important element of choice. Other countries' legal aid systems have been more experimental. It is difficult to see what the Legal Aid Board has got to lose in encouraging mediation, especially in cases such as personal injury when the litigation success-rate is over 90 per cent. Funding might be a barrier to mediation in some privately funded cases. The costs of mediation can add to the expense of litigation, if the case does not settle. This was one of the Lord Chancellor's concerns.

A practical problem is the link between a mediation agreement and an enforceable court order, particularly in cases mediated before the commencement of legal proceedings. As mediation agreements can include a number of issues which are outside the power of the court to control, only part of those agreements might be incorporated into court orders. Objections have been raised in some quarters to the idea of the parties using the court as a convenient 'rubber-stamp' to a mediation agreement. However, in my view, this objection is more apparent than real, as in many disputes that are litigated the court currently has minimal involvement, often routinely approving consent orders when the parties reach a settlement.

The development of mediation is currently limited by the restricted pool of trained mediators available. These come from a number of different disciplines, including some lawyers. Difficult questions remain to be decided. For example, is it essential for mediators to know the law in the area of the dispute they are mediating? How should mediators be trained and accredited? If the courts were to sanction mediation as part of the litigation process, would it be necessary for there to be regulation and even insurance for mediators? Answers to these questions are not straightforward.

At present, evidence and research into mediation, particularly in the litigation context, is sparse. The two main private providers of mediation services publish newsletters with brief details of their work, but not fully evaluated studies. There has been a little more progress in family mediation research and the Bristol Law Society scheme does include a research project by local universities. Research from other jurisdictions, although interesting, is of limited value because of their different legal cultures and costs regimes.

Mediation in the UK may be too much in its infancy to support settlement weeks on the New South Wales model. However, unless and until there are some carefully monitored and researched mediation projects, the real benefits of mediation will be difficult to assess. Without this, the development of mediation is likely to continue in an *ad hoc* and unstructured way, available only to certain parties to disputes. This increases the risks of 'privatised litigation' which currently concern some commentators. 'Rent-a-judge' Californian-style may not be immediately attractive in the UK. However, unless litigation in civil disputes can be made speedier and more financially accessible to those other than the legally aided and the affluent, then more disputes will be resolved outside the courts by other means, including those which are not suitable or by means which are not in the public interest.

Is rough justice better than no access to justice at all, or is there a middle way? Appropriate dispute resolution in the future, in my view, should include a broader range of options than is currently available: one of the difficult questions is who decides which option; it ought to be the parties and their advisers, but will it be 'fund-holders' and court staff?

## A selected bibliography

Law Society Legal Practice Directorate memoranda, *Alternative dispute resolution first report* July 1991, and *Second report* June 1992.

General Council of the Bar's Committee on ADR (the Beldam Committee), *Report*, 1991.

K Mackie, *Handbook of Dispute Resolution*, Routledge and Sweet & Maxwell, 1992.

H J Brown and A L Marriott, *ADR Principles and Practice*, Sweet & Maxwell, 1993.

Law Society of New South Wales reports: *Settlement Week October 1991*; and *Contemporary Developments in Mediation Within the Legal System and Evaluation of Settlement Week 1992–3*.

National Consumer Council, *Settling Consumer Disputes: A Review of Alternative Dispute Resolution*, 1993.

Legal Aid Advisory Committee, *Report to the Lord Chancellor of the Conference held on 4th June 1992*, 1993.

N Armstrong 'ADR and the Public Interest in Personal Injury', *Journal of Personal Injury Litigation*, September 1994.

CHAPTER 18

# Lessons from tribunals

MARTIN PARTINGTON

*Martin Partington is a barrister and professor of law at the University of Bristol and also director of the Bristol Centre for the Study of Administrative Justice. He is a member of the Legal Action Group and was on its management committee for a number of years. He has written widely in the areas of social security law and housing law. He was a part-time chairman of social security appeal tribunals from 1990–94. He has recently been appointed a member of the Council of Tribunals. He is a member of Arden Chambers, London.*

In writing this chapter, I wish to consider whether, when thinking about the future of the civil justice system in general and access to justice in particular, there are any lessons that may be learned from the work carried out within the British tribunal system which might be carried over into the civil justice system.

For the last 20 years I have had a considerable personal involvement in the work of tribunals, especially social security appeal tribunals: as an advocate in the early 1970s; as a trainer of tribunal chairs and members from 1978 onwards; and as a part-time chair (from 1990). For the last six years I have been a member of the Tribunals Committee of the Judicial Studies Board. In 1994, I was appointed to the Council on Tribunals. The comments which follow are based on, but necessarily limited by, this experience. They are, of course, made in a purely personal capacity.

## General considerations

Before dealing specifically with lessons from tribunals, I would like to start by considering two general matters, which, while they may cover ground described elsewhere in this volume, nevertheless need to be borne constantly in mind.

# *Looking to the future: what are the problems?*

There seems to be a broad consensus that the system of English civil litigation has reached a point of crisis. It may be the case that the consensus view is correct; however, before accepting it, it may be worth at least asking what exactly is wrong. For if we are not clear about what is wrong, the chances of taking steps that will improve things will be less strong than they might otherwise be.

According to the latest official Judicial Statistics, 81 per cent of civil hearings are now disposed of using the county court arbitration procedure. Even in the High Court, many cases are disposed of by way of summary judgement. Is delay or cost or lack of court control – which are frequently stated to be the main cause(s) of the 'crisis' in civil litigation – the *real* problem in these cases? Put another way, are the problems, which are stated to be endemic to the system as a whole, in fact problems affecting a relatively small number of (admittedly) high-value or high-profile cases where the value of the litigation and the complexity of the law or facts means that there is always likely to be high cost and much delay? Furthermore – to play devil's advocate – is it not highly desirable that trials *should* be very expensive and subject to delay? Is this not the best way to ensure that people settle their differences rather than have them resolved for them by a court?

There are important questions to be considered, before we accept the consensus view that there is a crisis within the modern civil justice system, about what exactly the crisis is, and what its causes are. If we are to consider the reform of the process of civil litigation, there must be greater clarity as to what are the deficiencies of the present system.

While the scope of the current review of civil litigation being undertaken by Lord Woolf is not wholly clear, the following matters have clearly been put onto the agenda: what is, and what should be the role of the court in the handling of cases; what are, and what should be the methods used to resolve factual issues; and can disputes be handled in different ways? This selection of matters gives an indication of what the Woolf inquiry thinks may be wrong.

The aims of the review are stated to be: the improvement of access to justice; the production of a single set of rules for handling general business in the High Court and county courts; and provision for specialist jurisdictions and procedures in each court. The review team has defined the main focus of its work as searching for ways to reduce the costs of civil litigation. The principal ideas being considered are: whether more court control would be desirable, to reduce both delay and cost; whether there could be rationalisation and streamlining of procedural rules; and whether extension of the small claims jurisdiction in the county court and other alternative institutional arrangements would be a good idea.

There are, however, other issues which are not presently at the forefront of the inquiry, but which arguably should be put into the frame. For example: should there be far less reliance on the principle of orality as the basis of the procedural rules for civil litigation? What would be the impact on the civil justice system of fundamental change to the substantive law, eg, on accident compensation? Is judicial competence a problem, and if so how major a problem is it? These matters do not appear to be on the current reform agenda at all.

Furthermore, there should be much more openness about the interests of those arguing that there is a need for reform. The interest of the civil servant is likely to be different from that of the High Court judge; that of the district judge, different from that of the circuit judge; that of the solicitor, different from the barrister; that of the rich litigant, different from that of the poor. Indeed, in relation to any policy, questions should always be asked: is the English civil justice system working? If not, how might it be changed? If it were to be changed, whose interests would be affected?

A valid working hypothesis is that the problems identified are caused by a rather complex mix of factors but with different factors contributing differently in different types of case and also in different courts in different parts of the country. It will be difficult to know precisely what reforms will work unless we know precisely what the problems are, what the causes of those problems are and whose interests are likely to be affected by proposals for reform.

## Alternative models

One suggestion on the Woolf agenda is that we should consider alternative models (or as they are described in the most recent literature, 'appropriate models') for the resolution of disputes; the Woolf enquiry is said to be examining systems in continental Europe. Two points need to be stressed.

First, we should not forget the variety of models in existence here. They include: complaints procedures of various degrees of complexity; ombudsmen; mediation and conciliation procedures; inquiries; and tribunals. These can all be regarded as alternative or 'appropriate' forms of dispute resolution. If we think less narrowly about dispute resolution, we may be able to redefine our own legal system to include these alternative models, before we look to other jurisdictions for inspiration.

Second, and related to the last point, there is the fundamental problem that the legal system tends to be defined by reference to what lawyers do and the places where lawyers do it. Certainly in lawyers' minds, there may be questions as to the legitimacy or authority of alternative models which will need addressing positively if such alternatives are to be regarded as attractive in their own right, rather than as some form of second-class justice. Achieving this will involve changing the attitudes of people, including practising lawyers and the judiciary, who are powerful opinion-formers in this context, towards the courts and their relationship with the other institutions listed above.

## Lessons from tribunals

With these general considerations in mind, I turn now to the more specific question of what lessons might be learned from the operation of tribunals. There are two main issues to be considered under this head: management and informality.

Management raises a considerable number of sub-issues which go beyond management in a narrow sense and enter other areas such as training, policy and quality control. The matter of informality will be considered more briefly.

## *Management*

One of the central issues on the Woolf agenda relates to the question of who should be responsible for the management of the courts. Management is not a simple concept in this context: it involves a number of separate issues, including management of the financial resources available to provide judicial services; management of court personnel (eg, clerks and other staff); management of judges and the use of judicial time; and management of the case list.

Although practice does differ in different courts, it is probably true to say that the bulk of management responsibility lies with civil servants from the Lord Chancellor's Department working under circuit administrators. The Woolf agenda implies that there should be a substantial transfer of management responsibility to judges. While this will be anathema to some, it is arguably the case that, far from reducing the role and importance of the judiciary, it is only by taking clear responsibility for management that the judiciary will be able fully to assert the constitutional independence which a number of senior judges have recently suggested is under threat.

It may be helpful to have an account of the management of the Independent Tribunal Service (ITS) in thinking about the question of judicial management, and how it might operate. This is a personal account from someone who has had some external involvement with ITS as its management strategy has developed, rather than a true 'inside' view.

When what is now known as the Independent Tribunal Service was first established under the Health and Social Services and Social Security Adjudication Act 1983, the senior figure in the Service was the President – a circuit judge – together with a number (originally seven, now six) of regional chairs. They in turn were supported by a number of full-time chairs. The President, with the support of his administrative staff, was responsible for putting together a budget under the normal public expenditure principles, which was negotiated with and progressed through the Department of Social Security, which is the sponsoring department of the ITS.

Funding is based on assumptions on the overall case-load, combined with assumptions on the number of cases that can be cleared within any sitting period. It also has to take into account the creation of new jurisdictions – where relevant – and anticipated case loads associated with them. In addition, funding has to be provided to enable the President to undertake his statutorily prescribed training duties in relation to both tribunals chairs and their members.

In the early days, ITS' responsibilities extended only to the social security appeal tribunal – a blend of the former supplementary benefit appeal tribunal and national insurance local tribunal – and the medical appeal tribunal. Since that time jurisdiction has been expanded to the disability appeal tribunal (1992) and child support appeal tribunal (1993). In terms of the judicial structure, there has been a significant increase in the number of full-time chairs and a reduction in the use of part-time chairs.

Although the enabling legislation makes the President responsible for the work of the ITS, in practice it has always operated on a more collegiate basis. HH Judge Holden, the ITS' second President, developed a complex management structure, with a main board, chaired by the President and consisting of the regional chairs together with the chief executive, supported by a number of committees. The committees were responsible for a range of topics: new policy and legislation; procedure and adjudication; judicial recruitment and conditions; training; and publications and literature. The procedure and adjudication committee itself had a number of sub-committees on forms, judicial performance monitoring and listing and adjudication.

The following are some examples of the work of the committees.

(a) The Publications Committee developed the new *Journal of Social Security Law*, replacing the rather more informal *ITS News*. It monitored the need for new texts such as the annotated versions of the relevant legislation. It commissioned a new version of the Procedural Guide. In short, it was responsible for ensuring that relevant material was available to enable the tribunals to perform their work.

(b) The Policy and Legislation Committee played a significant part in the development of policy on adjudication where new legislation was in contemplation, such as child support or dasability appeals.

(c) The Judicial Recruitment Committee kept an overall watch on the numbers of new members and chairs needed, and for which tribunals. It took active steps to advertise the availability of full-time chair appointments to the part-time chairs. It endeavoured to ensure proper balance on panels of members and part-time chairs and in particular to ensure that adequate numbers of women were appointed.

(d) The Training Committee was responsible for monitoring and developing a training plan for the country as a whole, though with considerable scope for regional initiative. It was directly responsible for the provision of national training courses for tribunal chairs, both induction training and refresher training; and also for arranging 'roadshows' to introduce major new legislation. As a part-time judge in the system, I received, on an annual basis, at least one one-day training conference in my region; and once every four to five years (or so) a two-day national training conference. There were special training days to accommodate major new jurisdictions such as the arrival of disability appeal tribunals and child support appeal tibunals. At the training conferences themselves, considerable effort was put into training, not only on questions of substantive law, but also on the skills required to chair tribunals and on the implications of taking certain procedural decisions. For example, considerable emphasis was put on the costs involved in adjourning hearings or allowing postponements; chairs were not prohibited from taking these steps, but made to realise that such decisions had a cost. In addition, it was stressed that, often, such decisions were unlikely to produce any worthwhile results.

(e) The procedure committee took certain procedural decisions designed to ensure that appellants did in fact turn up to the hearings, by providing that appellants had to give an indication they were going to come to the hearing. My personal experience suggests that this has had a marked effect on attendance rates at hearings. When I started to sit, a list of six cases would often have only one attender. By the end of my time, it was relatively rare to have a case in which a claimant did not attend. This committee has had a major impact on the working of the tribunals.

(f) The sub-committee on judicial performance, monitoring and listing has been possibly the boldest of all, for it has laid down standards[1] of competency which tribunal chairs are expected to meet, procedures for monitoring the performance of chairs against those standards, and procedures for removing – after due process – chairs who, despite remedial effort, remain below those standards.[2]

In short, what was created was a management structure not dissimilar to that which might be found in certain companies, and certainly very different from that underpinning the courts. Although the details of the committee structure are currently under review, and the fourth President, HH Judge Bassingthwaite, is in the process of putting in place a revised structure which will rely less on the work of committees and more on devolution of responsibilities to individual judges within the ITS structure, nevertheless the *principle* of the judiciary in ITS being responsible for the management of the service is now clearly entrenched.

I suggest that the following lessons may be drawn in relation to the issues of judicial responsibility for management.

(a) The level of resources available to the ITS to perform its statutory functions involves an annual negotiation – which can be difficult – between the President and the sponsoring department within the usual framework for public expenditure bids.

(b) A crucial element in determining resource levels – namely assumptions as to the number of cases to be heard in a session – is still in the hands of the Department of Social Security.

(c) Once that level of resource has been determined, however, responsibility for the efficient use of those resources is in the hands of the President and the management board.

(d) While detailed management of ITS support staff is carried out by the civil servants appointed to support the ITS, they still work to the philosophy of the tribunal system (eg, on questions of customer care, and the enabling role) determined by the President and the board.

(e) Considerable emphasis is given in training and monitoring to the efficient dispatch of business; this guidance, however, comes from the full-time judicial office holders in the ITS, not the civil servants.

(f) Judicial management has taken a step further and set up standards of competence for the work of tribunals in general and of chairs in particular. Arrangements are now in place to monitor performance against those standards.

These lessons cannot be taken over in simplistic fashion into the civil justice system. Apart from anything else, there are differences in operating a jurisdiction in which the state is always a party, from one where the jurisdiction involves – typically – two private parties. The model of the industrial tribunals *may* be more relevant. Nevertheless, there may here be the basis of a new kind of management style and structure for the civil courts. For this to be achieved, however, there would need to be major changes in judicial attitudes and a willingness – while retaining the fundamental principle of 'independence' – to accept that the task of judicial management goes beyond basic tasks of allocating court work,[3] and should include a leadership role in relation to the setting of standards and the maintenance of those standards which the civil service should certainly not engage in. In addition, there would need to be a substantial realignment of the relationship between the Lord Chancellor's Department and the judiciary.

The difficulties of this approach cannot be overstated. For example, the fact that the full-time judiciary are appointed 'during good behaviour' – a principle of fundamental importance in the preservation of the independence of the judiciary – may mean that the ability of any senior managerial judges to regulate performance and improve 'under-performers' will be limited. However, if it is accepted that the courts are providing a public service, ought there not to be standards for such services? Should they not be able to be monitored and enforced in some way?[4] The ITS has, from its early days, recognised that it would have to operate within fixed budgets.

It has sought to ensure that the ways in which judges perform in the system means that judges are used in a cost-effective fashion. From time to time, part-time chairs have been heard to complain that the emphasis on throughput of cases is inimical to notions of justice. But here we see one of the fundamental debating issues – what should be the relationship between getting to a result and the time and cost of reaching that decision?

My own personal view is that the fundamental judicial principle of independence – which was always emphasised in training – is not compromised by a clear lead from the senior judicial members within the organisation. Indeed, I suspect that there will certainly be some cases where the plea for judicial independence is simply a mask for judicial incompetence or laziness, given that in most court systems there are no proper mechanisms of accountability. On the contrary, as noted above, it can be argued that only by the judiciary taking greater responsibility for its own management can independence be enhanced.

What is not clear is how a management system developed primarily in the context of a tribunal system that relied heavily on part-timers, whose appointments were renewable every three years, will adapt to a system in which there will be increasing numbers of full-time appointments. In particular, it is not clear whether the principles of monitoring and appraisal applicable to the part-timers will also apply to the full-time chairs. Nevertheless, the ITS model does raise the prospect of the court system being run on quite different lines to those which currently apply.

## Informality

One of the claims frequently made about tribunals and their approach to adjudication has been that they are 'informal'. Most commentators in making this observation have focused on the fact that – usually – tribunals do not have formal rules of procedure, or formal rules of evidence. It is the informality of the *hearing* that is usually highlighted. There is now a growing literature that throws doubt on the notion of procedural informality and whether it is self-evidently desirable. Discussion about informality has focused less than it should have done on the informality of the preliminary proceedings before the stage at which the hearing takes place, in particular the documentation needed to launch proceedings before tribunals. Tribunal proceedings are often launched simply with a letter, perhaps the completion of a form. In the case of social security appeals, the background to the case is provided by the DSS in its submission to the tribunal. The appellant is not required to respond to this but can come on the day with new evidence to be evaluated by the tribunal itself. By contrast, the civil justice process is extremely complex – with pleadings, affidavits, discovery, bundles of evidence and so on – even though each part of the process has the object of trying to define the issues and identify the areas of contention, whether of fact or of law.

Many traditional judges might find the procedural informality of social security tribunals hard to cope with. Practice suggests, however, that it is still possible to define the issues and come to a decision, despite the informality of the preliminary written proceedings. Those currently operating the civil justice system – both judges and practitioners – would no doubt look askance at an informalisation of process. But if, on the whole, tribunals can manage, why not the courts?

A fundamental question that will have to be faced is whether it can be accepted that there are two 'tiers' of justice – reserving the highly procedural tier for those that can afford to pay, or for cases which involve fundamental constitutional legal issues, and using another, more cheap and cheerful, user-friendly if you will, for dealing with more routine cases. Many will argue that to accept this would be a retrograde step; but can it not be argued that this would be a positive development? I have argued in the past that tribunals should not be regarded as second-class courts, but as first-class tribunals – doing a different but complementary job to that being done in the courts.[5]

What is more, many litigants might actually prefer it. That gets us back to fundamental questions about whose interests the civil justice system is there to serve.

# References

1 Independent Tribunal Service, *Monitoring Performance in Tribunals*, 1994.
2 The idea of setting standards of competence is not unique to ITS chairs; a similar approach has been adopted in the context of selection of magistrates to be chairs of local benches.
3 Surprisingly little is known about the work of the various circuits' 'presiding judges'; it may be that they might form the basis for the possible managerial structure implied by this analysis.
4 For hints of judicial acceptance of these views, see the comments of Mr Justice Brooke, 'Address to Conference of Tribunal Presidents and Chair-

men', *Council on Tribunals Annual Report, 1993–1994*, Appendix C (HMSO, 1994, HC 22).
5   M Partington, 'Lessons from Tribunals', May 1990 *Legal Action* 9.

# CHAPTER 19

# Filling the void in civil litigation disputes – a role for empirical research

TERENCE PURCELL AND GILLIAN McALLISTER

*Terence Purcell is the Director the the Law Foundation of New South Wales, Australia, a position he has held since 1973. He is the author of chapter 5. Gillian McAllister, a lawyer with a strong policy background, was appointed Executive Director of the Civil Justice Research Centre in 1993.*

## The Australian response – the Civil Justice Research Centre

Are lawyers the source of all evil, and are New South Wales lawyers the source of even greater evil than their counterparts in other states? Who uses the courts – are litigants only the very rich and the (legally aided) very poor? Why do civil cases take so long to get through the courts? What factors are causing this delay? Does alternative dispute resolution work and are some cases more suitable for procedures such as conciliation than others? These are some of the questions that the Law Foundation of New South Wales' Civil Justice Research Centre (CJRC) has been called on to examine in the last few years. The projects themselves will be described a little later in this paper, but, first, here is some background information about CJRC itself and what led the Foundation to establish it.

The impetus for the establishment of such a centre came from a recognition that, while there was much debate on issues in the civil justice area, this debate was not based on factual information, but on impressions and anecdotes. Everyone had a story to tell about lengthy court delays and high legal costs but none of these anecdotes were based on solid empirical research. What was even more disturbing was that programmes, aimed at reducing costs and delays, were being implemented in the courts without any sound research to back them up.

The Law Foundation has had a long-standing research role, and    257 has been at the forefront of socio-legal research in New South Wales. For example, in 1983, at the request of the New South Wales Law Reform Commission, the Foundation financed and supervised a study of accident victims in receipt of lump-sum compensation. This provided a much-needed factual basis for the Commission's report on accident compensation, and led in time to the introduction of accident compensation schemes for people injured at work and for those injured in motor vehicle accidents.

The Foundation had also established links with RAND's Institute for Civil Justice in California. The Institute for Civil Justice was established in 1979, and carries out independent, objective policy analysis on the American civil justice system. Throughout the eighties, the Foundation had kept in contact with researchers at the Institute for Civil Justice and had monitored its various research reports. Our interest in establishing a similar specialist civil justice research body in Australia was further stimulated when the Foundation's Chairman paid a visit to the American institute in 1987.

These different threads were drawn together at the Law Foundation Board's policy retreat in 1989, when civil justice research was identified as a major priority. It was decided to establish a research centre which would be capable of providing objective empirical information about the civil justice system. In defining the centre's charter, the Foundation emphasised the necessity for the CJRC to take on policy-relevant projects: that is, projects which would feed into the policy making process, and which would assist in creating a fairer, more accessible civil justice system.

In its short life, which commenced when the CJRC was established by the Law Foundation of New South Wales in November 1989, the CJRC has undoubtedly made a significant contribution to the debate about the civil justice system. The purpose of this paper is to illustrate the type of input to the policy process that the CJRC has been able to have by referring to several of its projects.

## Is conciliation effective? Establishing a methodology

The first major project conducted by the CJRC examined the role of conciliation in resolving workers' compensation claims. Our interest in this area had been stimulated by discussion with insurers about the role poor claims handling often played in triggering unnecessary litigation and thus causing unnecessary legal costs to be incurred by insurers, as the plaintiff won in the great majority of cases. The choice of this area of research was also influenced by two other factors. First, a new system for workers' compensation had been introduced in New South Wales in July 1987. When we started to look at the subject of the workers' compensation scheme almost three years later in 1990 we found that there was no information available on the operation of the new system. This was in spite of the apparent importance of such an initiative, particularly its use of the early intervention of conciliation with disputed claims. So, there was a real need for some current factual information about the workers' compensation scheme. A second reason for examining the use of conciliation in workers' compensation matters was the growing interest in alternative dispute resolution (ADR). While ADR has been in use in Australia for many years, there has been little systematic evaluation of ADR programmes. The innovative use of conciliation within the new workers compensation regime provided the opportunity to do just that.

Although the CJRC set out with the aim of providing a full assessment of the role of conciliation in the workers' compensation system, we discovered a problem which was to become very familiar to us over the next few years: the absence of useable data. For example, there was no current information on the total number of claims for workers' compensation in the state, and there was no comparative information available on the previous system. To quote the report itself, 'our approach was severely constrained'. Thus, the research became more of an exploratory study which looked at how matters were referred for conciliation; how they were resolved; the amount of time taken; and the characteristics of the claims which were referred for conciliation. In the end, we adopted an approach which would provide the foundations for further work in the area, if improved data collection policies were ever implemented.

As socio-legal research of this type is something which is not familiar to many people, it may be useful to provide a brief description of the research methodology adopted for this project. The best possible source of data for the study was considered to be the case files which existed for each individual matter referred for conciliation. A sample from these files was selected and data was extracted manually. Preliminary discussions with the authority responsible for administering the workers' compensation scheme had identified a wealth of possible study variables. The suitability of these for inclusion in the study was assessed during a pilot study, when a small number of files were perused. Variables were selected for the study if they could be retrieved from the files easily and on a consistent basis.

A coding sheet was prepared to ensure the standardised recording of the required information by research assistants. A coding sheet is a type of data entry form, which research assistants are asked to complete for each file in the study. They must answer a series of questions about the file, and then record the information by means either of ticking a particular box, or entering details such as the date on which the claim for compensation was lodged or the amount of compensation awarded. This information is then entered onto a computer record, and the principal researcher is able to use different means of analysing the information.

The sample to be studied was chosen by examining first of all the archived conciliation files. This showed that there had been over 16,000 matters referred to conciliation during the period 1987 to 1990. The cases for 1990 had to be eliminated from the study due to the large number which had yet to be finalised. The total number of cases thus amounted to some 13,000, and a simple random sample of 10 per cent was taken.

From this sample, the following issues were examined.

*How are matters referred for conciliation?*

By far the greatest proportion of referrals were received from insurers fulfilling their statutory obligations to refer matters which involved a dispute over a claim for weekly benefit payments. Only 4 per cent of referrals came from other sources.

*Did conciliation resolve the matter?*

In approximately two-thirds of the sampled cases, conciliation resulted in the successful resolution of the matter, with the insurer agreeing to pay (63.7 per cent), the claim being withdrawn (3 per cent) or the insurer being directed to pay (0.1 per cent).

*What types of injuries are typically referred for conciliation?*

Some 63 per cent of cases resulted from sprain and strain injuries. No other injury category dominated the picture to quite this extent.

*Are particular industries or occupations more likely to be involved in conciliated disputes?*

Sectors such as health, education, community services and public administration appeared to be over-represented in the sample, suggesting that claims from these industries were more likely to result in a referral for conciliation.

The results, which were published by the Centre as *The Role of Conciliation* in November 1990, provided the workers' compensation authority with a very useful assessment of the operation of the conciliation scheme. One lasting benefit of the study was the fact that the authority now knew how to go about collecting data on a periodical basis which would help in monitoring the efficiency of the scheme.

Using this groundwork, the CJRC then decided to study those matters which were not resolved successfully by conciliation, that is, about one-third of the cases which were in the sample. This was undertaken in order to provide a better understanding of the flow of matters through the workers' compensation dispute resolution system, and to consider whether claimants are pursuing matters unresolved by conciliation in the courts. We found that around one-third of the matters which were not resolved by conciliation were followed by litigation. Within this group, the typical litigant was an employee of the private sector who had made a claim for continuing weekly benefits in respect of a sprain or strain injury. No relationship was found between the frequency with which litigation was commenced and the litigant's occupation or industry.

This follow-up study was not the subject of a full report but was reported in a periodical bulletin which the CJRC publishes called *Civil Issues*.[1] This bulletin began to provide a means of reporting and publicising smaller studies which, while not meriting the cost of a formally published report, are, nonetheless, extremely interesting. It also gives the CJRC an avenue for providing progress reports on long-term studies to the civil justice community. The centre's programme allows for quarterly publication of this bulletin. By producing a regular bulletin like this, the centre ensures that its activities are visible, and that stakeholders are well informed of current research projects.

One lasting benefit of the study was the fact that the authority now knew how to go about collecting data on a periodic basis which would help it monitor the effectiveness of the scheme. One overwhelming conclusion which came from this study and which has been consistently reaffirmed in a number of other studies, is that the information collected by administrators, whether in insurance companies, government agencies or courts and tribunals, is invariably of very limited value for research purposes. This is partly because the data collection practices used are of a poor standard, and thus the information is invariably unreliable, and partly because such data is usually collected for management or other purposes, so that it is the 'wrong' information for empirical research purposes.

## Disparities in settlement rates in the Family Court

A more recent project undertaken by the CJRC, which also highlighted the inadequacy of available statistical records, involved the Family Court of Australia. The Family Court is a national court, with registries in each state and territory of Australia and deals with marriage breakdown and its aftermath. The court produced some figures towards the end of 1993 which apparently showed that cases filed in the registry in Sydney had a much higher likelihood of going through to a trial rather than settling at an earlier time. Not surprisingly, the implication was drawn that this was the fault of practitioners in Sydney, who were tying up more than their fair share of the court's time and resources. The Law Society of New South Wales, which represents Sydney practitioners, asked the CJRC to investigate why it was that Sydney lawyers were apparently so much more litigious than lawyers in other parts of Australia.

The centre's inquiry was divided into two parts. The first part involved assessing the court's statistics. The second part of the proposed research was then to involve a more qualitative style of research, interviewing court officials, judges and practitioners to try and establish why cases in Sydney are so much more likely to go to verdict. The CJRC never in fact got to the second part of the project. We began to have some suspicions about the statistics which had been published when we found that each time we met with someone from the court, the figures had always 'just been revised'. After examining how statistics were collected and analysed at the Family Court, the centre concluded that the statistics were neither reliable nor an accurate measure of the way that cases were finalised in the court. Discrepancies were found in the way that statistics were collected across the different registries and the final percentages produced were a fairly dubious means of measuring case disposal in a particular time period. The most disturbing aspect of this research was the realisation that the court was prepared to allocate its resources based on information of this quality, and may well have ended up throwing dollars at a problem which may not in fact have existed.

The outcome of this project was a recommendation to the court that measures be taken to ensure that their collection of statistics was standardised. In addition, it was suggested that a systematic sampling of cases be undertaken to discover the truth about how cases were being finalised at different registries.

In the course of conducting this study, the CJRC was asked to provide a briefing on the research to Peter Duncan, Parliamentary Secretary to the Federal Attorney General. In his role as Parliamentary Secretary, Mr Duncan has responsibility for the Family Court. He was particularly interested in the implications that our study had for existing measurements of the workload and performance of the court and individual registries. Inaccuracies in such measurements could also feed through to the budgeting process. Mr Duncan undertook to raise the problem with the Attorney General. He was also giving consideration to our recommendation that a study of a sample of court files be undertaken, to provide an accurate picture of the disposition of cases between registries.

## Surveying court users – the use of market research techniques

Another important type of information that court policy-makers and administrators are beginning to request is feedback from court users about their experience of litigation. It is very rare that consumers of legal services are systematically surveyed to ascertain their views, but this is what the CJRC did with one recent piece of research. Over 400 plaintiffs (55 per cent of the sample) responded to the CJRC's questionnaire, which asked them about their satisfaction with different aspects of the litigation process. Many plaintiffs were so keen to make their views known that they telephoned the centre to elaborate further on their experiences, even though there was no suggestion that they should do so. The questionnaire asked the plaintiffs to answer quite specific questions – for example: 'Were you satisfied with the time it took to resolve your case?' – and also gave them the opportunity to write in general comments about their experience of litigation. The responses to the questionnaire provided the CJRC with both quantitative and qualitative data. Thus, we could measure both the proportions of plaintiffs who were dissatisfied or satisfied with the outcome of their case, or with the court, and also bring out some of the reasons for these reactions.

As might be expected, there were large numbers of plaintiffs dissatisfied with the length and cost of their case, and with the legal system in general. However, more interesting was the finding that much of this dissatisfaction was related to the expectations held by plaintiffs. For example, where plaintiffs were told that their case would take a long time and it did, they were much less likely to express dissatisfaction with the duration of their case than was a plaintiff who had been told at the outset that the case would take a much shorter time than it had. A clear message coming out of this project is that lawyers need to give their clients good information at the outset of their matter, and need to keep their clients up-to-date on the progress of their case. It is when unrealistic expectations are created that clients are most likely to express dissatisfaction with their lawyer and with the legal system.

The results of this research must also give court administrators pause for thought. Considerable time and money has been devoted to implementing measures designed to reduce court delays, and this is particularly true of the New South Wales Supreme Court, where this project was conducted at the instigation of the Chief Justice. However, this study shows that simply reducing the amount of time it takes for a case to go through court may not improve consumer satisfaction. There are more important factors at work, and one of those is the expectations held by plaintiffs. It may be that at least some of the court's efforts would be more usefully devoted to providing litigants with better information about the court process.

One issue relating to this project which must be taken into account when considering these survey results is the special nature of the cases included in the study. The project examined the cases involved in a programme of Special Sittings at the New South Wales Supreme Court. The Special Sittings were a case management programme introduced by the Chief Justice in an attempt to reduce the backlog of cases in the Common Law Division of the Court. The cases selected for inclusion in the programme were the oldest cases on the court list. They were all also claims for compensation for personal injury. While the special measures introduced for these cases made them a particularly interesting set of cases to study – for example, parties had to supply the court with quite detailed information about the case – it also means that some caution must be used in interpreting the results. Many of the cases could be considered to be the intractable cases which had been in the system for a longer period than usual. In addition, the unique procedures introduced to finalise the cases may have had an impact on plaintiffs.

## How much does litigation actually cost parties?

The CJRC finalised a study of the costs of civil litigation at the beginning of 1993, a topic which is likely to be of more immediate concern to legal practitioners.[2] This study had its origins in a request from the Law Society of New South Wales for the CJRC to conduct research on the issue of speculative fees. In particular, the Law Society wanted to know about the desirability and feasibility of various alternative speculative fee arrangements. The interest in speculative fees reflects the formal recognition of the fact that for many years solicitors acted for personal injury clients on the basis that they would only be paid if the client won, hence the term 'speccing' cases.

In researching the speculative fee issue, the CJRC discovered that there was very little information available on the operation of the current legal fees system in New South Wales. As we went further into this project, it became obvious that we had to reconsider the objectives of the research. If informed debate was to take place about possible changes to the legal fee system, information was also needed about the operation of the current system. Thus, the project developed into an examination of the current mechanism for setting legal fees, as it was possible that the proposed scheme might in fact be irrelevant. The CJRC interest in studying legal costs coincided with work being undertaken by the Victorian Law Reform Commission, and we saw a long-term benefit in coordinating similar research in both states. The methodology was settled in consultation with the Victorian Law Reform Commission, and parallel investigations were undertaken in both states. Thus, the CJRC was able to use identical information from two states – New South Wales and Victoria – and a comparison was made of a sample of cases on such questions as the length of time to completion of a matter, the legal costs to both plaintiffs and defendants and the proportion of those costs to overall payouts.

The report showed that the sheer length of a litigated matter did not influence its cost. Rather, costs were lower for matters that reached settlement and higher for matters that went to verdict. On the state-to-state comparison, the time taken to completion of a matter in New South Wales was significantly longer than in Victoria, as was the proportion of matters that proceeded to verdict. While the difference between legal costs in New South Wales and Victoria was not statistically significant, there was a consistent trend for both legal costs and amount recovered by the plaintiff to be higher in New South Wales.

The release of this report in January 1993 proved to be very timely. There is currently very lively debate in Australia over the costs of justice. There has been a major inquiry by the Trade Practices

Commission (the body which investigates monopolies and unfair business practices), the issue featured at a summit meeting involving the Prime Minister and all the state Premiers, and there has been, of course, much discussion in the media. However, something has been missing from this debate – factual information. This report therefore went at least part of the way towards filling a serious gap in the information available to policy-makers in Australia. It also provided some pertinent information to those in the legal profession, judging from the number of requests for the report received from law firms.

## The causes of case delay

Apart from costs, the next most-discussed issue in the area of civil justice is probably court delay. Debate on the causes of delay has been heated, and accusations of inefficiency have been laid against all the key players in the system. However, empirical data addressing the issue has been sparse, and a systematic understanding of the process of settlement is lacking.

The CJRC sought to fill this gap in its study entitled *The Pace of Litigation*, released in December 1991. This study asked two main questions about delay: what is the current level of delay in civil matters, and what factors cause this delay? It focused on cases in one area which had become known for unacceptably high levels of delay – third-party motor vehicle claims. This area was also an interesting one to study because of the attention it has received from policy-makers. Since 1987, there have been two major changes to the system for claiming compensation following motor vehicle accidents. In spite of this, motor vehicle claims continue to exert considerable pressures on the court system.

The CJRC took a 7 per cent random sample of finalised compensation cases, and examined the insurers' files on these matters. This amounted to 1,053 files, and it was acknowledged that it would be too costly and time-consuming a process to collect information on all the possible causes of delay from every one of these files. To overcome this, the data collection phase of the project was split into two. Initially, general details were collected from all the 1,053 files in the sample. Information collected included the dates of key case events, details of the claim, plaintiff characteristics, initial offers made and the stage of disposal. After a preliminary analysis of this information, more specific issues were then addressed by a further data collection focusing on a subset of the 1,053 matters.

To consider aspects of the processing of claims in more detail, 100 matters which took a 'typical' time from commencement to disposal were selected. These matters were examined in order to collect information on the activities of key players in the settlement system, and the relationship of these activities to court events.

The first question that the study looked at was: When do matters settle? The sample showed that the majority of the claims in question were litigated, yet only a small proportion of these required judicial determination. A high proportion of the sampled matters were settled either on the day allocated for the hearing or after commencement of the hearing. These facts are obviously of particular concern to court administrators, as resources are allocated to these cases unnecessarily. The sample also revealed that litigation significantly increased the amount of time claimants had to wait to obtain damages. This was the case regardless of the stage of disposal. That is, even where settlements occurred in the early stages of litigation, matters which were litigated were considerably longer than those which were unlitigated.

The study then looked at the different factors to which delay is often attributed: court procedural requirements, claim characteristics (eg, age and injury) and claim processing (that is, the activities undertaken to collect information and medical details relevant to the claim, leading up to the resolution of the matter). The report drew the conclusion that the pace of litigation was largely in the hands of the parties themselves. In particular, it was found that the parties took significantly longer to provide information to each other than did other sources. While factors such as issues of liability and the size of the amount claimed may have had some impact on the time taken to resolve particular matters, their value in influencing the pace of litigation overall was minimal. Thus, for the first time, objective, empirical information was available to policy-makers and administrators, to allow for a better-informed debate about the issue of court delay.

# Economic impact analysis of changes in court rules

Another innovative piece of research relevant to court administration in which the CJRC is currently engaged is a cost/benefit analysis of a new system of case management recently introduced into the Supreme Court of New South Wales. This system – known as differential case management – is aimed at encouraging more cases to settle early and reducing the amount of time it takes for those remaining cases to go through to a hearing. The government department which administers the courts commissioned this research with the long-term aim of devising a model which will measure the economic impact of changes in court procedures. Previously, research on the costs of justice has been focused on lawyers' fees. This project is taking a much broader view, and is trying to establish a way to assess the impact on the whole community of changes to the administration of justice.

In tackling a project like this, the CJRC is breaking new ground, as, to our knowledge, a study like this has never before been undertaken, at least not in Australia. However, this project also represents the fulfilment of one of the Law Foundation's goals in establishing the CJRC – that of bringing a multi-disciplinary approach to research into the administration of justice. This project was also one that required the CJRC to offer briefings to Members of the New South Wales Parliament. In a rather unusual move, the Supreme Court Practice Note which introduced differential case management became subject to disallowance by the New South Wales Parliament, in the same way as may occur with subordinate legislation. An article in the press alerted us to the fact that there was a considerable amount of lobbying by legal practitioners going on to bring about the disallowance of the Practice Note. They were apparently concerned that the new requirements would add significantly to the costs of conducting an action.

The CJRC felt that it was important that the key players in this debate know about the research being undertaken, but did not wish to become involved in the political debate. Accordingly, as both the Attorney General and the Chief Justice were fully aware of our project, we wrote to the shadow Attorney General with details of the research. He then invited us to brief him and some of his parliamentary colleagues on the research programme.

## Do only the rich and the poor use courts?

The final research project to be described here is one that considered the question: so, who does use the court? This study reviewed approximately 1,000 files from the Common Law Division of the Supreme Court of New South Wales to produce a snapshot of the users of the Court. It described the legal representatives, the defendants and the plaintiffs involved in the Common Law Division of the court. The study then went on to compare the plaintiff population with the general population of New South Wales. It found that there was not equal usage of the court across the community of New South Wales. For example, there were disproportionate numbers of men taking claims to the Court, and residents in certain parts of Sydney were far more likely to be involved in cases than were residents in other parts of the state. However, a more interesting point to emerge was that the plaintiff population was similar to the state-wide population with regard to average income levels. This runs contrary to the belief that only the 'rich' and the 'poor' can afford to have their disputes resolved in a court of law. This study therefore made a valuable contribution to our understanding of court usage, particularly about the plaintiffs who use the court. The significance of the research was such that the Chief Justice of the Supreme Court made extensive reference to this report in his speech for the opening of Law Term at the beginning of 1994.

## Completing the CJRC story so far

This chapter has given a brief tour of the work of the CJRC. There are several other interesting projects currently on foot, and the CJRC is increasingly being approached to carry out new research projects. This is the best indicator of the value of the work it has conducted so far. Requests for research are coming chiefly from government authorities responsible for the administration of the courts, and statutory authorities responsible for administering such schemes as the workers' compensation scheme. The CJRC has not only filled a gap in the information available to policy makers, it has also established a leadership position in this type of socio-legal research. A complete list of the centre's published research reports is annexed to this chapter.

One of the defining principles of the CJRC is the independence of its research work, and this has become an important issue as the centre takes on more projects for external bodies. To ensure this independence, the CJRC insists on retaining the rights to all work produced. This means that research results will always be published, and that a commissioning organisation will not be able to suppress a report if the CJRC does not produce the 'right' answer. While this might, at first glance, seem a difficult position to maintain when it comes to negotiating a research contract, it is, in fact, a selling point for the CJRC. The commissioning body is always able to point to the fact that independent research has been carried out to evaluate a programme or that independent research has led to the implementation of certain policy measures.

Some details of the resources required to run the CJRC may be of interest. At present, the CJRC employs an executive director, a lawyer with a policy background, a research manager and three researchers. The researchers, who are all social scientists, are all equipped with computers, and use several software packages which are designed for social science research. The total annual budget for the CJRC is approximately $450,000 (about £210,000). At present, the Law Foundation provides most of the money to run the centre, although revenue from commissioned work is increasingly forming an important part of the budget. Expenditure on salaries, equipment and administration accounts for around $320,000 (£150,000), while specific project costs and the cost of employing outside experts to review reports account for a further $120,000 (£56,000). The CJRC has gradually been able to build up a panel of experts in areas such as sample structuring, statistical analysis and qualitative research, who can be brought in to work on particular projects to ensure the high quality of the reports produced.

The continuing relationship with the RAND's Institute for Civil Justice is highly valued with great assistance being obtained through a number of recent visits to the centre from senior Institute researchers.

## Conclusion

The CJRC is fulfilling the Foundation's original purpose for it through having clearly established the value of sound, empirical research. Without an accurate knowledge of what is happening in courts and in the civil justice system, large amounts of resources may well be allocated to address problems that either do not exist, or which are not properly understood. Without solid, factual information, there can be no assurance that measures taken to reform the civil justice system will achieve their goal.

## References

1  'Matters unresolved by Conciliation', *Civil Issues*, 1991.
2  Deborah Worthington and Joanne Baker, *The Costs of Civil Litigation*, 1993.

# Appendix

## Civil Justice Research Centre publications

### Reports

Terence W Beed, R William Fitzgerald and Deborah Worthington, *The Role of Conciliation,* 1990.

Terence W Beed and R Ian McEwan, *Lawyers in Civil Litigation,* 1990.

Deborah Worthington, *The Pace of Litigation in New South Wales: Lessons from the Tail,* 1991.

Elsina Rasink, *Demands on the Compensation Court: Preliminary Thoughts and Suggestions for Empirical Research,* 1993.

Elsina Rasink, *Investigation into the Resources of the Dust Diseases Tribunal,* 1993.

Tania Matruglio, *So, Who Does Use the Court?* 1993.

Deborah Worthington and Joanne Baker, *The Costs of Civil Litigation,* 1993.

John Schwartzkoff, *Matters Going to Trial in the Family Court of Australia,* 1994.

Deborah Worthington, *Compensation in an Atmosphere of Reduced Legalism: A study of the legal costs of workers' compensation claims made under the New South Wales WorkCover Scheme,* 1994.

Joanne Baker, *Who Settles and Why? A study of factors associated with the stage of case disposition,* 1994.

Tania Matruglio, *Plaintiffs and the Process of Litigation: An analysis of the satisfaction of plaintiffs following their experiences of litigation,* 1994.

### Reported in 'Civil Issues' Bulletin

Deborah Worthington, *Matters Unresolved by Conciliation,* Volume 1 1991.

Tania Matruglio, *Insights from the Tail: The Other View of Activities – a study of third-party claimant solicitor files,* Volume 2 1991.

Deborah Worthington, *Insights from the Tail: Costs incurred by the plaintiff in third-party litigation*, Volume 2 1991.

Tania Matruglio, *Some demographics of accidents*, Volume 2 1992.

Deborah Worthington and Tania Matruglio, *Access to Justice: Food for Thought*, Volume 2 1992.

Elsina Rasink, *Supreme Court Special Sittings – The practitioner's perspective*, Volume 4 1994.

Marie Delaney, *Plaintiffs' Perceptions of Procedures: Perceptions of trial, arbitration and pre-trial conference in the New South Wales District Court and private mediation*, Volume 5 1995.

# Part VII

# The way forward

# CHAPTER 20

# New directions

ROGER SMITH

Carrie Menkel-Meadow begins her contribution with the quote from Dickens: 'It was the best of times; it was the worst of times'. This provides an apt text for the book in general and this concluding chapter in particular.

In England and Wales, as in many other jurisdictions around the world, apparently irresistible pressures are now at large. These will lead to fundamental change to the legal system in order to accommodate the new demands of changing societies. This makes possible the kind of structural reforms that have hitherto been resisted, largely by the deeply entrenched conservatism of the legal profession, the judiciary and those who govern them. So much is good news.

The bad news is that not all change makes things better. Attacks on legal aid, for instance, have increased over the period in which this book has been in preparation. The demand-led nature of legal aid, at least in civil cases, has founded the analysis that solicitors were a major determinant of rising cost (see p25). The media generally have led an assault on legal aid for the undeserving, particularly in large fraud cases. This has precipitated a recent Lord Chancellor's Department consultation paper suggesting, among other solutions, that legal aid could simply be a loan rather than a grant.[1] The Chief Secretary to the Treasury has begun to argue publicly that legal aid needs to be cut.[2] The parliamentary opposition offers no hope of greater resources. Labour Party spokespeople have stated categorically that no more money will be made available.[3]

One of the worst consequences of this negative publicity is the loss of the optimism that briefly flowered in the 1970s. LAG was founded in 1972 on the crest of a wave of demand for improvement in the legal system and legal services. Considerable achievements have been made, the greatest of them a legal aid system that still provides 275 adequate cover in criminal cases, at least in terms of financial eligibility, and acceptable civil services, at least for the poor. The extent of this success may well even account for some of the pervading pessimism among those concerned for the future of legal aid. Significant sections of the legal profession are now dependent on the income that legal aid generates, as reported in chapter 3. Legal aid practitioners complained about cuts in their remuneration during the 1980s and early 1990s (see p25). The next decade is likely to see many of them lose this source of income completely.

A similar loss of faith in the prospect of beneficial change can be seen in the progress of reform of the courts. As Cyril Glasser describes in chapter 15, the Civil Justice Review was hyped as presaging a revolutionary approach to reform of the civil courts. In fact, its most radical suggestion, the creation of a unified court structure which amalgamated the High Court with the county courts, had been killed shortly after its birth in an early consultation document. The policies that flowed from its report amounted to little more than moving cases down the system. Lord Woolf's review of civil justice, due to give birth to an interim report in May 1995, is already being attacked as unlikely to meet the expectations that have been raised of its possibilities.[4] The recommendations that will actually be implemented from its proposals could well amount to little more than the Civil Justice Review revisited. An élite High Court will be preserved at the expense of overloaded lower courts.

## The opportunities for advance

For all such justified pessimism, the contributions in this book retain, as promised in the introduction, an essential optimism. This is true even of the chapters that deal directly with the form and structure of publicly funded legal services. Both Geoff Budlender in chapter 9, dealing with South Africa, and Gerry Singsen in chapter 11, covering civil legal services in the United States, present an upbeat assessment of what might be possible, though both are clearly aware of the pressures on resources that may stunt the prospects of new services. The election of a Republican-dominated Congress since Gerry Singsen wrote his contribution underlines the difficulties of obtaining adequate levels of finance that will be faced in both those countries and, increasingly, our own.

It remains particularly important, even if the political tide appears currently to be running with those who wish to restrict public funding for all services, that public debate is not simply confined to resistance to, and the mechanisms for, cuts and caps to expenditure. Study of the position of legal aid or its equivalent in the United States and South Africa, very different societies from our own though they may be, provides valuable encouragement to reconsidering the fundamental objectives of our own legal aid system. Legal aid is not just a tiresome head of public expenditure: it provides what should be seen as essentially a constitutional right that forms a necessary support for a fair society.

Legal aid is, however, only part of our legal system. It is also, in historical terms, still in its infancy, having existed in its modern form for less than 50 years. Much more fundamental components of the rule and the role of law are under threat of change. The two themes of Part V are relevant in this context. Indira Jaising in chapter 12 explains how the Indian courts responded to the challenge of observing many evident causes of action but no litigants, in part because of the lack of any legal aid. The judges themselves moved into the consequent vacuum. A parallel judicial invention with similar motives can be identified in the British judiciary's opening up of judicial review since the early 1980s. Behind both developments is the recognition that the courts can, and should, be the arbiters of the public interest as well as the deciders of private grievances. This begins to challenge the core of the individualistic economic liberalism that underlies much legal theory. Society, as a whole, has interest in how some cases are decided.

Martyn Day and Sally Moore argue in chapter 13 that multi-party actions also raise questions of the public interest in litigation. They also raise the issue of the collective interest in litigation. Multi-party actions are defined by reference to the participants' membership of a particular class with common characteristics. They cease to be atomised individuals. As discussed in chapter 3, our legal system has singularly failed to grapple with these problems. Insurers, and those lobbying on their behalf, wish it to be even harder for such cases to be taken and have launched a strong counter-attack on multi-party actions, alleging that they are a waste of money.[5] The present system is, however, unsustainable and some new mechanism will be required. George Pulman QC argues in chapter 14 for a new form of public inquiry. Martyn Day and Sally Moore, as plaintiff litigators, prefer the courts. In any event, reform of this area is overdue. LAG hopes to undertake more work in this area over the next year.

## Challenging the professional model

One of the implicit themes that runs through a number of contributions to this book is the growing challenge to the traditional model for the delivery of legal services. These services have, hitherto, been dominated by the legal profession. A classic description of the attributes of a profession was provided by the Law Society in 1968 and quoted with approval by the Royal Commission on Legal Services in 1979:

> The learned professions have not suddenly come into existence, but have developed over the centuries as a result of needs generated in all advancing societies . . . a profession . . . may be described as a body of men and women (a) identifiable by reference to some register or record; (b) recognised as having a special skill and learning in some field of activity in which the public needs protection against incompetence, the standards of skill and learning being prescribed by the profession itself; (c) holding themselves out as being willing to serve the public; (d) voluntarily submitting themselves to standards of ethical conduct beyond those required of the ordinary citizen by law; (e) undertaking to accept personal responsibility to those whom they serve for their actions and to their profession for maintaining public confidence.[6]

This model of a profession faces a number of threats. For instance, the doctrine of personal liability has been muted by the development of professional negligence insurance. More importantly, the level of skill required by professional bodies from their members has come under question. Academic researchers have questioned the degree of competence of lawyers, at least in some areas of their work.[7] An important aspect in the development of legal aid franchising has been the development by the Legal Aid Board of mechanisms for controlling the quality of legal aid practitioners in response to the perception that the profession itself was not doing this adequately (see p30). The board and not the profession is setting the standards for the level of competence to be expected in undertaking legal aid cases and it will be the board, therefore, that regulates this aspect of quality, not the profession.

The contributions to this book concentrate, however, on the consequences of the high cost of conventionally organised legal services. Gerry Singsen in chapter 11 describes how the Legal Services Corporation in the United States has, from the beginning, been disposed to use salaried services rather than funding private practitioners. Terry Purcell in chapter 5 details how the Law Founda-

tion in New South Wales is developing new technology in an effort
to allow lawyers to bring down their costs. Forrest Mosten in chapter
4 takes another approach. He argues that there is a market solution.
Lawyers can divide up their work so that they only offer to clients
what they want and can afford. He uses the term 'unbundling' for
this process: it originally described the division of hardware and
software in the early development of computers. His experience
suggests that, at least, for some clients and some cases, there is
potential in offering clients a choice in the level of service to be
provided.

The most obvious challenge to the legal profession comes from the
increasing use of paralegals in substitution for fully qualified lawyers. Considerable impetus in all jurisdictions is given to such
substitution because paralegals have been, in most countries,
cheaper. It remains to be seen whether this is still true, given
growing unemployment among lawyers in jurisdictions like the
United States and Britain where this tendency is becoming an
increasing phenomenon. The relative cheapness of paralegals
remains the major attraction in South Africa, as Geoff Budlender
indicates in chapter 9. This is enhanced by a political argument,
advanced by Thandi Orleyn in chapter 10, that paralegals exist in
community-based advice centres otherwise faced with closure as the
result of the withdrawal of foreign aid. This trend of thought echoes
that of the Legal Aid Board in England and Wales in its exploration
of franchising with non-solicitor agencies (see p34).

## Reviewing the courts

The courts have traditionally largely been considered separate from
the legal services available to, or needed by, those that use them. The
two chapters by Cyril Glasser and Carrie Menkel-Meadow, chapters
15 and 16, contribute to the process of redressing that balance. Both
provide an overview of developments in this country and the United
States, respectively. Both show the value of careful consideration and
research in guiding change. Chapter 19, written by Terence Purcell
and Gillian McAllister, demonstrates in very practical terms what a
coherent research agenda might look like by reference to experience
of the Civil Justice Research Centre in Sydney, Australia.

From these and the other chapters in Part VI come three themes
that need to be further explored in both practical experiment and
thoughtful research. Cyril Glasser points to the importance of roll-
ing back the principle of orality and replacing it with more written

procedures. He stresses, however, the need for very carefully considered reform, pointing out how the move to exchange of written
witness statements, implemented after the report of the Civil Justice
Review in 1989, has backfired. These are now drafted by counsel at
great cost; have become almost like pleadings; and have probably led
to an increase in expense rather than any saving.

Martin Partington in chapter 18 suggests that the management
structure developed by the Independent Tribunal Service may have
lessons for the organisation of courts. Its corporate nature might be
anathema to many judges and smack of too great a judicial involvement in what should be the role of the executive. There are, however,
already some signs of a new relationship between courts and judges.
The work of the Children Act Advisory Committee brings together
groups of court users in a way that could be a prototype for a
national structure of committees that involved judges much more
proactively than has traditionally been the case. Interestingly, this
committee has reached the same sort of conclusions, though involvement of practitioners, as have the senior judiciary and Lord Woolf,
in particular. The foreword to its 1993–94 report states: 'There is
undoubtedly a need for more formal intervention by the courts in the
interests of good case management . . .'[8]

Both Carrie Menkel-Meadow in chapter 16, and Suzanne Burn in
chapter 17, deal with the topic of what in the US is given the
appealing name of 'appropriate dispute resolution'. This will
clearly be considered by Lord Woolf in his review of civil justice. It
is also likely to be promoted in the context of legal aid because, by
removing cases from the courts, it offers the promise of doing
without lawyers. Carrie Menkel-Meadow considers the issue of the
privatisation of justice implicit in American 'rent-a-judge' schemes.
Similar trends can be identified in the UK with the development of
private-enterprise mediation and arbitration schemes. Examination
of the consequences will form part of one of LAG's next projects.

## Empowering the citizen

Unbundling theory raises directly the extent to which people can be
empowered to undertake their own cases if given appropriate assistance. Forrest Mosten makes use of a client library to allow people
to help themselves. The People's Law School in Vancouver, described
by Gordon Hardy in chapter 6, and the Citizenship Foundation in
this country, the subject of Jan Newton's contribution in chapter 7,
provide two other examples of how information and education can

be disseminated. As noted in the introduction to Part III, the role of both organisations is strikingly similar. Both emphasise the way in which the need for legal information shades into broader education in the legal elements of citizenship. Finally, John Richardson in chapter 8 shows how, in law centre experience, legal information can be linked to individual casework. He gives the powerful example of the way in which the centres linked together to meet the need for information revealed by a sudden explosion of cases relating to the enforcement of the ill-fated poll tax.

There are obvious dangers in promoting the idea that DIY can solve the problems caused by lack of qualified assistance when it is necessary. Nevertheless, there must be opportunities to obtain more benefit from a greater emphasis on information and education, leaving aside the general benefit of a more legally and constitutionally literate society. This is particularly so in the light of the tremendous possibilities of new technology in disseminated information and skills. Expert systems are being developed in the United States, like QuickCourt described on p82. This is an area where there needs to be experimentation of a very broad kind about what can be achieved. We need also to ensure that there are channels of communication by which the results of different approaches can be compared.

## Next steps

There is an obvious danger in asserting too easily that lessons can be learnt from abroad. The different histories of publicly funded legal services in different countries, as noted in the introduction to Part IV, bear evidence to how varied experience can be, even within countries sharing the same common law foundation to their legal systems. Nevertheless, the contributions to this book, particularly those from abroad, show a number of opportunities for innovation and experiment. For the reasons set out in the opening chapters, our legal system is very much at a crossroads. Whichever way it goes forward, it will be in a new direction. That direction will be much determined by the decisions of government over the next five to ten years.

To return to a point made early in chapter 1, our aim for reform should not be that currently articulated for itself by the Lord Chancellor's Department, 'to ensure the efficient and effective administration of justice at an affordable cost' (p14). Rather, we must place people and their needs at the centre of our objective. The current government aim should be replaced, therefore, by a form of words something like: 'to ensure for all members of society appropriate access to justice'. The emphasis on administration should be relegated to becoming the means of achieving and not the object of policy. The difference is more than semantic. We need innovative experiment and active change to widen access to justice and fairness.

## References

1   Lord Chancellor's Department, *Legal Aid for the Apparently Wealthy,* December 1994, para 4.19.

2   See, eg, 'Legal Aid Faces Curbs', *Daily Telegraph*, 14 February 1995.

3   Eg, Lord Williams of Mostyn at Law Society conference, 8 October 1994.

4   M Zander, 'Are there any clothes for the Emperor to wear?' *New Law Journal*, 3 February 1995; R Smith, 'An open question of justice', *Guardian*, 1 February 1995.

5   Eg, 'Greed is not for you, lawyers told' *Daily Telegraph*, 3 February 1995.

6   Quoted in Royal Commission on Legal Services, *Final Report* Volume 1, HMSO, 1979, Cmnd 7648, p30.

7   See, eg, H Genn, *Hard Bargaining: Out-of-court settlements in personal injury actions*, Clarendon Press, 1987; and M McConville, J Hodgson, L Bridges and A Pavlovic, *Standing Accused: the organisation and practices of criminal defence lawyers in Britain*, Clarendon Press, 1994.

8   Children Act Advisory Committee, Annual Report 1993/4, Lord Chancellor's Department, 1994, p3.

# Index